SHE HAS
A STORY FOR
EVERYTHING

by
Flo Samuels

TABLE OF CONTENTS

PREFACE

When life slaps you down, slap back… with laughter. For 68 years my disaster stories, some disasters being self-created, have made others laugh while demonstrating it's how you react to problems not the problems themselves that defines whether you'll succeed or fail. Bad marriages, an out-of-wedlock child (big no-no in the '60s), job discrimination, serious back problems (doctors viewing my spinal MRI have said they didn't know how I could walk), deaths, losing a house (and jobs), bankruptcy, numerous sports injuries and other calamities (such as a four month battle with a skunk) could have resulted in depression or giving up. But after I calmed down I saw the funny side.

She Has a Story for Everything is the first of a two-volume humorous memoir demonstrating that the fire that burns the wood really can harden the steel, that nothing is certain but unforeseen (got that in a fortune cookie) and 'no guts, no glory' will get you a lot more out of life than being afraid to take risks. The first book, all 400 pages, covers 1944 to 1998 and ranges through three states (Michigan, California and Oregon), three marriages, moving to California with two sons and no job, taking up motorcycling and white-water rafting in my late 40s and using exercise to overcome multiple injuries and back problems that would have left others disabled. The second volume due at the end of 2012 covers 1998 to the present. To those who have said over the years, "Flo, you need to write a book," here it is!

THE SWEET SMELL OF SKUNKS

(or Coping With The Wilderness In The Big City)

San Diego, California, 1982

I never thought about skunks except when I passed areas where they had signaled their presence. Consequently, when I moved back to my home in 1982 and my old tenant mentioned seeing skunks in the back yard I was not worried. Phil, who rented a room from me, installed bricks and chicken wire along the back fence. We assumed the barriers combined with my house being two streets from the canyon's edge would eliminate any problems with our odoriferous friend. We also proved the old saying, 'Ignorance is bliss.'

Late at night in the second week I heard my dog, Penny, growling in the back yard. As I let her into the house I noticed she smelled a little ripe. The pungent aroma spread rousing Phil from his second floor room. Racing down the stairs he asked who had died. Recognizing the odor's source he went to the local Safeway for help. Tomato juice was recommended. Penny's white coat turned a distinct shade of pink, eliciting many curious stares when we took her for her daily run.

Reinforcing our barricades we assured each other there would not be a second occurrence. Stupidity reigned supreme. Two weeks later Penny was hit again. So was Safeway.

Deciding that neither my house, my renter, my two boys, my dog nor my nose could take a third onslaught, I called the Wildlife Center for help. The lady asked why I wanted to remove the skunk. When I pointed out the damage I was scolded.

"Why do you want to harm that poor, innocent creature?"

"But," I protested, "it keeps spraying my dog."

She responded, "Then keep your dog inside. The skunk was there first."

Realizing I was headed in the wrong direction I called the County Animal Shelter. They would furnish a cage for twenty dollars and, when I had captured the skunk, they would remove it. Being the thrifty sort and considering my sons were in Boy Scouts, I decided to save money and put their training to use.

All day Sunday they sawed, nailed, glued and tested. The skunk trap was ready. Hot dogs were carefully prepared for bait. (They suggested steak but I vetoed the idea. We may live in a higher income area but I didn't feel the skunk had acquired tastes that expensive.) The trap was set, night arrived. We waited for the sweet sound of the falling lid. And fall it did. A black and white creature sat entrapped within the cage's confines. Unfortunately it was our cat. Dutifully the trap was re-baited and reset. After two hours with no results we all said the hell with it and went to bed.

The next morning we checked to see if the bait had been taken. It had. Of course the trap door had not fallen but the bait was gone. At least we knew it liked hot dogs.

The trap was left out, baited, denuded of its bait, reset, retested, kicked a few times then relegated to the garbage. I called the Animal Shelter again resigned to paying the twenty dollars. This call brought a new suggestion. Why not try the old mothball trick? I was assured that people who liberally sprinkled mothballs around their yards had been spared further visits by the striped devil. At least, said the Shelter Lady, they never called back. Considering the smell of mothballs I wondered if the lack of calls was due to success or that the people had simply been asphyxiated.

Before I could stock up on ammunition we went to the Del Mar Fair. The day stretched into early evening when I suddenly remembered. Penny was outdoors. Rushing back to the house I prayed Luck was on our side. Hearing Penny's shrill bark I realized Luck was somewhere else. As I ran out the back door I also realized I needed more than Luck.

Penny was a wire-haired fox terrier. A big wire-haired fox terrier, two feet tall and weighing twenty-five pounds. She was charging an animal that, by my estimate, could have taken on a bobcat and won. The skunk, with its tail pointed directly at her head, was at least half again as big as Penny.

Penny charged, was rebuffed and charged again. I screamed at her to come at me. Since her response to my commands had always been minimal if non-existent, I have no idea why I expected instant learning under such conditions. I finally grabbed her tail and dragged her away but not before I was a party to the action. At least I had Penny and the skunk had a chance to leave.

I immediately went to Safeway, cleaned out their mothball shelves and added some cans of tomato juice. As I stood in the checkout amid politely gasping shoppers, the bagger looked at the fifteen boxes of mothballs and four cans of tomato juice then loudly observed, "Oh, now I know where that stink came from when you came into the store." I thanked her for her astute observation.

We mothballed the fence, the yard, the deck and the dog. A day went by, a week, a month. It appeared our problem child was gone. We all heaved a sigh of relief. Victory at last.

Hah!

Penny was a show dog and we wanted her to have puppies. Along with a graphic description of how Penny would be bred, which was of great interest to John, my fifteen-year-old son, the breeder mentioned that they used a woman's personal cleanser as an antidote for skunk spray. No stain, pleasant smell and anything left over could be used for other purposes. We returned home with the smug self-assurance we would never need to use it.

The winter rains hit and Penny was confined to the house. On good days we would leave her out as long as possible. Unfortunately one day was too long.

The sun had long set. I was busy and Penny started to bark. I raced to the door. Too late. Since the stores were closed I called my 72-year-old mother, explained the problem and asked if she would bring some feminine cleanser the next day. She agreed although somewhat confused. I locked Penny in the garage and went to bed.

That incident taught me one valuable thing about skunk smell. It can penetrate doors, closed windows and walls. The next morning I let Penny outdoors (rain or not, she wasn't coming into the house) and went to my office at the shipyard. As I entered the office people greeted me warmly. Their warmth soon turned to wrinkled noses and questions such as, "What the hell is that smell?" My coat and scarf that had been hanging on a chair near the garage had absorbed the skunk odor.

Not wanting to slowly suffocate ten people I sprayed the offending clothing with room deodorizer (industrial strength) and hung them outdoors. Since they were cleaning the chemical toilets at the time I wasn't sure the new smell would be much improvement over the old.

Returning to the office where everyone had opened windows and moved desks to "give Flo more room to work," I sat down and my long hair swung into my face. I instantly realized the skunk odor had transferred from my scarf to my hair. Gasping I grabbed the industrial deodorizer and gave my hair a liberal shot. At that moment my boss entered the office. For some reason, for the rest of the day he relayed messages to me through my clerical staff.

That night my mother greeted me with her little black purse, her sturdy shoes, her sparkle-framed glasses and four cans of feminine cleanser.

"I wasn't certain how much you needed," she said, "so I got four just to be on the safe side." She paused then looked at me with a curious expression. "The check-out lady asked if I was expecting to have a good time this weekend. Now what do you suppose she meant by that?"

The next day I asked my 10-year old son, Josh, to use the feminine cleanser and wash the rugs Penny had slept on. I heard the sound of running water and a low, sing-song murmur from the front yard. Glancing out the window I noticed women and men walking by with very offended looks on their faces. Curious I opened the door to hear Josh's little ditty. "This is the way we douche the rug, douche the rug..."

We re-mothballed and re-barricaded the yard. Phil moved out and was replaced by Joe, a used-car salesman with questionable connections. I didn't realize how questionable until the night we spied the skunk under the backyard deck.

"Hey, Joe," Josh called, "come see our skunk."

"It's out there, eh?" Joe responded, "Well, I'll get the little s.o.b."

Glancing up from the deck I instantly took in Joe and the unmistakable gun in his hand. Now guns are all right in their place but brandishing them in the house is not it. Joe immediately recognized my discomfort when I let out a scream that brought on the next-door neighbor's lights. Evidently the skunk didn't like guns either because it instantly scooted out a previously unknown hole in the fence. After that Joe kept the gun at work.

Things remained quiet for a few months. Joe moved out and Sean moved in. Sean was a displaced lawyer from Vancouver with no office, 'rich foreign clients' and an expensive wardrobe. One night Sean was in the kitchen when John took out the garbage. This rather pedestrian chore quickly became a night to remember.

The garbage cans are along my neighbor's five-foot brick wall that the previous owner built to contain the rats she said were feeding on my garbage. (After ten years in my area I have seen dogs, cats, coyotes, snakes and, obviously, skunks but never a rat. Perhaps she had found a new substitute for pink elephants.) In any case nothing can get over that wall.

John was gone about thirty seconds when I heard pounding feet (John is 6'4"). He burst through the front door.

"The skunk is at the garbage cans. Where's my spear gun? I'm going to get that bleep this time."

Grabbing his spear gun John raced back out the door closely followed by Josh. Well, maybe not that close. Within seconds I heard the zing of the spear gun, a cry of "I got him" then the pounding feet. Again John burst through the front door. Followed by Josh.

"Where's the shovel? I think I only stunned him. Now I'll finish him off for good."

Grabbing the shovel he ran back out the door with Josh a respectable distance behind.

The following sounds drifted through the open door.

'Whomp, whomp.'

Crashing of cans.

'Whomp.'

Ringing of a shovel on the driveway.

John's voice.

"Where is he? There he is. Josh, head him off."

"Head him off?" Josh cried incredulously. "Are you crazy? You head him off."

"There he is," John yelled, "now I've got him. No, he's headed for the front door. I'll get him now."

Sean became very attentive. Although he had been drinking prior to arriving home John's words led to instant sobriety.

"Is that skunk heading towards the house?" he asked.

"Sounds like it," I replied as I read the newspaper. Keeping up with the news is very important.

"What are you going to do?" he asked uneasily.

"I guess I'm going finish my newspaper," I replied. "They're the ones chasing the skunk."

"Oh, no," he cried, "what if it gets in the house?"

"Well," I suggested, "since you're closest to the door maybe you'd better close it."

Leaping from the chair he ran to the door to see a black and white creature bearing down on him. Slamming the door shut he screamed at its blank face, "Don't chase it towards the door. Keep it away from the door."

Dashing to the window overlooking the front step he watched the skunk run under it, releasing its heavy perfume on the way by.

Turning to me he yelled, "They're chasing it under the window. Why are they chasing it under the window?"

I calmly replied, "Probably because you told them not to chase it towards the door. Under the window is the only other place it can go."

Returning his attention to the drama unfolding in the front yard Sean screamed out the window, "Get it away from the house. Keep it away from the house."

Turning to me again he railed, "The smell is coming in the windows. What should we do?"

"Well," I responded, "since you're standing at the windows why don't you just close them?"

As he closed the windows we heard a blood-curdling scream from the front yard. Within seconds Josh exploded through the front door proclaiming the news of the night.

"It got John, right in the face."

We could hear water running from the outside hose and an undercurrent of words. It appeared John had a low opinion of skunks. When he staggered through the door, face dripping, his only comment was "I didn't know they could spray that far."

The odor slowly filled up the kitchen. Sean looked at me and pleadingly asked, "What are you going to do?"

Rising from my chair I picked up my purse and started for the door. "I'm going to do what I usually do. I'm going to Safeway."

The ladies at Safeway had become old hands at this. As I moved through the checkout line with my six cans of tomato juice the clerk's only remark was "Well, who'd it get this time?"

Arriving back home I placed the tomato juice where John could reach it (from a distance, of course) and turned to Sean who was still quivering in his chair.

"The smell," he whispered, "the smell. What should I do? My clothes will smell. I can't see my clients with that smell on my clothes."

Brightening he sprang from his seat, ran to his room and feverishly began to pack.

"What are you doing?" I asked.

"I'm going to put my clothes in my van and park it away from the house. That way the smell won't be on them."

I wondered how he was going to keep the smell off his bed sheets, towels and hair but kept my questions to myself.

During the next hour Sean paced from his room to the door through the living room and kitchen and back muttering about the smell. Finally he turned to me and demanded, "What are you going to do about that smell?"

With an incredulous look I asked, "What would you suggest?"

"Well," he faltered, "can't you do something?"

I soothingly replied, "Aside from not breathing for the next three days I sincerely doubt anything can be done. However I do have one solution."

"What's that?" he asked.

"I'm going to bed. It's not too bad up there and you're driving me crazy."

When I reported John's absence from school the Attendance Clerk asked the reason.

"He stinks," I replied.

"He what?" she asked.

"He stinks," I answered.

"Oh," she responded, "he stinks."

"Yes," I continued, "he was sprayed by a skunk."

"Oh," she gasped, "tell John we all thank him for not coming to school and he can stay home as long as necessary."

How the skunk escaped the spear gun and the shovel is beyond my understanding. Perhaps it had a survival instinct beyond that of mere mortals. Or, since we still received visits, maybe its ghost will haunt us forever. In either case my encounter with the wilderness has left me with a deep appreciation of the resiliency of nature's children and the sweet smell of skunks.

Postscript:

Penny was bred and had two puppies that the breeder immediately determined were physically unsuitable for either show dogs or sale and was going to put down. Her contention was their jaws were under slung, they would eventually be unable to eat and they would starve. Neither I nor my sons found this acceptable so we took the puppies and bid her farewell. We sold one, kept the other and named him Gil.

Gil was not trainable nor was he amenable to coming when called. He had no problem eating. He also tended to dig holes where he disappeared and all the dirt went into our pool or Jacuzzi dependent on where he had decided to build his bomb shelter. So when I heard a ruckus one night and went out to investigate, it didn't surprise me to see Gil walking toward me with the leg of a skunk in his mouth. And not a drop of spray on his body.

A few days later I noticed the Jacuzzi was dirty so asked Josh to clean it. Josh went out, took one look then returned to the kitchen.

"No way am I cleaning that!" His eyes were dancing with laughter.

"Why, what's wrong?" I asked.

"Take a look you'll see what's wrong." He returned to the Jacuzzi with me and we both stared at the drowned skunk at the bottom.

"Well," I said, "now we know why we haven't had any visits lately."

And that truly was the end of our skunks. They finally found something faster than they were.

MOM AND DAD
Michigan and California

Since this is my memoir I'm not addressing my Mom and Dad's relatives. However, for those who have seen my book-related picture album on Facebook, I have added an Addendum to briefly explain who everyone was and what happened to them.

My mom and dad met and were married in New York in 1942 or 1943. I was born in 1944 at Camp MacKall, North Carolina where my dad was a parachute instructor. And a boxer. At one time he had a 44-inch chest and a 32-inch waist making it difficult to fit him with regular clothes let alone Army issue.

Before they were married Dad kept leaving Mom at home when he went to dinner with his parents (the word 'shiksa' seemed to be his parent's issue with Mom). After I was born he continued to accede to his parent's wishes that Mom and I never darken their door so she moved herself and me to Michigan, home to most of her family. Dad had two choices, his parents or his wife and child so the three of us ended up in a small area in southeast Michigan west of Pontiac called Waterford Township. That my mother's not being Jewish was the major reason for his parent's disdain was supported when I met them for the first time in 1962. My grandmother's first words were, "That woman took my son. She ruined my Sammy." That was also the last time I communicated with them.

I remember one story my mom told about when they were still in the Army camp. My birth had been pretty trying, lasting through 24-hours of labor. (I was born as they sounded the camp morning reveille.) My mom told me that I came out with a head that went to a point with the slope starting at the eyebrows. My dad had had a screaming fit to which the doctor had barked, "You'd look like that too if you'd been banging against a bone wall for twenty-four hours." After assuring my father that my head would return to normal the doctor noted that my right eye was squinty and only time would tell if there was any damage. There was but it didn't manifest itself for years.

After a few days I did not look like a cone head. Mom said when I was brought home Dad sat her on the bed in front of the crib, held her tightly and said, "Mommy, I will love you the rest of my life for this beautiful baby you've given me." Dad kept his word.

Being a little overprotective, Dad required anyone coming to see the baby to wear a mouth and nose mask. Mom didn't argue as she was more involved sitting in her sitz baths necessitated by the long labor. Unfortunately in those days the bathroom facilities in trailers were a tad cramped so she had resorted to using a wooden bucket in the middle of the living room floor. One day Dad brought home some friends to see his new daughter. As Mom recalled he did have the presence of mind to throw a towel over her after he had ensured the visitors' face masks were in place.

While she engaged in the cooking, cleaning and child care normal for the 50's she also was pretty handy with a hammer and saw. When I was maybe eight or nine they bought a two-bedroom house built on a slope with the basement opening to the back yard. The lot was on a canal that led to a lake. She now had her canvas and she was ready to create. Her house improvement projects took weeks and Dad just wasn't into her ideas of what passed for perfect.

One time she kept at him about the shelves in the laundry room and he finally went downstairs to help. A few moments later I heard a scream, her cursing my dad and his calm footsteps coming up the stairs.

"She was holding the nail. I told her I should hold the nail but you know your mother." It took over a month for the nail on her thumb to heal.

Another time Dad was helping with painting the two story high exterior at the back of the house. He was on the scaffold working on the window trim when he stepped back to check his work (or admire the great job he was doing). The solid 'THUMP' brought my mom running from the front of the house. There he was on his back the paintbrush in his hand pointing upwards like the proverbial final lily laying the dead to rest. Hearing my Mom's scream he sat up, shook his head, looked at the paintbrush then climbed back up the scaffolding as if nothing has happened. Surprisingly enough the only glitch to the fall was some dirt in the brush evidently dislodged and sprayed from the force of his body hitting the ground.

Dad worked in the auto factory and often filched a few dollars from Mom's wallet to pay for lunch or the occasional beer after work. In the days before credit and debit cards this filching often resulted in Mom going to pay for gas or groceries and finding herself abysmally short. After numerous requests that he stop this smalltime pilfering she finally took action.

On Fridays the guys went out for some serious beer-drinking. As Dad was getting ready for work Mom relieved him of every dollar and coin in his wallet. His 'This round's on me,' caused him enough embarrassment that her oft-depleted purse never was hit again. Dad said his buddies' response that they would pound their wives if they ever tried such a thing was greeted by his laughter when he pointed out how often he had done it to her.

Soon after his missing money incident he brought these same friends over late one Friday night to see how Mom had finished off the basement. The walkway alongside the house led to the bottom level via a stone stairway. Inside the house were stairs leading up to the main house.

Of course they had had a number of beers. After their tour they started up the inside stairs then quickly turned around, almost knocking my dad down, fled through the basement door and up the outside stairs to the road. My dad turned to watch them run then looked up to the top of the stairs where my Mom stood in her bathrobe and curlers holding a 12-inch cast-iron frying pan. The guys never did believe my mom wouldn't have used it.

Another time, again a Friday night, the guys had left Dad off and he was leaning on the closed car door rehashing the events of their boozy night. Suddenly the car sped off and Dad continued to lean for a few seconds until he realized the car wasn't there. Recovering his balance he turned around and there she was in the doorway, frying pan in one hand now accompanied by a rolling pin in the other.

I had been in a tuberculosis sanatorium for two six-month stretches when I was five and seven. With all the medical bills my parents were not well off. But by fifth or sixth grade it had become very apparent that I needed glasses. Not just normal glasses but ones with bifocals. The squinty eye at birth had come back to haunt me. My left eye was slightly near-sighted in the 120/20 range. But my right eye, in the words of an ophthalmologist, had a cornea that looked like a mountain range. With 750/whatever I could see neither distance nor close. This had been masked for years by my left eye doing all the work. The doctor hoped that wearing glasses with a special bifocal lens for the right eye would train that eye to become stronger. My parents got me the glasses at considerable cost.

Within two days I was pitching a softball game with a hardball and the batter drove it straight back into my face. The glasses prevented the ball from obliterating my eye but the glasses were toast. I think the school paid for the second pair since they had allowed us to use a hardball. Even in those days parents could scream liability and get results. (How a softball, when making contact off a bat and into an eye socket, could have any less damaging results is beyond me but I'm sure my mom convinced them of the harm.) Sadly that summer I fell off my bike and re-rammed the same eye with the bike's handlebars. At least this time my parents had insurance on the glasses.

During this same time period a female friend who was taller than I decided to demonstrate how girls could protect themselves. She used a judo move to throw me over her back and to the ground. When she did, something in my back came out of it for the worse. I was twelve at the time and have had back problems throughout my life. The gift that keeps on giving. This is only brought up now so you'll understand what happened later.

Being from the Bronx in New York City my dad wasn't the outdoors type. On the other hand my mom was willing to try camping if it meant a low-cost vacation. After numerous arguments (my dad's idea of a vacation was a pile of books, the television and a case of beer), he finally relented. Not, however, without a final attempt to prevent our going. While packing he discovered the lapel to a suit was creased so he went off on one of his temper tantrums.

"What's this?" he screamed. "Look at this! That damn cleaners bent the lapel. I can't go anywhere in this. How can I go anywhere with a bent lapel?"

As my mother led me out the back door she said, "Fine. You can stay here and cook, clean and take care of the dog. We're going on vacation."

We sat in the car for about five minutes until my dad exited the house and put his bags into the back of the station wagon. "I had to change shoes. Those thongs hurt my two front feet."

Off we traipsed to a campground near Glen Lake and the Sleeping Bear Sand Dunes in the northwest part of the Lower Peninsula. Based on the photos I must have been 14 or 15 at the time. I remember a dunes buggy ride where the driver swung in a sharp arc that made it appear you were going over the edge of the dune into the lake. But the thing I most remember was my dad trying to put up the tent.

Mom had gotten a big family sized tent that was set up with two center poles and six side poles. Dad, the ex-Army paratrooper-boxer with biceps so big I couldn't get both hands around them, would be the tent-putter-upper. He laid out the tent, grabbed the two poles and crawled into the tent. Watching the material rise and fall in the flattened tent as he crawled around had my mom and me in such hysterics we didn't realize he was really in trouble. When he started yelling, 'Get me out of here, get me out, I'm suffocating,' Mom opened the tent flap, calling him to follow the light. He did, rising from his tarpaulin grave and turning the air blue. (Being ex-Army and an automobile factory worker he had a rich vocabulary.)

As other campers gathered near, some to watch and others to ask him to tone down his feelings about the tent, he stared at the tent with center poles in hand. With a gleam in his eye and hatred in his heart he strode toward the tent, the center poles aimed to smite the evil in its black heart. And he re-entered the flat tent. This time his comments were about being unable to see anything and he needed help to get out. At least he wasn't suffocating.

As my mom guided him to safety a little guy, maybe 5'4" (Dad was 5'10"), walked over and softly said to my sweating father, "Having trouble buddy?"

He then proceeded to put up the tent corner poles then the center poles in the now half erect tent. In his still quiet voice he asked my dad, "Do you know how to stake the poles?"

My Dad's nod and thank you confirmed that he would be able to accomplish this complicated task. As the guy walked away my dad grumbled, "Why did that little squirt have to make it look so easy?"

Another vacation we headed north with a trailer and our route took us through Bay City. At the time a good portion of the downtown highway system was being reconstructed so there were a few detours. My college friend, Nettie, was accompanying us on this adventure.

Dad drove, Mom tried to navigate and Nettie and I sat in the back seat. After a number of turns Nettie whispered to me, "I think we've been by here already. I recognize that tree."

I relayed this information to my dad who promptly denied this was the same street, all trees look alike and he was not having any problem.

The second time I too realized it was the same tree. The third time my dad checked to see if it was the same tree and started heading *towards* the tree. (One problem with my dad's driving was you really couldn't point out interesting things along the road as he would inevitably steer that direction.) At our chorus of screams he corrected his path, pulled over to the side and told my mother to drive. She got us out of Bay City on the first try. You can take the boy out of the city but...

The summer between my baccalaureate and starting grad school I got a job working for the AT&T LongLines Group in Chicago. This was in the day when live operators completed long distance calls and I was there as an Assistant Group Operator Trainee. My senior year I had acquired a small calico cat I named Buffy. Notwithstanding that my Dad hated cats the only place for Buffy while I was in Chicago was with my parents. A stray Russian Blue had shown up the winter before. My mother had fed it but was only allowed to sneak the cat into the basement when it snowed or rained. So over my Dad's objections, "What do you suggest Daddy, I have her put down?" Buffy was brought to her new home. Where she immediately climbed the curtains and perched on the cornice.

"See," yelled my dad angrily, "see, now how are we going to get her down?"

"If she figured how to get up she'll figure how to get down. Just leave her alone she's scared of everything new and Dizzy *[our wire-haired fox terrier]* isn't helping any."

"She'll fall and hurt herself. You can't just leave her up there." With this he got a kitchen chair and tried to reach her only to receive a hiss and a swipe from her tiny paw. As he grabbed at her he almost fell off the chair. Angry because she wouldn't let him save her and turning the air blue he watched her run across the cornice, down the curtain at the other end and under the davenport.

"Trust me Daddy she can look after herself," was my only comment as he clambered off the chair with a scowl on his face.

When I came back from Chicago at the end of the summer to start graduate studies I noted that the refrigerator had a large dent in the upper freezer part. I looked at the dent with a raised eyebrow then at my mother.

"Buffy likes to sit on top of the refrigerator and Daddy closed the door on her tail one day."

"And that put the dent in the refrigerator?"

"Well you know his temper. He was just so mad at himself for hurting Buffy that he hit the refrigerator with his fist."

As I packed up for school my dad came in my room. "Are you taking Buffy back with you?"

"Well first I have to find someplace where I can keep her."

"You know she's made friends with Blue. And she gets along with Dizzy. She's got the yard and the field across the street to hunt in. Not that she can catch anything she's so small."

"Blue?"

"Well I figured since we had one cat in the house there was no reason to make the other one stay outside."

"OK Daddy you can keep my cat even though I know how much you hate cats."

His shamefaced grin told me he would have been very unhappy to lose Buffy.

One other instance showed how much he hated cats. This was after I had decided not to get my MBA but instead move back home and get a job. One day Blue got his head caught between a leaning fence post and a brick wall. We tried moving him up and down to get his head out but the more he fought the tighter it seemed his head was caught. My dad was almost in tears he was so afraid Blue would get hurt. Finally we used some cooking oil on his head (Blue's not my dad's) and he was free. But his head and body were soaked with the oil. We brought him into the basement to clean him up and at that point Buffy spotted him. I have never seen a cat's coat get that puffed in so short a time. She hissed, expanded to twice her size then took off up the stairs. It took two days before she'd get near him again.

Dad was a softie for just about any animal. We had parakeets when we didn't have cats. Often my dad would sleep in his Lazy-Boy chair with the leg rest up and Dizzy sleeping in his lap while one of the parakeets was walking around on top of my dad's head. Dad's hair was pretty much gone by then so it was comical when he had just gotten out of the shower and his head was wet. The parakeet would come in for a landing and skid off onto the dog.

Luckily Dizzy and the parakeets were good friends although one parakeet got too friendly and started acting like a dog, running alongside Dizzy, eating out of her dish, using her water bowl for a birdbath. They somehow got into the bathroom one day and Dizzy stepped on the budgie. After that all new parakeets were encouraged not to emulate their four-footed friends.

One day one of our parakeets flew out of the house. Dad couldn't bear the idea that the bird might not be able to live in the wild so he set off to hunt it down. The bird was in a big tree so my dad climbed the tree holding out his finger trying to get the bird to 'come home to Daddy.' I had a big fishing net that I was to throw over my dad's hand when the bird took the bait.

I have never been overly hand-eye coordinated so I bagged my dad's head instead of his hand. The bird took off while my dad untangled himself from the net and saw the drops of blood from where I had cut the bridge of his nose.

"Thanks but I think I'll do this myself."

Eventually he coaxed the bird to his finger and carried it back to the house to be caged for a few days until we had time to do more training. It took a week for this nose to heal.

Dad did have a temper. He never beat up my mom or tried to intimidate her but he did do a number on walls, doors, and, of course, refrigerators. Rumor was he could have risen far in the factory had he been able to control that temper. Having to work two full-time jobs for ten years probably contributed to his irritation level.

One night he was in a bad mood and we were at the kitchen table eating our dinner of salad, meat loaf, mashed potatoes, gravy and corn. I said or did something he didn't like and he lashed out and hit my arm. My mom yelled at him for hitting me. Sweeping his salad bowl to the floor he started to get up. My mom said, "If you can throw things so can I." As he left the kitchen for the bedroom where he could take a nap she nailed the back of his head with her plate. The contents of her plate were dripping down the wall so we lifted Dizzy up for an early dinner.

About an hour later my father came into the living room and sat down in his Lazy-Boy to watch TV. My mother waited expectantly for an apology. She got one but a little left-handed. "I couldn't sleep. Too much corn in my ears."

Years later I learned how really unusual wire-haired fox terriers are. In Michigan our house was on the road to the neighborhood beach. My mom and dad owned three terriers during the 25 or more years they lived there. Mom was also an elite gardener with people stopping by in the spring and summer to view the displays.

I moved to San Diego California in 1974. In 1984 I was at the America's Finest City All-State's picnic in San Diego's Balboa Park browsing literature at the Michigan table with my fox terrier, Penny, at my side. A woman walked up and said, "You used to live on Watkins Lake didn't you?"

I was flabbergasted. "How did you know?"

"I had an aunt who lived near the beach and I remember seeing a dog like that in a yard that was full of flowers and flowering trees. Your mother was quite a gardener. But it was the dog I remembered. You don't see many like that breed anywhere."

So many miles and years apart.

The most memorable event while I lived in Michigan was the Fourth of July party my husband and I threw in our house in 1971 before we got divorced.

My husband had a brother and numerous friends, most of whom were into drugs of one variety or another. Larry, a tall, well-built, good-looking blonde, was the least drug addicted. He was more into beer. He was also the most irreverent person I had ever met. He had been kicked out of all the public schools in Royal Oak (Michigan) and many military academies. One expulsion resulted from his being tasked with a speech before all the teachers and students on the wrongs of swearing, a speech he ended with, "Got that mother-fuckers." Another expulsion turned on his bringing a friend up the steps into the school medical facility on horseback, a ride that broke the friend's leg. The original injury that had initiated the ride, a slightly sprained ankle, was overlooked by medical responders.

Larry had been scheduled as Best Man for our wedding but due to a slight brawl the night before and his wife's emergency makeup job not being timely enough, he missed the wedding. Luckily my friends, Linda and her husband Don were available.

That was Larry and he was invited to the party along with his wife, many of our friends and my mom and dad.

I never knew if Mom had been drinking before getting to our house (she was not a frequent drinker) or if she was in one of her more expansive moods (doing something just to see what reaction she'd get) but soon after she got to the party she latched onto Larry. She hugged him. She followed him. She asked him for kisses. Larry appealed to my Dad, "Sam, can't you control her?" to which my Dad replied, "Hey, you're bigger than I am." By this time Larry was pretty much into his cups so his evasive moves weren't always as evasive as he would have liked. He disappeared.

My husband brought out his accordion thinking for some strange reason that the dulcet tones of a polka might settle down Mom and a few of our other inebriated friends. He hadn't meandered through half of one song when my mom grabbed the accordion saying, "Here, give me that. We need some modern music." This lasted for maybe fifteen seconds when we heard a shrill scream. "Owwwww, I got my tit caught in the accordion."

At that my Dad and I exchanged glances. "Yeah, I guess it's time to take her home."

As she was ushered to the car she let loose one last plaintive plea.

"Won't Larry kiss me goodbye?"

"Sorry Mom we can't even find him."

"Tell Larry I love him."

"Will do Mom."

Later that night we found Larry passed out under the outdoor heating oil tank. He hadn't noticed all the oil on the ground (the tank line leaked and we had not been able to stop it). The next morning he wandered around moaning about his head and the smell of oil in his hair and clothes. He did feel much better after we threw him into the lake although the smell didn't dissipate from his hair for a few days.

Dad died in 1975 at age 60 while racing the younger workers to the lunch wagon. It happened ten months before he was set to retire. His meat and potatoes diet had never made him fat but really did a number on his arteries. A typical meal was two steaks for Dad and one steak between Mom and me. A pound of bacon and a dozen eggs at breakfast were normal. Two fried chickens for dinner. I was told his blood pressure had topped out at 300. The medication made him impotent so he stopped taking it, which contributed in part to his having a heart attack and a stroke at the same time.

People told me that the whole plant was in mourning especially blacks who cried at their places on the line. Dad had taken them under his large biceps to train them for the skilled and semi-skilled jobs that had finally opened due to the Civil Rights Act. (Prior to this legislation the only jobs open to blacks at the auto plants were janitorial.) While racism ran rampant in the factories, at Pontiac Motors you didn't mess with my Dad. For years, rather than call for a forklift, they called for Sam. That had paid off with muscles that basically said, 'Cause problems for my friends, you contend with me.' No one did.

Mom said she had as many kids come to the door in tears as she did adults. They used to call him Mr. Clean due to his powerful build and almost bald head. During the summers Dad would go to the beach at the end of our street and swim for hours. (His retirement dream had been to teach handicapped children how to swim.) He would let the kids climb on his broad shoulders for hours and dive off or he'd race them to the dock and back. I can remember him saying, "Tschk, tschk," as he pretended that they were exhausting him. The spelling is the best I can do to simulate the sound.

Fifteen years later at a motorcycle rally in San Diego I spied a bike with Michigan plates. We got to talking and the guy said he came from Pontiac.

"Wow," I exclaimed, "I wonder if you knew my dad, Sam Jharmark?"

"Sammy? Oh my God are you Sammy's daughter? Of course I knew Sammy. Everyone knew him. We were all so devastated when he died. Everybody loved him."

I still miss my Dad after all these years. Even though he had worked two full-time jobs for ten years and I didn't see a lot of him while I was young he still was the perfect father. He taught me to swim urging me to swim across the lake with him, wrestled me to show women could be as strong as men. I'll never forget his wanting me to get an education not to find a rich husband (my mother's aim) but so I would never be dependent on someone else. Nor will I forget his constantly having to borrow lunch money from me when his beloved Yankees kept losing to my Detroit Tigers. Despite the continual losses, he really loved to bet on those games.

Mom moved to California to be near me and the grandsons. Over the years, she had lost all her hair from alopecia. While it was an embarrassment she had early learned to roll with the punches.

When gardening outdoors, she wore a scarf with flower-like petals. One day she felt something picking her head like being tapped with a pencil point. She put her hand up but felt nothing. Returning to her gardening she again felt the tapping. Stepping back she looked up to see a very frustrated humming bird who could not figure out why those flowers didn't have any nectar.

Her greatest triumph however was with the Jehovah's Witnesses. Despite her repeated requests to be left alone they continued to ring her doorbell. One day they were back and she answered the door dressed in shorts and a stretchy tube top. Opening the door, at the same time she opened her mouth and dropped her false teeth to the carpet. Leaning over to get her teeth she let her wig slide off. As she bent down further she loudly proclaimed, "God I hope my tits don't fall out." When she straightened up the Witnesses were gone and did not darken her door again.

SPORTS – WHEN I WAS YOUNG
Michigan, 1960 to 1965

The summer of 1960 when I was 16 I tried to water ski. My dad was friends with the ski boat owner, a fellow worker in his 20's for whom I had a massive crush. My father recognized this and made sure his friend did not take advantage of it. But I did want to learn so one day the friend tried to get me up on skis. First try I floundered. Second I floundered. By the fifteenth try I was so waterlogged inside and out that he called it quits. I don't think it was the pain of seeing me plow a deep furrow in the water it was the fear that I would eventually drown and my dad would beat the shit out of him.

That winter I tried to snow ski. My first attempts had the same results as the water skiing. However, unlike the water skiing I finally did make it down the not-so-steep slopes at Pine Knob near my home.

The ski slopes had been developed by cutting into some small hills to build up others. This left some runs being very close to the raw dirt where a hill had been sliced in half. In addition, in those early years of resort development, the parking lot and chalet were directly at the bottom of the runs with no separations.

One day I witnessed not one but two totally incongruous ski accidents.

First a guy skied into the cutout in a hill. While his arms were partially buried in the dirt it wasn't quite as bad as Wiley Coyote. His skis, however, were much the worse for wear.

Within a half hour I heard someone yelling, "Help! Help! I can't get up." This unfortunate had fallen backwards and was sitting on his skis headed toward the chalet. Someone opened the door either to enter, exit or give the guy clear sailing and he went into the chalet. The screams kind of indicated where he landed.

The high school's ski club planned a weekend at Caberfae a ski resort with the second largest vertical drop in the Lower Peninsula. 485 feet. Having since skied on real mountains I now find that vertical drop laughable. But in those days to a new ski bunny…. After numerous tries I could actually stop by turning both skies rather than snow plowing and figured it was time to challenge myself. I was going to Caberfae.

By the time we arrived I was in the middle stages of laryngitis. My skis were a little unwieldy. Keep in mind this was the era of heavy wooden skis, barely release bindings and cords that held the skis when the bindings released so there would not be the dreaded 'runaway' ski on the slope. Ski brakes were still in the future.

Off I set on the ski tow confident that I could handle the now steeper slopes. After a few runs I realized I couldn't and sought more gentle declines. I side-stepped over a ridge. As I stood above a run that looked really well groomed and straightforward one of the chaperones skied next to me.

Quietly he asked, "What're you doing here?"

"Getting ready to go down that slope."

"Really? Why?"

"Well it looks pretty smooth. No bumps or big turns."

"Hmmm," he muttered, "could be because it's the beginning of the ski jump?"

I looked at him flashes of incredulity and sheer terror flitting across my face. "Ski jump?" I whispered.

"Yeah looks like I got here just in time."

"Guess so," I murmured as I started side-stepping back up the hill.

On the other side I stood at the top of a mogul-strewn slope that ended short of the chalet. For non-skiers moguls are different sized bumps in the terrain with some as small as a turtle and others as large as an upside-down wash basin. Skiing moguls takes lots of skill in sharp turns and hopping, neither of which I had. At the bottom of the run people were gathering to head inside. As I started down I realized that not only could I not ski moguls the hill was steeper than I had calculated. The moguls were putting a serious dent in my ability to stop even when snowplowing. As I barreled down I tried to yell 'Track' the danger warning for a loose ski (or skier) in those days. But the laryngitis had now taken hold and all I could manage was a croak.

"Track, track," croaked before me as I headed towards a male threesome directly in line with my out-of-control body. Suddenly one of them looked across the baseline and cocked his head as if trying to hear something. He then looked up, saw me and his eyes and mouth opened wide. Frantically pushing his friends they all dived for cover. I hit something before embedding myself in the chalet wall. Thankfully my left ski disengaged preventing my leg from turning where no leg should turn. I knew it had disengaged because I had felt the ski when the cord had snapped it back onto my shin.

"Why the hell didn't you yell Track?"

"I did," I rasped, "I have laryngitis."

As they listened to my mangled voice along with seeing the snow stuffed into every crevice in my ski pants and jacket they took pity. They helped me disentangle from my skis and invited me in for a hot chocolate. As we sat near the fire with me nursing my hot chocolate while they drank beers one said, "What's that in your pants under your knee? Did you get snow that far up your leg?"

Looking down I saw that my left leg had one regular knee and one below it that was twice the size. Pulling up my pant leg I revealed a black and blue lump about the size of a grapefruit. One of the guys looked a little ill. "Hmmm," I muttered, "the ski must have hit me harder than I thought." They wanted me to get an X-ray to see if the leg was broken because to these experienced skiers it sure as hell looked like it was. I replied that if I could still walk it must be OK. I never did get an X-ray but my 'ski wound' got a lot of attention.

The next summer I was able to get up on water skis the first try. I could even slalom (stay up on one ski) though I had to drop a ski rather than start off on the slalom. Despite the lump and the pain it caused as it healed learning to snow ski did have its advantages.

My other sport experiences were restricted to being the last person selected for teams even though I could hit the ball out of the park and the athletic classes I had to take in college my freshman year. My grades were the lowest allowable to ensure I wouldn't have to retake the class. As one instructor noted after I had almost speared her with an arrow in archery class, she could tell I was really trying but did have a slight issue with hand-eye coordination. My score of 53 on a three-hole golf course sealed the deal.

COLLEGE DAYS – U. OF MICHIGAN
1961 to 1965

I had two dates in high school one of which I think was paid for by my Dad when I went to the Senior Prom with a college sophomore. Being tall, pudgy and the antithesis of the cutesy-submissive-little-girl role expected in the early 60's was not a recipe for garnering boyfriends. Nor was I a favorite with the in-crowd particularly after I gave a speech at the high school oration contest and got to Regionals. The speech addressed high school cliques and how they froze out and demeaned those who were deemed unworthy. Names were not named but people were easily identifiable. College brought me into a new environment where I could let myself go although maybe not always in the right direction.

During the 60's women were required to live in dormitories or sororities until seniors. Men only had to stay in purgatory their freshman year. Of course the dormitories had their housemothers and their rules but it never dawned on me that the housemothers could be, ahhh, pliable.

I was returning from a well-liquored party during an ice storm when I fell and slashed my leg. The cut was bleeding rather profusely and my gait was a little unsteady as I staggered up to the desk to sign in. The housemother smiled with grandmotherly approval her hands clasped at the level of her waistline.

"Did you have a good time dear?"

My enthusiastic but slurred reply evidently assured her of my positive experience.

She replied, "That's nice dear. Have a good night's sleep," as I staggered off to the elevators dripping blood along the way. Since coming in drunk happened more than once I never quite figured out what the real purpose was for the housemothers. (On the being drunk part my inability to drink beer was my downfall. Had beer been my beverage of choice instead of hard liquor I think the level of inebriation would have been a lot less. Despite my dad going through a case a week I got sick at the slightest sip.)

You had one way out of the dorms before senior year and that was to live in a co-op. The co-ops were organized as women-only or men-only residences with members of the opposite sex allowed in for meals supplied in exchange for work. I had met a girl named Nettie while in the dorms and our junior year we decided to try the co-ops.

My room was on the third floor with the bed next to the window. The window that opened onto the fire escape. Curfew was at midnight but the fire escape was open all night. It didn't take me long to realize that keeping my bed next to the window probably wasn't a good idea. But I did get to know Nettie better as she was a frequent window user.

Using fake IDs Nettie and I frequented the bars in downtown Ann Arbor. I can't remember who first met Bob but we soon determined that his roommate, Jake (not his real name), was with Bob because Bob had a different woman every night and Jake had never had a woman, period. Somehow Jake figured if he stuck around Bob long enough something might rub off.

The only problem was that Jake had a tendency to black out when he over-indulged. No matter what happened, if he was drunk enough he wouldn't remember it. Unfortunately for Jake his abrasive manner and remarks had made it quite clear that Nettie and I were not in his league as dating material. His conceit gave us the perfect reason to play the joke of the year. We just needed the materials and a little cooperation from Bob.

We started keeping our cigarette butts, Nettie's with lipstick and mine without. That torn nylon? Put it in the bag of tricks. Nettie had been dating someone but they had broken up somewhat amicably. We turned to him for the piece-de-resistance: a used condom. I can still see her 'Eeww' face at the ex-boyfriend's house when we picked up our stash neatly wrapped in a small sandwich bag.

By this time Bob was a little tired of Jake tagging after him every time he went out since Jake's 'style' tended to drive away some of Bob's female targets. Bob set the night. He would take Jake to a bar get him plowed and bring him back to an already staged setting. Nettie and I were to gain entrance via their second-floor back patio.

On the appointed night as we started up the stairs Bob came out of the apartment. "No," he hissed, "I couldn't get him out. Some kind of test coming up." He flapped his hands whispering, "Leave, leave."

At that point Jake started to the patio door asking Bob who was out there. Nettie and I flattened against the apartment building wall and slid around the side toward the front. Where someone had parked the gate shut. The only way out was behind the hedge that ran along the property line. The short hedge that ran along the property line. We had to get on our hands and knees to scurry out commando style and hope for another day. Keep in mind this was the 1960's when nylons and skirts were 'de rigueur' for class wear so our commando style was definitely on the girlie side.

A week later Bob got Jake out and fully loaded. Nettie and I snuck in and laid our trap. Cigarettes in the ashtrays in the kitchen and Jake's bedroom. Partially filled wine glasses with and without lipstick. The torn nylon hanging over the bedroom doorknob. Nettie was quite well endowed and donated a bra. The pillows and sheets were smeared with perfume, eye liner and eye shadow. We dabbled some watered down glue on the sheets and left the now dried out and starting to crack condom on top. As we left we sniggered at what would happen the next day when Bob had invited us to a small party.

Jake was in his glory. The lady was a fireball. Kept him up all night if you know what I mean, wink, wink. He had her phone number, was going to get with her tonight. Wouldn't be a problem she thought he was a complete stud. And she was gorgeous unlike some of the other women he'd recently met (firmly looking at Nettie and me as he made this pronouncement).

I turned to Bob. "Well Bob just what did this gorgeous lady look like?"

Shrugging his shoulders Bob replied, "Beats me I never saw a woman here last night."

Jake's voice got smarmy, "What's the matter Bob? Jealous of the dish I got? Did you get any last night?"

Bob looked at me. I looked at Nettie. She looked at me. We and the others in on the plot all burst out laughing.

"What's so funny?" Jake fumed.

After Bob told him he'd been in one of his drunken blackouts I recited to him all the things that had greeted his eyes that morning. When I got to the condom I asked, "Wasn't that condom a little dry Jake? Did you think that's how used condoms looked?"

Jake never talked to Nettie and me again. He also stopped accompanying Bob to the bars. Soon he moved into his own place and we never did hear if he lost his virginity. Assuming he would have remembered it.

Another memory of school was the day President Kennedy was shot in Dallas. Nettie and I had gone to the MUG, the cafeteria-grill that was in the basement of the Michigan Union. Connected to the West Quad dormitory the MUG was the most popular meeting place on campus. Naturally it was always loud enough that you had to shout to be heard over the din. That day Nettie and I were sitting at a booth and yelling at each other over the roar. Suddenly the roar stopped. The old cliché about dropping a pin would have been totally accurate. That sudden quiet was like a punch to the stomach.

Televisions throughout the MUG were quickly turned to Walter Cronkite. Horrified we sat there as he read from his statement then started to cry. Seeing Walter Cronkite cry was the proof of what he was saying. Walter Cronkite would not be crying if President Kennedy wasn't dead. Now that punch to the stomach spread to a knife in the heart. We were all crying. Remember this was our President. He'd started the Peace Corps on these very steps. And he was dead.

I was in the School of Business Administration at the time and had an appointment with my finance professor. I can still see myself walking across the Quad, in front of Angell Hall, up the steps of Tappan Hall, the main building for the business school. And doing this practically alone. No students hurrying to class, no one playing Frisbee, no one walking their dogs. No one. The silence was absolute. My finance teacher, a stout Republican, commented that while he didn't regret Kennedy being gone he didn't like the manner of his going. "No matter what his politics he was still a man with a family." That never set right with me even after all these years.

During the funeral my back went into spasms. The pain ran from the small of my back to my ankles and while it wasn't too bad when I was lying down, getting to and from the bathroom required a little floor time on my hands and knees. I remember watching Kennedy's funeral lying on the floor while my roommates stepped over me. I dragged myself to classes for about a week but soon the pain lessened to an unpleasant memory.

Since my father slept on a hard mattress with a piece of plywood as his box springs, I should have known there was something wrong genetically. But his back problems were supposedly from landing wrong when he parachuted out of a plane while giving instructions. I was twenty and was going to be healthy forever so what did I care. When something heavy needed to be moved, I was right there doing the work. That back pain was just an anomaly, wouldn't happen again. Was I wrong.

That summer I worked as a waitress in a semi-fancy restaurant near Pontiac. One night we were short wait-staff and were slammed with full tables. I had dinners piling up on the racks and had to serve wine to a couple. I uncorked the bottle and handed the cork to the man. He sniffed it more than once then offered me his glass. I poured it half full while glancing at the dinners waiting for my pickup. He swirled the wine in the glass then sniffed it. At this, his date (or wife) said, "Cut the crap Harry you don't know anything about wine and she's got food to serve. Let her do her job." I tried to keep my laughter in check as I hurried back to the kitchen.

In my senior year I rented one side of a duplex with an old high school chum and her female friend. We were having a get-together one night and I was loading records on the spindle. One record had multiple streaks of some white substance and I asked the chum what it was so I could have some idea of what I was going to be removing.

"Shhh," she hissed, "stop talking about it."

"About what? I just want to know what this is so I can get it off without ruining the record."

"Quiet," she hissed again, "just give me the record."

"But this is not only my record it's my favorite record. What's the problem?"

Grabbing the record from me she hissed again low enough that only I could hear. "My boyfriend was here last night. We were using that foam contraceptive when the cat jumped in the window and landed on him."

I looked at her. She looked at me. "Is that why he was acting funny when he sat down this morning?"

Another night an old high school friend called asking if he could come over. He was just visiting the area and thought he'd stop by to say hi. We chatted for a while about local and national politics, gossiped about people we had known in high school and parted around midnight. The next morning my mother called.

"Turn on your television! Turn it on! Pete (not his real name) is in jail. They arrested him for arson."

As I turned the set on I replied, "You must be mistaken Mom he was just here last night."

With that announcement my mother went bonkers. I could have been killed. He could have burned the duplex down, the world could have ended. By that time I had found the station and sure enough it was Pete. Of all the high school guys I had known I wondered why he was the one who had wanted to visit. I started to get a small inkling that I might be the type to attract men who were a little out of whack. In 1982 when a guy I had dated in 1968 was arrested as a Tylenol-Cyanide copycat I was convinced. (Before the days of tamper-proof bottles and capsules someone had put cyanide-laced capsules into bottles of Tylenol and left them on grocery shelves in Chicago. Seven people died before the source of the poisonings was determined and all bottles of Tylenol pulled from shelves nation-wide.)

My dad hated guns and killing animals for sport. To him hunting was just killing Bambi to prove you were a man. (At his size he certainly didn't have to prove anything.) I was ambivalent. I had eaten venison and liked it and we were all big meat eaters so killing a cow to eat wasn't that much worse than killing a deer. As long as it wasn't Bambi's mother. In my mind gun ownership was OK.

My attitude was changed forever when a college date took me to his apartment to get a book on anarchy he was going to loan me. (We used to kid that he was an 'anarchist' with a small 'a.') Instead he pointed a target pistol at my forehead telling me how easy it would be to shoot me. After I pointed out the flaws in his plan such as getting rid of the body, the blood, the noise bringing others to the room, he decided not to shoot. I can't remember what I did after that. Hopefully I had enough brains to report him to school authorities but from that point I was against guns and have been ever since.

I went on a personal ads date over thirty years later and my blind date met me at a table outside a fast-food place. We discussed our likes and dislikes. When we hit guns I noted I did not like them. I would not allow them in the house, would not allow the boys to have them or shoot them. I think I had a few more 'not allows' but at that point he began screaming at me to the point other customers ran into the fast-food place to call the police. I was a Communist. I was sick. I was a bleeding heart liberal (music to my ears) and on. Guns were the supreme object on earth and I had defiled them. He only left when he heard the police siren. Meeting guys like him kind of reinforced my feelings about guns and their owners.

I decided to go for my MBA at Michigan since it would only take one more year. As I've noted between June graduation and the September start of the fall term I went to Chicago as a trainee for AT&T LongLines. I found a sublease of a cozy two bedroom apartment in South Chicago. I later learned it was in a semi-ghetto area but either I was on the fringes or ghetto dwellers were reluctant to engage me.

The L from downtown stopped running at 12:30 a.m. and started again at 4:00 a.m. If I (and later Nettie and I) were imbibing at a bar that was lots of fun we had the choice of leaving early (midnight was early) or staying until the bar closed, which in Chicago was generally never. I remember one night I had taken the 4:00 a.m. L and was walking home when I noticed someone following me. At that time I was almost 5'8" (aging and collapsed spinal discs have shrunk me a few inches) and still a tad hefty. Clenching my hand into a fist I fiercely turned around.

"Why are you following me?"

The guy put up his hands. "Don't hit me lady, please don't hit me. I'm not going to try anything."

"Then why the hell are you following me?"

"Women have been attacked in this area so some of got together to kind of keep an eye out for any women walking home late at night. But I don't think you need much protection."

"You're right," I replied, "so you can go protect someone who needs it."

He looked pretty relieved as he walked away.

After Nettie joined me we checked out as many bars in downtown Chicago as possible to find one that had a band, dancing and men who were fun but had some respect for us as intelligent females, i.e. who wouldn't try to maul us during the first dance. Finally we found our gem. The guys didn't leer, they loved to dance and they kept their hands to themselves. Heaven! We later found out it was the biggest gay bar in Chicago.

At least they loved to dance.

Our most interesting experience was the night I cut my hand. I was dressed for bed in a baby doll nightgown that ballooned around my body and reached about mid-thigh. While doing the dishes I pushed the towel into a glass to wipe the inside. Unfortunately the glass broke and sliced a two-inch long gash in the fleshy part of my palm under my thumb. Trying to seal the cut with band aids did no good; it continued to bleed. Wrapping a towel around my hand I threw on a robe and raced to the sidewalk to hail a cab. One miraculously appeared and as I started to open the back door I said, "Please take me to the nearest hospital."

Looking at my voluminous nightgown he started to move the cab away. "No way lady. I ain't letting no one have a baby in my cab."

"Wait, wait," I cried thrusting my towel-wrapped hand towards him. "I'm not pregnant. I cut my hand. I just need to get to a place where they can sew it up."

He looked at me a little dubiously then agreed to let me in his cab. "There's a first aid station for the L a ways down the street. They can probably fix you up there."

Today I can't imagine anyone doing this kind of first aid without requiring I complete a hundred forms but this was the 1960s. The cab left me off. The resident on duty took a look and said I needed stitches. I think he was thankful for something to do that late at night. Of course I had to accidently insult him when I said, "If you're just a resident how can you do this? I want a real doctor."

"I am a real doctor," he sputtered. "I'm putting in my required time before I get my certification. Do you want me to sew this up or not?"

Embarrassed I agreed to his ministrations. As I look at the scar today, 46 years later, I realize that plastic surgery was not going to be his specialty. I know the glass didn't do a clean slice but the little bumps and divots that still show indicate his sewing job was not the best.

At least it was free.

That fall while I was living in a new campus apartment building everyone called the Penis I sliced open my leg using a razor. In those days the razor's head opened up for placement of double-sided blades. While I had been shaving the head had come lose so I had laid a track of cuts all the way up my leg. Across the hall Arnold heard me scream and came rushing to my room – we didn't lock doors much in those days – saying, "I'm studying to be a doctor. Let me help." He got big band aids to keep the cut sides together then wrapped my leg in gauze then tape. No matter how much I protested he was going to be a doctor and that was what doctors did. When I took the wrappings off the next day to take a shower he was pretty sad that I had destroyed his work.

BEING FEMALE IN THE '60s WORKFORCE

Michigan, 1966 to 1968

I didn't get the MBA. Too much partying and too little attention to my books resulted in some incompletes that I wasn't going to make up. Tired of school I got a job distributing industrial tool catalogues throughout the southeastern United States. I saw a lot of interesting places including colorful rivers that stank from all the chemicals being dumped in them and meat and paper processing plants where I seriously thought I was going to need a respirator and/or a barf bag.

When the company decided to distribute the books by mail rather than in person I came back to Michigan and tried to find work in the automobile plants. Unfortunately in the late '60s even with a business degree from one of the top ten business schools in the nation if you were female you had to know how to type. Being a clerk was not what I wanted to do with my degree and being unexpectedly pregnant sans husband kind of put a damper on my job hunting. (The guy never said word one to me during the pregnancy until he learned he had a son. Then he was all eager to renew acquaintances. No deal.)

I found work teaching Physical Education at a middle school. I stuck it out until I was getting serious back pain from wearing girdles to hide my pregnancy. The day one of the other teachers asked why my stomach was moving I knew the masquerade was over.

I returned home shaken and ashamed. Dad wasn't that ashamed and vowed to support me all the way. Mom was maybe a tad less supportive but took me to the family doctor who said he could have done something if I had come in sooner. I guess deep down I didn't want to do anything. Although I support the rights of any woman to get an abortion I had too much curiosity about how this child might turn out.

My obstetricians were a partnership mating a sixty-year-old doctor with one who was maybe thirty. Each visit that included the older man's ministrations also included constant exhortations to give the child up for adoption. When I mentioned this to the younger doctor, a taciturn man but quite supportive, he noted that the older doctor came from a different era.

When I went over the expected due date I was not happy. My friend Joyce had a motorcycle and we took a ride over the hills in the nearby state forest hoping to shake the baby loose. No dice.

A few days later after a doctor's visit noted by zero dilation I returned home totally bummed. My mother suggested a movie at the local drive-in that I watched but didn't really see. Back at home she lay on the couch watching TV while I trundled off to bed wondering if this kid was ever going to come out. After five trips to the bathroom she looked at me dragging back to the bedroom and said, "I think you're in labor." My water hadn't broken but I dutifully called the doctor to report events. He suggested I wait awhile but by four in the morning it was pretty clear that I didn't have normal gastro-intestinal issues.

At the hospital I went through labor pains while a woman in other bed quietly read a book. Soon a doctor appeared at my side. He wasn't my doctor but I figured maybe my doctor wasn't there yet.

"I just need to ask a few questions."

"Fine," I panted, "ask away."

"Is this your first pregnancy?"

"Yes," I groaned as a contraction hit.

"And how has the pregnancy progressed in regards to morning sickness, illnesses, etc."

"Except for getting really nauseous when I smelled hamburger cooking it hasn't been too bad." This was complimented by another contraction.

"And when did your contractions start?"

"I don't know maybe midnight, one in the morning?"

"And when did they stop?"

I looked at him aghast. "Stop? What do you mean, stop? What do you think I've been having the last five minutes?"

"You're having contractions? Aren't you Mrs. Wilson?"

"No, you idiot, she's in the bed over there. You mean you can't tell when someone's in labor?"

His face turned red as he swung to the next bed and I exclaimed, "Good lord what kind of hospital am I in?"

My doctor was in and out during the next few hours checking my dilation and noting that it wasn't much. This was not encouraging. Soon a mid-wife came in to help me in my misery.

"Here, roll on your side. It will make the contractions easier."

My bad back definitely did not like this arrangement. I had had two more incidents of muscle seizures and back pain that literally brought me to my knees, one in college and one after graduating. The contractions were aggravating my back and rolling on my side only made it worse. I noted that to the mid-wife.

"Don't be ridiculous. This will make the contractions easier. And stop being such a baby the pain isn't that bad." As she said this she was rolling me onto my side.

Looking over my shoulder I asked, "And how many children have you had?"

"Why none at all. I've never been married."

As I rolled back to my back I yelled, "How do you know what the pain is like if you've never had children? Get the hell out of here and don't come back you idiot."

A few minutes later my doctor re-appeared with a grin on his face. "I hear you've been a little upset with some of the staff."

"Jesus what do you expect? A doctor asks when my contractions stopped while I'm having a contraction. Some moron tells me the pain isn't that bad when she's never had a baby. Make sure she doesn't come back I was being polite."

His eyes lit up as he laughed and assured me she would not return. What was really amazing was that this taciturn doctor who rarely looked me in the eye during the months I had visited him was now becoming a jazzed up human who was literally clapping his hands. When we finally went to the delivery room I remarked to him about the change.

"Oh yeah all the rest is pretty boring. Delivering the baby is the fun part."

John, my 8-pound 7-ounce boy, finally made it outdoors at one in the afternoon screaming all the way. Two days later I was walking to the public telephone booths to call my mom and dad about when they would be picking me up. (I remember Mom had to drag Dad away from the nursery the previous nights. John was the son he had never had when Mom quit at one.) I ran into one of the upper-level in-crowd girls from high school who had been a target for the clique speech.

"Bunny (my nickname in high school) what are you doing here?"

"I had a baby, the same as you."

"But, I didn't hear you had gotten married."

Smiling I replied, "I didn't."

Luckily no one was between her and the telephone booth. She ripped the receiver off the phone so hard I thought she was going to break it. A half hour later she was still making calls.

As a note to the younger set, in the '60s women who had a child outside marriage were considered 'table meat' by most men, an attitude I was introduced to when I refused dates. I'm sure she had many interested in her tale.

I stayed with my parents and tried again to find work. As usual the auto plants wanted a clerk. Men in my class with the same degree were working as Foremen-in-Training. At my third rejection my Aunt Joy, who worked at General Motors, sniffed out the cause. This was the same aunt who when she found out I was pregnant clapped her hands and said, "I don't care how it happened we're going to have a baby." My Aunt Joy was the greatest person in the world and her early death from heart problems due to scarlet fever when she was a child was a tragedy. At any rate the reasons for my non-employment were that I had a child, would not be able to find suitable child care (my parents evidently were not suitable) and would cause safety issues when I walked across the factory floor in my mini-skirts. That I could dress differently was not an option.

I found work with the Detroit AT&T LongLines Division as an Associate Group Chief Operator Trainee with the promise that the training would be very short since I already had four well-praised months in Chicago under my belt.

Unfortunately at this particular time the operators were up in arms about AT&T hiring college graduates into the supervisory ranks instead of making the graduates work their way up (five to seven years if not more). I was shifted from one office to another while management dealt with the unions.

During this shifting I learned that a Management Operations Trainee position was opening so I applied only to learn that women were not allowed in that program. Women could only go to the Chief Operator level a position mostly supervisory in nature. Woman couldn't be managers. The man who got the job was fresh out of college (and not a college at the academic level of the University of Michigan) with no work experience. I thought, "This Operator job will have me working nights, weekends and holidays and I can't go higher because I'm a woman. Bullshit."

I went back to college at Wayne State University to get a teaching degree. The pay wasn't what I would have been making in the job I was suited for but it meant no weekends or nights and no discrimination. I thought.

I continued to substitute teach while taking extra coursework so I could finish the program early. My diligence worked as I completed the two and a half year program in fifteen months. The difference between the University of Michigan and Wayne was evident in my first class, Data Processing. I had taken the class at Michigan but not completed it. Wayne was on the quarter system (twelve weeks) while Michigan was semester (sixteen weeks). In the quarter allotted for the class at Wayne they covered the material the Michigan class had covered in three weeks. I saw this again when I took a Statistics class at San Diego State University many years later. SDSU was on a semester basis and they took the whole semester to cover the same material covered at Michigan in the first four weeks. I had a degree from a prestigious school and no way to use it.

One little glitch in obtaining my teacher certification was my student teaching. The mentor was a woman in her late fifties who was stuck in the 1950s. My skirts that ended a few inches above the kneecap were far too short. The proper length was below mid-calf. I told her that I did not have the money to buy new clothes for a five-month program so she gave me a C. No amount of protest could get the grade changed even when that protest came from the school administrators where I'd student taught. My first run-in with the power of tenure.

Around this time my Mom finally got to remodel the house. The house wasn't the mansion she had been aiming for all her life. Out of three marriages, two to rich men, only the poor man, my Dad, was the one that lasted. The unfortunate thing was that she had the skills to start businesses that would have allowed her to buy her dream home herself but never the intestinal fortitude to take the plunge.

She had taught a neighbor to sew but refused to join the neighbor in starting a bridal gown business. It might fail. The neighbor ended up owning three shops and a gorgeous house. The gown my Mom made for my Senior Prom prompted the photographer to take front and back shots, the only gown out of close to 350 so honored. She had the opportunity to start a pizza restaurant, a food item virtually unheard of in Michigan at that time. Those who got into pizzas at that time made fortunes. Again the fear of failure stopped her. After she moved to California she took up painting but refused to show her work because people might not like it.

The remodel was the best she could do in following her dreams. The living room was doubled with a large storage closet, sliding glass doors and a huge deck that overlooked not only the canal but part of the lake. The day the red carpet was laid she was in her glory. It was the first expensive, thick, luxurious carpet she'd ever had in a house. That night John reacted to a bout of the flu and I had to meet her at the door and prepare her for the results. John had inaugurated her carpet as Dad had run him into the bathroom from the living room spewing every step.

While I was getting my teaching degree I met Mike who was to become my first husband. We lived in a basement apartment with John who my Mom and Dad were still caring for during the day. John was my Dad's world and every day he was telling someone at the plant about what John had said or done. Even about the time he had changed John's diapers and forgot to put a diaper on top during the process. John got him right in the eye.

At any rate, back to our basement apartment. The woman in the apartment above had a habit of coming home from work, starting her bath then falling asleep allowing the bathtub to overflow. The overflow drain was plugged and while we called the landlord each time it happened he did nothing. The final straw was the night the tub overflowed and the landlord hung up on us because the moon walk was being televised.

Mike was furious. Placing buckets under the various falls he raced up the stairs and banged on the woman's door. She did not reply and the water kept running. Finally she responded with cursing about how he had woken her up and what he could do with the buckets of water in our kitchen. (What he could do is what one does during a rectal exam.)

She didn't know who she was dealing with. In those days cars were made very solid, very water tight. Tight enough to pour five buckets of water in through an open window. We heard her scream the next morning when she opened her car door. The overflow drain was fixed that afternoon.

TEACHER, TEACHER
Michigan, 1968 to 1972

While I was getting my Masters I substitute taught for the Pontiac school district. It was through substituting that I realized what school districts were doing to people of color. The white schools had everything, the black and brown schools nothing. And I mean nothing, not even books. One white school where I worked had brand-new books for every student. The black school had ten to fifteen books for each classroom to meet the needs of 25 to 35 students. The white schools had clean halls, bathrooms and lockers. The black schools had dirty halls and bathrooms and less than half the lockers needed for the number of students. The differences in the science equipment provided each school was inevitable.

I was appalled but my voicing my outrage when I subbed at the white schools only served to ensure I would be mostly subbing at minority schools. Keep in mind this is the school district that distinguished itself as the first in the nation where buses were burned when the Supreme Court ordered busing for racial integration in education.

One day I was called to take over for a teacher who had suffered a nervous breakdown. When I got to the middle school I realized it was on the edge of the ghetto and this particular teacher had been assigned the math and science classes for the slow students, i.e. those of color. And they weren't happy about being in the slow classes. Which was why the teacher had suffered a nervous breakdown.

My first day one of the black students slouched into class, refused to take his seat and looked at me with a smirk on his face. The other students were waiting to take their cue from him.

"We ran that other teacher out and we're going to run you out too."

"Oh yeah?"

"Yeah!"

"So how are you going to do that?"

"I ain't telling you nothing. You'll see what we're gonna do when we do it."

"I bet I will. But you got a problem."

"Oh yeah, what's that?"

"Well, it's a piece of paper."

"Piece a' paper?" he responded, looking around at the floor and smirking. "I don see no piece of paper that gonna stop us from running you out."

"You won't see it here. It's a paycheck. I get one every two weeks and as long as I get one I'm staying. So sit down."

Momentarily hindered he thought for a minute. Then a light bulb went on. "You won't want that check when we get done."

Shaking my head I resorted to my kind of reasoning. A threat. "You do not want to be on my bad side until the end of school because it will get very painful."

His smirk started to fade. "Yeah, why?"

"First I know they use the paddle here and the principal is the one who uses it. *(The principal was a 6'2" black man who brooked no misbehavior when the miscreant could be identified.)* Second I have no problem going to your house and telling your parents what you're up to in trying to get rid of me. Third, if those don't work, I'll tell my boyfriend's biker pals where you live. So take your pick or sit down and let's get started with today's lesson."

I had no further trouble with him except the usual acting up with kids in seventh and eighth grade. As the year progressed I helped a number of them get out of the slow classes into the regular school program. When they realized I didn't care what color they were as long as they were willing to do the work more came around and stopped causing problems.

I think another incident also created some trust. I had a paddle that I sometimes rapped on my desk to get attention. One day the kids had their desks all turned around before I got into the room. After repeatedly asking one boy (who, at 15, was a tad too old for 8th grade) to move his desk, I rapidly brought the paddle down on his desk to make my point. Just then he decided to straighten his desk placing his hands at the top to swing the front around. My paddle connected with his hands.

He screamed, I screamed. The class became totally silent. I started apologizing almost to the point of tears. He said to forget it the fault was his for not moving the desk sooner. I said it was my fault I shouldn't have slammed the paddle down. This went back and forth for a few minutes until I offered to take him to the nurse or emergency to check his hands. He declined but I think he and the others had an attitude change because I admitted being in the wrong and basically asked him to forgive me. In my experience not many black students had heard that from a white teacher.

The principal was pretty smart relative to handling the students and garnered a lot of respect from most. I had heard that on the last day of school students would damage the cars of teachers they didn't like. So the day before the last day the principal mentioned to all the teachers that they might want to leave their cars elsewhere the next day. I asked him if he left his car elsewhere. He said he didn't have to because he always picked one or two of the worse kids and told them if anything happened to his car he would come to their houses and personally beat the shit out of them. He noted that in ten years his car had never been touched. So when two girls who I had been totally unable to reach threatened to damage my car I responded with the same words as the principal. My car wasn't touched the last day either.

One thing that puzzled me while teaching at that school was the seemingly political ignorance of the minority parents. When I heard Robert Kennedy was assassinated in 1968 I was driving to work and arrived in tears. After JFK Bobbie was my hero. While civil rights activists accused me of being apolitical because I wouldn't go on the road to fight for black rights (in the fall of 1963 my college co-op was SNCC headquarters), I felt I was contributing something by getting blacks into the main-stream classes in school. So when I got into the classes and heard kids cheering that Kennedy was dead I was flabbergasted. Pointing out that Kennedy was fighting to get the Civil Rights Bill passed fell on closed minds. It left me shaking my head in disbelief.

I received my teaching certificate and in 1969 ended up in the same all-white junior high school I had attended years back. But all-white definitely did not mean all-OK. A small number of students lived in houses with dirt floors and no central heating (this was Michigan remember) or with relatives in over-crowded conditions. The teachers, particularly those from the area, knew who the drunks and child/wife beaters were. These students had few chances and acted-out accordingly. However, by the second year I had few difficulties in the classroom. Grabbing a taller student's arm and physically lifting him off his feet to make my point about not terrorizing a fellow teacher may have had an impact.

That is not to say I didn't have difficulties with the principal. This was the era when women did not wear pants to school. No slacks, no jeans, no matching pant suits. Skirts and nylons (you got demerits for no nylons). The school counselor with twelve years of tenure had tried to rally the women teachers to oppose this dictum but none had the nerve. Then there was me.

This was my first year. Two weeks into classes the counselor and I showed up in pants suits. We were told by the principal to go home and change. We both replied that forcing us to wear skirts when the men did not have to wear skirts was discriminatory. The principal backed off but got back at me my second year by writing a performance report recommending I not get tenure. I fought, he lost. From that point we rarely saw him outside his office.

Students wanted to take my business classes because I didn't use the assigned book (totally boring). The book's subjects were covered but differently. Explaining capitalism was accomplished by reading books, both positive and negative, about Carnegie, Rockefeller, Morgan and presenting reports to class. Economics included simulations where the students started businesses, sold products and services, hired each other, had to pay for rent and food. For them, the topics were eye-openers. I even got two of the worse slackers in the school to do projects. My reading to the classes from The Jungle by Upton Sinclair was done to illustrate what prompted the passage of Federal and State laws such as the FDA and EPA.

That created a few waves. The first wave was the students who took the class before or after lunch particularly when I hit the parts about rats being included in making sausage. The second wave was the parents who did not appreciate that I taught the truth about how business owners and government had colluded to oppress Native Americans, immigrants, minorities and workers. A number wanted me removed for Communist leanings. Another trip to District headquarters squelched that.

The annual Ninth-Grade Spring Trip to Washington D.C. was the most interesting. The criteria for admission on the trip were decent grades and no bad behavior during the school year. But the vice principal, some other teachers and I wanted all the kids to go. For some it might be their only opportunity to see a world other than the hovels where they lived. The year I went on the annual trip the vice-principal and I had all the rejects on our bus. Interestingly enough our bus was the only one that did not have problems with alcohol, smoking or sex. As one kid said, "You and Mr. X had faith in us. We couldn't let you down."

Mike and I were married in 1970 I think and around April of 1971 I was pregnant with Josh. The only problem was that women had to leave teaching when they started to show around the fourth or fifth month. Too much negative influence on these impressionable youngsters you know. They might see a pregnant teacher and start fornicating under a desk.

That summer Mike and I went to a party at the house of a fellow teacher. I was definitely showing by then as the baby was due in late December.

The principal took one look and said, "You're pregnant. You can't start this fall. Why didn't you tell us so we could get another teacher?"

"I didn't tell you because I intend to work until I have the baby."

"But you can't work. No district in the state allows women to teach past the fifth month."

"Then I'll sue the district and the state. The Civil Rights Act of 1965 covers women and being pregnant doesn't make me any less capable of teaching."

The president of the union piped up, "But it's in our contract."

"Then I'll sue you too."

The principal shrugged at the union guy. "I guess we have another item for negotiations."

I was one of the first teachers in Michigan to teach to my last month but that year I had plenty follow my footsteps. The union and district had negotiated that the teacher had to provide a medical report every month confirming that she was still capable to teach. When I presented my first report no one knew what to do with it so I had to write the procedure for the district.

Before the first one was due however my principal noted that the monthly report was probably going to be overkill. I think it was after I participated in the Teacher-Student Exhibition Basketball Game. The students kept threatening to use me as the basketball. When I got tired I just lay down on the court. It was a good ploy, helped us get a few points.

HUSBAND NUMBER ONE
Michigan, 1970 to 1972

Being the typical '60s male Mike didn't believe in sharing the housework. He hadn't made the mess why should he clean it up. Since I was working full-time as well as taking care of John plus Mike's two kids on weekends I didn't cotton to this mentality. One day he went to get dressed for work but had no clean underpants, socks or shirts. Turning to me with a puzzled look he asked, "Where are my clean clothes?"

I innocently responded, "I didn't dirty them so I didn't wash them."

We had no more arguments about sharing the work.

His kids were Little Mike, a seven-year-old boy and Sheila, a five-year-old girl. Due to his inability to hold onto a job or money, which suddenly appeared after we were married and I started teaching, he was constantly behind on child support. His ex-wife used this to stop visitation.

Unfortunately for her she didn't know who he was married to. I had only taken business law classes at Michigan but I knew how to read the statutes. I did some research, contacted an organization fighting for men's rights in divorce and started documenting the visitation problems. After a month or so we had the evidence and presented it to the Friend of the Court, an office designed to advocate for the children in a divorce. She was ordered to cooperate with visitation.

It was obvious Little Mike was under tremendous stress from his mother. Stress that included memorizing and reciting poetry or being beaten with a coat hanger if he didn't.

Intelligence-wise he was superior to most kids his age and had an almost photographic memory. That was the talent his mother was attempting to display. Mike had tested out at 135 IQ so it figured some would rub off on his son. When Little Mike was over he would write plays that he and John would act out. (John was also pretty advanced having learned to read and count when he was four.)

The daughter had problems and expressed them by sitting on a couch and banging her head against the back of it or staring at you while she peed her pants. I cured her of both habits in a hurry. When couch pillows are removed and you hit your head on the frame or the wall it hurts. You stop banging your head. When you have to sit on plastic pillows in your own pee or go outdoors wearing plastic bags under your clothes you stop peeing. The mother handled the problem by changing her every time she did it. I didn't. Nighttime 'accidents' took more time. Mom had revolving mattresses. I had a dry mattress or blankets on the floor. She quickly learned how night-time drinks and refusing to use the bathroom before bedtime contributed to having accidents so they soon stopped.

Mom didn't like the fact that her daughter didn't mess herself at our house. Nor did she like that when she sent them over in rags, particularly during the winter, I bought them new clothes. In one instance, for which I took pictures for the Friend of the Court, the kids were at our snowy front door dressed in undershirts, underpants, socks, sweaters and shoes that were too small – their toes were sticking out. When they returned from visitation, she promptly burned the new clothes. At least I understood why the daughter had issues. (After the pictures, rags and shoes went to Friend of the Court, the kids were decently dressed when picked up.)

Despite getting visitation and having a responsible, mentally-stable wife, Mike wouldn't stop drinking or using uppers and downers. His brother, Bob, was a heroin addict who had nailed his Christmas tree to the ceiling and took it down in July. Staying around those two was not in the cards.

I tried to work with Mike by insisting he get medical care. The medications to stop him from drinking worked for a while but the urge was greater than the desire to resist. A few days after he bought a Mustang Mach I from Bob he crashed it and took out someone else's brand-new Cadillac. A year later he said he had been trying to commit suicide but the reasons were so flimsy that I was sure it was purely due to drinking.

That little escapade reduced me to driving an ancient convertible. It was so bad that the police officer who stopped me walked around the car, approached the driver side, looked at me then said, "Lady, this car has so many violations I'd be here an hour writing them up. Don't let me see you in this car again or I'll have it towed." Luckily a few months later my parents purchased a new sports car so I got the old station wagon. (That red Pontiac Firebird did make my Dad's heart sing.)

While I was driving the convertible Mike was driving a car that was in better condition. But it was a stick shift and I couldn't drive a stick. One day we were at a friend's house and, as usual, he was drunk. I told him we needed to leave as he was getting to the point where he'd be too drunk to drive. Laughing he said, "If you want to go why don't you drive yourself." Snicker, snicker, she has to stay. She can't drive a stick.

I got in the car, started it, promptly stalled it then restarted, re-stalled. The friend's husband, who had known me a lot longer than Mike, gave me some basic instructions. I restarted, went a few feet, stalled, started, went a few more feet, stalled. The driveway was pretty long and Mike was walking by my side ridiculing me at every stall. By the time I had jerked and shuttered to the highway I was driving further and stalling less. As I pulled out on the highway I flipped him the bird then looked in the rearview mirror to see him with his mouth hanging open.

A few hours later my friend's husband gave him a lift home. He said, "I never thought you'd do it."

I replied, "Yeah and now that I know how to drive it you get the convertible and I get the stick. And you know I'll take it because I always leave for work before you even wake up." (At the time he worked nights and he did indeed get stuck with the convertible most of the time.)

In the end Mike's inability to handle the booze did him in. We had dragged his ex to court so many times she left for Oklahoma. Using my super-human sleuthing techniques (going through her garbage) we found her after a few weeks. Mike was able to get Little Mike back but not Sheila. Considering she had to see a psychiatrist at age five I don't know that I would have wanted her back.

Mike was in and out of jail so often on drunk-driving charges that I got tired of bailing him out. One time I had his bags in the car. After I bailed him out I drove to a lonely highway near his mother's house then threw him and his bags out in the middle of a snow storm. Took him over half the night to get to her house.

At one hearing while I was pregnant I had John with me and when I left, knowing Mike was going to spend a number of days in jail, I was so angry I was crying. Poor little John was holding my hand crying along with Mama with his teddy bear firmly clutched in his hand.

A guy in the parking lot asked, "You don't have the money?"

I responded, "I'd let the bastard sit in jail but he'll lose his job and this crap has gotten us on the edge so much it's bail or food."

The guy handed me the bail money and said, "Get rid of him, he isn't worth it to make your son cry like that."

The next day I discovered he hadn't paid the mortgage on the house for four months. (I wondered why he had been so diligent in getting the mail.) When he finally got home I told him I wanted a divorce because he was too expensive. He moved out a few weeks later. Pregnant or not I wasn't putting up with him any longer.

The union had also negotiated that the teacher had to start the term to keep her place so that meant I had to be ready for school when the second term started February 6. By January 2 when the baby was still happy in his/her little cave I started getting nervous. Finally my doctor agreed to induce labor on January 15. She wore really long false eyelashes and while I was delivering I asked if she had ever lost any in the childbirth (or in the child). She assured me they were on very tight.

When my soon-to-be-ex-husband saw Josh, his 10 pound 2 ounce boy, he wanted to sign him up immediately for the Detroit Lions football team. The doctor said it was lucky we had induced labor as we might have had to blast him out. My mother, who was hoping for a girl, was quite disappointed and had to take back all the pretty little new-born dresses she had bought. Not that they would have fit a baby that weight anyway boy or girl.

The day I had Josh the temperature had dropped to minus 18 degrees and the outdoor pump at the house had frozen. I did the old thermometer in hot water trick a few times to keep my temperature high enough that I could stay in the hospital until the cold snap ended. Finally they threw me out and I went to my mother's house. But she was a clutter hound and I'm a semi-neatness freak (although I hate to dust) so after two days I went home. I made certain a very large, very new light bulb was in the pump cabinet.

Mike was gone by then but not the bills. I had to borrow close to $8,000 to get the mortgage payments up to date and install a gas heater. (Some mornings when we got up both the oil line and the pump had frozen meaning I had to bundle up two hungry, crying kids, drive 20 miles to my parent's house, take a shower then go to work. It's very discouraging to look at a thermostat where the bottom number is 40 and the needle is hanging off the end.)

With John I had been 175 pounds when I got pregnant (on a 5'8" frame) and weighed 165 when I left the hospital. With Josh I had been 160 pounds at impregnation and 185 when I left the hospital. In addition to feeling like a cow I also had nothing to wear. My mother was heavy so I could wear some of her clothes but the wardrobe was limited and I am not into being overweight. I dieted stringently. As little as possible passed my lips.

Then I had some standing blackouts. When it happened I had no idea what was going on. I'd be in front of the class giving instructions. A black circle at the edge of my peripheral vision would start narrowing until all I could see was a point of light. Within what felt to me to be a few seconds the pin-point would expand back to normal range and I could see everything again.

After the third time the students began asking me what was wrong. I asked them what had happened. They said I would be talking then my speech would start slowing. I would stop for a second or two then start speaking again although slowly. Then my speech would speed up until it was back to normal. I wasn't slurring my words I was just getting slower and slower. And I hadn't slouched or looked like I was going to faint.

A few tests with the doctor revealed I was extremely anemic. After a series of iron and B12 shots in my bazoo three times a week I was OK. But that was one of the weirder experiences I've had related to a medical issue.

Despite it all Mike and I remained in touch because Josh was his son. Toward the summer of 1972 he started talking about going to California with his brother to check things out. Did I want to come along? Josh would be seven months old,

John five years and Bob's wife would be along to help care for the kids. I started making plans and sure enough he got another DUI and ended up in jail again.

I decided the hell with him I'll go to California myself. I asked one of my students if she wanted a trip to California in exchange for babysitting and she jumped on it. Josh still was not sleeping through the night yet. (He didn't until he was a year old. At times I had to go to bed at 6 p.m. just to get six hours sleep because he cried so much. Then my mother would say he slept like a log all day with her.) Even with the sleep issues the trip was fun and I gained a good impression of the cities lining the coast from San Diego to San Francisco. I particularly liked Costa Mesa in Southern California. On the way back to Michigan I set my sites on eventually moving to California.

When I got the divorce I had asked for the minimum on child support, $10 a week. Josh started walking, went on visitations with Mike and came home stumbling and smelling of beer. A visit to the house where Mike and his new girlfriend lived revealed pills on a coffee table within reach of little hands. Rather than fight with him about visitation I knew the perfect response. Even though I had not wanted it child support bestowed power. I took him to court for non-payment of child support knowing he would not show. He fled to Georgia where Larry had friends and effectively eliminated the visitation problem.

Based on comments from my old friends and Mike's mother Mike kept drinking and never held steady employment. He finally married a nurse who supported him. But she rejected Little Mike who ended up living with Mike's mother in Florida.

When I moved to California I did not tell Mike where because I was afraid he might try to snatch Josh just as he had snatched Little Mike. To me, considering his mother's issues, taking Little Mike was more like a rescue operation. Plus I would be there to provide the mothering he hadn't had. (That Mike's ex never put up much of a fight to get Little Mike back kind of proved the point.) But Josh in Mike's drug and alcohol lifestyle was not going to happen.

When Josh was eight I notified Mike's mother where we were. For some reason (her lame excuse was she lost the information) she never told Mike. Mike knew some of my co-workers and could have asked them for my address but hadn't made too big an effort to find them.

Around the time Josh turned 18 Mike tried to re-establish contact. Having three heart attacks in one year may have been the motivation. Josh said if he hadn't been interested for 18 years he could go to hell now. I was told Mike died when he was 55 around 1997. But doing a net search I found enough corroborating evidence to know he and Little Mike live in Port Huron, Michigan. I can't remember who told me he was dead. Maybe they thought I was still after him for the child support.

Years later someone said I was disloyal and didn't believe in the bonds of marriage. I replied that I believed in the marriage bonds but not as strongly as I did in self-preservation. Masochism just ain't my style.

NUDGED TOWARDS CALIFORNIA
Michigan, 1972 to 1973

Even though I sold the house Mike and I had bought, I still had major bills. I decided to stay in Michigan for two years, continue teaching, get the bills paid off then move to the land of sunshine. I remember a dream where I saw the word 'Michigan' in gray covered with white snow and the word 'California' in bright yellow with the sun shining behind it. Even my subconscious knew where I wanted to be.

By age five John was beginning to demonstrate his ability to get what he wanted, stay out of trouble or both. He was big for his age and active with dark curly brown hair and an impish grin. One night my Mom and I took John and Josh to the drive-in. The idea was that they would sleep in the back seat while Mom and I enjoyed the movie. As soon as we had parked John asked for a fountain drink. Since he had had a drink before we set out and I didn't want to spend half of the movie traipsing back and forth to the bathrooms I declined his request.

Within a few minutes I heard a tiny voice from the back seat.

"I'm so thirsty. Thirsty, thirsty, thirsty. I sure would like a drink. Just a little drink. Cuz I'm so thirsty. Thirsty, thirsty, thirsty." This went on for about five minutes until my mother, trying hard not to laugh, said, "I can't take much more of that. Get him a drink. I'll do the bathroom duty."

During this time period I took John on a horse ride. I've looked through my picture albums and racked my brain to remember where and when but the date just won't come. John was around five or six so it had to have been in Michigan. At any rate the events are crystal clear in my mind.

We had gone to a horse ranch where we were going to ride horses with John in the saddle in front of me. But before our group left one of the cowboys suggested we let John ride a little pony by himself. The pony would be in a corral on a rope led in a circle by the handler.

John was thrilled. The pony plodded in a circle seeming almost asleep as John kept pushing himself up and down in the saddle crying, "Let go of the rope, let go of the rope. I want to ride by myself."

So the handler let go of the rope and the sleepy, plodding pony took a sharp right turn and jumped through an opening in the corral where someone, unknown to the handler obviously, had taken out some of the crossbars. The handler flew after the pony and I flew after the handler.

That pony could run. John bounced around the saddle holding onto the pommel for dear life and screaming bloody murder. The handler soon tired and dropped out of the race while I carried on. To the side I noted a posse running to their horses pulling themselves into their saddles just like a real cowboy movie. The thundering herd took off in pursuit of the pony that began to not only run faster but into an area with lots of trees.

Realizing the posse was spooking the pony worse I yelled for them to back off as I ran closer. Finally the pony stopped, lowering its head to snip at blades of grass. By this time, John was in full flood crying for me to stop the horsie because he wanted off.

I snuck up to the horse and reached for the rope. The horse shied and moved off a few feet. I slowly snuck up again and again tried for the rope. No luck. The pony skittered away.

We went through this song and dance about five times until finally I was close enough to grab the stirrup with one hand and the bridle with the other. By this time I was crying, John was crying and the posse was slowly sneaking up on the tableau. (They later told me it was over a mile from the corral before that critter stopped.)

I waved them away because I now had control of the pony and didn't want it rearing before I could get John off. As I reached up John looked down with his excited, red, tear-stained face and said, "That was fun mommy! Can we do it again?"

While putting in my two years before moving I needed a place to stay. I've always looked at houses as an investment that provided living space so I bought a fixer within four miles of my parents. I have never bought a new or well-maintained house because I always intended to make a profit off what I could do myself to remedy the problems. Of course paying a much cheaper price was a big inducement. However I never imagined the consequences of some of the 'fixes.'

The beginning of each semester the teachers had a party. I offered my house that year not realizing the work needed to make it habitable. When the crowd arrived the put-together table and chairs I had bought were not ready. I assigned duties and soon the table and chairs had been assembled. Not, however, without major grousing by some of the teachers.

I rented rooms to make the payments and that created some interesting situations.

A guy I had met while he was substituting at my school was from Texas. He volunteered his truck to pick up a washer and dryer I had purchased. We loaded the appliances, started out then got stuck in the traffic jam that always occurred when the auto plants let out at 3:30 p.m. After fifteen minutes in the jam my friend-driver decided to take another route and inexplicably made a U-turn to get into traffic flowing the other way. Unfortunately he neglected to check the next lane and smashed head on into another truck buckling his truck's hood, front fenders and bumper. After we limped home and unloaded the washer and dryer downstairs he sat on the kitchen floor with a beer. My current renter wandered in.

Addressing the guy the renter commented, "I noticed the plates. Are you from Texas?"

My friend nodded his agreement.

"Wow," the renter continued, "they sure make trucks different in Texas."

My friend nodded his agreement, finished his beer and left, never to return.

That renter was not a long-time resident. He was evicted the day he came in drunk and said his friends had told him he deserved more than a room for the rent and when was I going to come across.

Another renter was a tall, lanky red-headed engineer whose degree, I soon learned, was not the mechanical variety. I can't remember why I wanted to apply acoustic tiles to the ceilings. Maybe the ceilings were water-stained from roof leaks or the plaster had gone bad. For whatever reason, the engineer was more than ready to help. We worked our way across the living room using black mastic to attach the tiles. At the last row the tiles were a tad too large and I suggested we trim them. The engineer responded that they only needed to be snugged in. There was plenty of room.

As he snugged them in I stood back and watched a slight ripple in the tiles become a full flood as they all started to part from the ceiling.

I yelled, "Stop, stop! The tiles are coming down."

He jumped off the ladder and moved it to a large bulge. Pushing on the bulge he yelled, "Help me, help me! We can keep it up."

Folding my arms I drily replied, "I don't think we have enough ladders or time. Look out below she's coming down."

"No," he screamed as he jumped off the ladder and moved it to another bulge, "we can stop it! We can keep them up!"

After moving the ladder again and exhorting to me to help he stopped and looked up in utter misery as down the ceiling did indeed come. Luckily most of the tiles landed mastic side up so putting them back was easy. Where they landed mastic side down, removing the mastic gave my carpet kind of a tie-dye pattern. (We had moved the drop clothes as we moved down the living room.) Looking at the mess I thought, 'What I would have given for a video camera.'

As winter set in I came home one day to find the floor of my dining room that was adjacent to the back door covered with carpenter ants. These ants aren't biting ants they are just really big. I can remember John on the porch crying because I wouldn't let him in the house and he was cold. I kept begging him to stop crying because cleaning up the ants was enough of a problem. Josh, still asleep from his nap at my Mom's, had no idea of what was going on but John sure did. It took me an hour to get rid of the ants and seal up the crack in the half basement where they had emerged. Trying to explain the problem to John didn't work too well because he cried every time he looked at where the sea of ants had been. This was not one of my better days.

That winter (January through March of 1973) we had some major temperature drops. On more than one occasion I had to bundle the kids into a car that was way too cold even though it had been in the detached garage. Driving to my Mom's with two shivering, crying children was a great way to start the day.

One storm resulted in school being cancelled and I was snowed in for three days with my little cherubs. On the fourth day I tried to get out of the driveway that had been torn up the previous fall for installation of the municipal sewer pipes. After an hour of effort in the mud and snow and a number of expletives I looked at my crying children and gunned the motor. (John didn't do well when I got angry and trying to get a car unstuck was not conducive to calm. Josh generally took his lead from John). After visiting with my mother and stopping at the grocery store I returned home to call the realtor who had sold me the house.

"Put the house on the market. I can't take this anymore."

"But, but, you just bought it in October. You've only been in there five months."

"That's five months too long. Sell."

The spring of 1973 I made plans to move to California. My Mom and Dad weren't happy about it but I knew that if I stayed in Michigan until my Dad was ready to retire in 1976 I might meet someone who wouldn't want to move and I'd be stuck in Michigan forever. Being celibate during that time was not an option.

Studying the crime rates and cost of rentals for cities along the coast I decided to head for San Diego. Preparatory to the move, I had been sending out resumes looking for business-related and teacher-related positions with no luck. As summer rolled around I decided to just go for it. My fellow teachers had a pool betting that I would be back in the fall because in 1973 there was such an excess of teachers in California that many were flipping hamburgers at McDonalds. I told them I would not return and as I look back on it, I should have joined the pool. It would have paid off some bills.

CALIFORNIA, HERE I AM

San Diego, 1973 to 1974

Ocean Beach

My parents came with me to take care of the boys while I looked for work and found a place to live. I don't remember if I had a job when they left after three weeks but at least we had found a small apartment over a garage in Ocean Beach, a small beach community in San Diego. The rental unit was like many in Ocean Beach at the time (and still is 40 years later). The front of the lot contained a small rented house with a small attached studio behind the house. Two apartments were over garages that were also being rented, mostly to people with motorcycles. My unit had one bedroom where I stashed the boys and I slept on a sofa bed in the living room. I think it came partially furnished but so long ago I'm lucky I remember it at all.

I found a job in the Purchasing Department of National Cash Register in Rancho Bernardo as their first female Material Planner. Another woman had been hired as an Assistant Material Planner Trainee but she didn't have a degree or much work experience. I was told her being married to one of the managers had a lot to do with her appointment and at first I relegated the remark to sexism. Soon she demonstrated that her ability to do the job, trained or not, was pretty limited so it had to be the marriage.

I later learned that NCR, like most companies with Federal contracts, was being chased by the Justice Department for sex discrimination in employment and she was their token female in Purchasing. When I came along, University of Michigan business degree and all, I was like manna from heaven. A woman who might actually be able to contribute to getting work accomplished.

NCR had been one of the companies to which I had sent resumes while still in Michigan. I got the job by seeing an ad in the paper for the Material Planner position then applying for the position in person. The day I applied I was hired. I later learned the hiring person was the same person who had sent me a letter stating they had no open positions meeting my qualifications. Of course the time between the rejection and the hire did include inquiries from the Feds about job discrimination.

I found a baby-sitter, a grandmotherly type in her fifties who would come to my apartment, and proudly went to work on a Monday. I was in California, I had a place to live and I had a job. I was going to make it. I came home and found John standing at the top of the stairs in tears holding Josh up so that he wouldn't sit in his obviously overloaded- not-changed-the-whole-day-diaper. Charging into the apartment I found grandma sitting in the chair, drunk, watching television in a bra and skirt and nothing else. If John had not been there crying I would have thrown her over the balcony.

The next morning when I was supposed to be going to work I had to call about my disaster. Luckily the Purchasing Agent was understanding. He told me to stop crying, get another babysitter and they would see me when I could get in. Two days later, mission accomplished, I was back to work. This time I chose a woman who had a child Josh's age and would be there when John came to her house after school. And she didn't drink.

NCR was a strange place to work. They had the most arcane personnel policies I ever encountered. The Purchasing Department (that I remember) was composed of the buyers, planners and expediters. To become a Junior Buyer you had to work a certain number of years as an Expediter. To become a Buyer you had to work a certain number of years as a Junior Buyer. Or have a college degree. Except if you were a Junior Buyer and got your college degree while being a Junior Buyer you still had to complete your quota of years in grade to become a Buyer. As one Junior Buyer (who had gotten his college degree) noted NCR was the training ground for buyers in San Diego County.

The Material Planners not only planned the purchase and delivery schedules of materials they also were responsible for ensuring the materials got to the production line. This was not always easy.

First, many normally common parts including fasteners (nuts, screws, bolts) were special design therefore not readily available as off-the-shelf items. To compound the fact that they had to be specially made they also had to use more exotic metals meaning any metal shortage could put the delivery schedule months down the road. Therefore an entire product line could be months behind delivery for want of a simple screw or bolt. This logic, or lack thereof, ran throughout the various NCR product lines.

Second, the warehouses were disorganized disasters. At Rancho Bernardo I planned fasteners. When the computer told me there were fasteners but the production line foremen told me there weren't I went to the warehouse, found the parts and wouldn't leave until they had been sent to production. This did not make me popular with the Warehouse people. A few times I was banned until my manager interceded noting that I was keeping the production line running and therefore ensuring their jobs. I often wondered if the tarantula I saw on the stairs leading into the warehouse was there by nature or design. (While walking up the stairs I noticed everyone giving a wide berth to this hand-sized black hairy lump. I made the same detour but took my time so I could really observe it. Another cool introduction to California.)

My modus operandi has always been completing my job efficiently so I would have time to learn new things. I was put in charge of a sub-assembly in a facility in the Southeast. The days for meeting critical points on the sub-assembly schedule kept getting missed due to, according to the facility manager, a lack of parts. I asked one of our buyers who was going to the facility to look for my parts. He found them in a pile ten feet tall in the middle of the facility's warehouse. The next day I talked to the facility manager and noted where the parts were and if they weren't on the assembly line by that afternoon he would be discussing the problem with the VP of our facility. The completed sub-assemblies were shipped within a few days. I learned later that I was a total emasculating bitch who had been hired because I was a woman not because I was competent.

The crowning touch however was the Industrial Engineer job.

After six months on the job I had been promoted to material planning for new products, an assignment that normally took two to three years of experience. Being analytical I just intuitively understood the planning process better than others who had more experience. The logic of the cycle and its risks had enabled me to find problems with the process, the way we took delivery and accounted for it, etc. My suggestions for change had been good. As a result I got new product planning.

But again I determined how to do the job efficiently and had to look for new conquests to fill up my time. An Industrial Engineer job came open and I applied. The requirements were a business degree (check), experience as a planner (check) and the ability to analyze process and improve on it (check, check). I was qualified. No. Wait a minute. I had one little problem. At NCR in order to go from one position to another you had to be earning within 5% of the lowest pay rung of the new position. I was earning 20% less than the lowest pay rung. Sorry do not qualify. At first I thought it was just a rather convoluted way to keep a female out of the classification but no it was true. One of the other Planners had applied and he was 10% below so he couldn't qualify either.

It was time to find another job.

During all this, adventures were occurring on the home front. The apartment across from mine over the garages was occupied by a woman (Jane?), her two kids, her boyfriend and friends of her boyfriend. They all wore leather vests, chaps, steel-toed boots and hair, lots of hair. And of course the friends and the boyfriend smelled because that is what all big, bad outlaw bikers do.

I'd been introduced to bikers while married to Mike. His brother, a heroin addict and dealer, also had grown marijuana for his buddies. At Bob's parties the bikers regaled us with tales of terrorizing towns, escaping from the cops, beating people up and threatening homeowners with guns up the homeowner's nose (some of whom were Bob's neighbors). So bikers were not new to me and I was not afraid of them.

The boyfriend and his friends liked to party. Until real late. Like four or five o'clock in the morning. After about two weeks of this I complained to the girlfriend (the apartment was in her name). Not only was I unable to get any sleep, which was affecting my job, but John was unable to sleep, was scared shitless with what he was hearing and it was affecting his attention at school. After keeping me awake for an entire year Josh slept through the whole thing.

"But they're Hells Angels. I can't tell Hells Angels to be quiet."

"I don't give a shit who they are. If they don't quiet down I'm reporting them."

"Reporting them? They'll kill you!"

"Maybe but then the cops will know who did it. At least they'll go to prison for it and it'll be quiet."

The noise did not abate. I was on the beach a few days later, saw a cop and noted the parties, location and, more important, the drugs. (After Mike and Bob I could recognize just about anything.)

"You know we're supposed to take names when people make complaints?"

"You know if you take my name and it comes out you may be making two kids orphans."

"I'll see what I can do."

Three or four days went by and it was the weekend. The woman in the front house, I think her name was Linda, was out in the yard playing with her kid. I noted how quiet it had been. Jane must have talked to her boyfriend and they had decided to be a little more considerate.

"Considerate? I don't think so. They were all picked up Thursday in a big drug bust. The cops hauled out bags of it."

'Thank you San Diego police' lit up my brain.

When they were let out the boyfriend stripped Jane's apartment and was never seen again. Now it was quiet all the time. What a relief. Within a few weeks Jane was in the yard talking to Linda. They were discussing telephones.

"I can get a long cord that will stretch to your apartment. I don't get calls after ten o'clock and that's when you'll be getting all of yours." This was from Linda.

Smiling I said, "Are you guys planning to string up one of those tin can communication systems?"

Linda laughed, "No. Jane can't pay her phone bill so they're disconnecting the line. And she needs her phone for work. Since I don't get late calls and her work calls are all late we can just move the phone to her apartment every night and she can move it back in the morning."

Me to Jane: "Oh you're on call at night? Are you a nurse?"

Jane looked at Linda. Linda looked at Jane. Both looked at me, I looked at Jane then said, "Uhhh, yeah, now I get it." Jane smiled. Linda smiled. I went upstairs and started looking for another place to live. (People revving their motorcycles in the garages day and night did influence my decision. Plus my babysitter not being home at times when John got out of school.)

But before we leave Ocean Beach we have to mention the pier. And Josh. The Ocean Beach pier was used by many to fish for bass, halibut, shark, stingray and other fish used to supplement diets that are made short by not having jobs. Ocean Beach was, and probably still is, known for its counter-culture population. Josh was about 20 months at this point and very capable of walking. When John and I went on the pier to fish Josh became everyone's mascot. To ensure he didn't become shark bait we tied him onto a long rope and let him wander. Many were the times when someone would hear, "Here fishy, fishy, fishy," and find Josh with his head in a bait bucket.

One day someone caught a small stingray. Josh was encouraged to get near the fish until he was very close when the catcher nudged the ray and it flapped its wings. Josh took off like a shot heading for the bait house. Unfortunately the rope was shorter than the distance to the bait house and Josh flew in the air and landed on his butt. That ended that night of fishing.

I think it was around this time that we went to San Ysidro. Not the San Ysidro on the border of San Diego County and Tijuana but the San Ysidro that is on the ocean halfway down the Baja Peninsula past where visas were needed to proceed further (or, as I was told, a little cash). My college Spanish was far behind me but I was assured by the neighbors that many in Baja spoke English. I soon learned they did near the border but not that far down.

Off we went, Mom and her two little cherubs. I bought Kentucky Fried Chicken on the way and it was the oddest tasting KFC I have ever eaten. I think it was liberally sprinkled with jalapeno peppers because the boys sure weren't impressed.

By the time we got to the place on the map that was supposed to be San Ysidro it was dark and I had to go to the bathroom. (John of course could just use the ditches alongside the road and Josh's potty needs were still contained.) We stopped at a little restaurant with three tables and ordered burritos. I asked for the toilet using my handy-dandy English-Spanish dictionary. Nothing was recognized. Finally I squatted and they all nodded their heads saying "Si, Si," as they indicated the back door.

Well it was an outhouse that had not been too well maintained. Using all my willpower we left the restaurant and drove back and forth along the road a few times until I spotted the little sign pointing down a dirt path with the words San Ysidro on it. We drove in a little way and I too utilized a ditch.

I kept driving on the pathway kicking up dust with just my headlights illuminating where I was. Suddenly I noticed a car behind me flashing its lights. Panic set in. Here I was with my two young children miles from nowhere being followed by some madman who was going to rape and kill me making my children orphans in a strange country with no one to care for them and how could I have been so stupid. I stopped the car, grabbed my flashlight, hopped out of the car and menacingly strode towards the other car yelling, "What the hell are you doing? Why are you following me?"

The driver hopped out of his car with his hands extended to ward off my imagined blows. His passengers peered out of the front and back of the car their eyes bright in anticipation. "It's OK lady I'm not going to hurt you. Don't swing that thing at me. I lived here a long time ago and can't remember the way in so I thought I'd see if you were going to San Ysidro so I could follow you."

Relieved and laughing I said, "Sorry it's the blind leading the blind. I'm only on this road because the sign said San Ysidro. Are there other little towns in the area?"

Breathing a sigh of relief that I wasn't going to do major damage to him or his car he laughed. "Yeah there are a few little places here. So maybe you should follow me. My Spanish is so-so but I can ask around to get on the right road."

"Great," I responded. I got back in the car, he drove around me and we started our little caravan down the road. After driving for about a half hour his brake lights went on. I noticed steam coming from the hood. I stopped, got out and went to his car to see what had happened. By that time he was out with the hood up cursing at the overheated radiator.

"Well you're going to have to let it cool down before you put water in it so maybe you could look around, see if there are any farms or anything where you can get directions."

He kept cursing his bad luck so I wandered ahead about 150 feet to the edge of a cliff that ended in a deep canyon. Had his radiator not overflowed at that minute he would have been at the bottom of a very long drop.

I ambled back to where he and his buddies were talking still pissed at the radiator.

"You need to kiss that radiator."

"What? What the hell are you talking about?"

"That radiator saved your life. Take a look down that way," as I nodded toward the cliff edge.

He and his buddies walked down the road. Within a few minutes I heard additional cursing but more the "Holy shit" variety. They came back, his face very pale in the moonlight and he mumbled, "Un-fucking-believable. We'll check around while the radiator cools."

I went back to my car and slouched down for a nap. Josh naturally was sound asleep. John was starting to calm down from all the excitement so he was getting ready to nod off. The guys came back and the driver leaned in my window.

"There's a farmhouse down the road to the right. The radiator is cooled off and I need to get water so we're going to push the car to the farmhouse and get water and maybe directions."

"I'll be behind you."

"And thanks for what you showed us. I might have started that car and tried to drive it to where I thought we were going."

"No problem. Let's hit the road."

He got his water and directions and soon we were at his stepfather and mother's beach house. The place was packed. They had not expected five more people plus two more kids. They were polite but short when they made it clear I would have to sleep in my car. Since it was a station wagon that was not a problem.

The next morning we woke to a clear beautiful day as we looked out on the ocean. I went to the door asking if we could use the bathroom and was invited in. After we'd done out ablutions and Josh was now in clean diapers we all sat down for a breakfast of boiled lobster. Five pots full. With fruit from the trees, mangos I think, and oranges. What a breakfast and what a trip.

WORKING FOR THE COUNTY
San Diego, 1974 to 1978

While I was looking for new digs I applied for the Administrative Assistant list that had opened for San Diego County. In those days the Admin Assistant was actually an Analyst responsible for division budgets, human resources, policy analysis, position papers, etc. In the late '80s when Administrative Assistant came to describe high-level clerical employees the positions I had held were retitled.

At any rate I was once again on the cusp of a Justice Department legal action, this time against the County for discrimination against women and minorities. The Admin Assistant series also included Management and Executive Assistants with the higher titles usually at the department or agency level. Of 105 budgeted positions county-wide, three were women and maybe four were minorities with two of the women getting double duty. In I walked with that handy-dandy business degree. I was welcomed with open arms. Well maybe not that open. My first position was at the Department of the County Engineer and when the County Engineer retired he told me he had to over-rule every (male) manager in the department to get me appointed.

I had a lot of interesting times at the County Engineer but these I remembered best.

The department was responsible for county-maintained roads including their construction. One day we had to send an invoice, approved by the County Engineer, to the County Purchasing Agent for 100 feet of telephone wire, a chicken coop and 55 Rhode Island Red chickens. Naturally the Purchasing Agent demanded an explanation. The reply was: 'A large stump had to be removed from a proposed roadway located near a farm and telephone lines. After three attempts to remove the stump, we had the option of calling-in more equipment or using more dynamite. The wrong option was chosen.'

The Board of Supervisors consistently criticized our department for its over-written bureaucratese. This verbosity probably was due to the high number of ex-military engineers we employed. One time I was reading aloud a particularly over-verbose document and noting all the unnecessary wording when one of the other Admin Assistants, with a red, angry face, noted that he had written it. This same person later went to the Veteran's Administration and reorganized some of the departments inadvertently eliminating his own job.

On the excessive language much of the problem was due to the new County Engineer's changes to staff material. To demonstrate his ability to respond to criticism he circulated a book on proper writing techniques. The letter of instruction, which he wrote to accompany the book, was soon returned with eighteen corrections properly referencing pages in the book addressing such bad prose. Changes to our reports mysteriously stopped as did the circulation of any more books.

(The critique was done by Powell Harrison the head of Traffic Safety who was one of the three or four funniest men I've ever worked with. He and I used to laugh so much his secretary brought charges against us with the union for creating an unprofessional work environment. One of his stories involved his reaction to a particularly pushy woman trying to get a traffic light or stop sign installed where studies indicated none was warranted. At her strident question, "How many people need to be killed before one is installed?" Powell, knowing none had been killed and tired of her constant barrage, responded, "Six!" He said he paid for that one many times over.)

My supervisor, Bucky, was a man close to retirement. Thin, gray-haired, face full of wrinkles, exuding confidence as he smoked his pipe and leaned back in his chair, he was the picture of a college professor in the wrong building. When the County Human Resources Department changed the criteria for promotion in the Administrative Analyst group requiring a college degree our protests got Bucky grandfathered in so he could compete for and win a promotion.

A stickler for being on time I was the bane of his existence. Getting a kid off to school, a toddler into day care and fighting traffic made arriving at work on time problematic. My lateness ran from five to fifteen minutes three to four days each week. One day, he took me to task for my tardiness.

"You have to be here at eight o'clock. I don't care what your home issues are I expect you here at eight o'clock."

I leaned back in my chair. "You know Bucky you're right. I will hereafter be on time at exactly eight o'clock. However I will then endeavor to be on time for everything else. I will leave for lunch exactly at twelve and return exactly at one. *(I often worked through lunch to get things done.)* I will also leave exactly at five. *(I often stayed to five thirty.)* I will be on time."

Bucky sat in his chair chomping on his pipe, contemplating. He removed the pipe from his mouth, looked at it, tamped down the tobacco in the bow, looked at it again, put it back in his mouth.

"Well at least be on time if we have any meetings that start at eight o'clock."

"Bucky you know I have never been late for a meeting."

He humped, nodded then looked down at the paperwork on his desk. Holding his pipe in his hand he waved me away.

After two years at the County Engineer I transferred to the Fiscal and Justice Agency, a significant step up if you wanted to get on promotion lists. The Agency was the conduit for all matters presented to the Board of Supervisors including budgets. There were four other Agencies although I can't remember their names but we had the big dogs. The Sheriff, the Courts, the District Attorney, the Treasurer, the Tax Collector along with smaller but not less important departments such as General Services, Purchasing and Revenue and Recovery. The departments reporting to our agency were divided up among three Administrative Assistants, including me, and one Management Assistant. I was the only female not in a clerical classification.

One of the men had the courts and the Sheriff primarily because he was married to the daughter of a judge. Therefore he had an inside line no one else had. He and the Management Assistant didn't like that I had been hired. First because I was female and second because in their opinion I wasn't smart enough or experienced enough to do the job. Women belonged behind a typewriter doing what others directed. When I started I was grudgingly given four or five small departments. As things turned out some of those small ones catapulted me into the spotlight much to the chagrin of the male admins.

The Agency director was a fussy man who had gotten to the level where his inadequacies were showing. At Board meetings he would quickly get lost relative to the subject matter and one of the Admins would have to take over to complete the presentation. But he loved to edit anything that was going before the Board. Unfortunately his editing often didn't include any understanding of what the document was trying to convey. At times he would end up with a product that took a contrary stance to what the document was addressing. If it made any sense at all. When I left the County, Donna, the long-suffering secretary who had to re-type our work due to his meddling wrote a full-page farewell with lots of editing.

The year Proposition 13, a tax-reduction measure, was on the ballot all the department heads were tasked to identify budget cuts that would have to be made if the proposition passed. Many suggestions were those that would affect the public the hardest whether those cuts were needed or not. The objective of course was to force the public to vote down the measure. It didn't work. Now real cuts had to be made and manipulating the public was not acceptable. The Board of Supervisors and many other department heads were elected and they were not going to screw their constituents.

A department with a female Executive Assistant who had obtained her promotion horizontally reported to our Agency. This particular department controlled the purchase and distribution of fuel for all County vehicles. At the preliminary budget meeting (if we didn't approve it, it didn't go forward) she came up with the brilliant idea to cut all department fuel supplies by half. As she announced this with a cutesy little smile her department head looked at her, chomped on his pipe then nodded that it was a good idea. Everyone in our group looked at each other in shock. We knew our director was fearful of making enemies but this was ridiculous. Two of the male admins hemmed and hawed trying to get the director and department head to see how stupid this was but they were the diplomats. I wasn't.

"If you cut the fuel supplies in half that affects departments like the Sheriff and the County Engineer. What do you think will happen when the Sheriff can't chase felons because his deputies won't have enough gas? Or the County Engineer won't have gas for heavy equipment to repair roads? That is the stupidest idea I've ever heard of."

The other admins tried to soothe the waters I had just roiled but the upshot was that a modest 5% reduction would be acceptable. After they left the Management Assistant said, "You will have to learn to be more diplomatic."

I replied, "Maybe you need to get some balls. If we play this game with every hair-brained scheme she dreams up we'll be in budget negotiations all night. You know she didn't get her promotion on her abilities."

He coughed then admitted that yes he had heard rumors. From then on he went to the department to review budget recommendations and cut her off at the pass.

One of my departments was Purchasing. An employee embezzling money was uncovered through his own ineptness. The scheme concerned fake purchase orders, receivers and invoices. Unfortunately for the guy (and fortunately for the County) he was careless about keeping track of things. A few of the receivers made it to a County Engineer Field Office where the supervisor noted he had never ordered the supposedly received goods. The employee's other embezzling was paid overtime to the extent that some weeks he wouldn't have had time to sleep. He also used department phones for long distance calls to South America for his home-based business. Because the guy had been doing this for months the Purchasing Agent lost his job. With maybe ten employees to supervise the PA didn't have an excuse for the lack of oversight. Being involved with discovering the embezzlement and the department's reorganization added to the experience shell I needed to keep the other admins at bay.

Another department was Revenue and Recovery whose mandate was to collect money owed the county particularly from fathers who wouldn't pay child support. This money was then used to pay fines levied by the courts, reimburse Social Services for the welfare paid the mother, etc. After Proposition 13 passed the Board of Supervisors imposed a hiring freeze. R and R wanted sixteen more employees and we calculated each employee would bring in a net of $160,000 in collections beyond the employee's salary and benefits. But this would violate the hiring freeze so the board nixed it.

In my opinion to give up $2.5 million in revenue (a good amount in the late '70s) for political posturing was pretty stupid. So I prepared a paper advocating for the positions. The Agency director almost had heart failure. In his mind taking something like this to the board was job suicide. He couldn't risk getting anyone mad at him.

Unfortunately for him I had the courage of my convictions if not the instinct for self-preservation. I met with Board of Supervisors' staff, dropped some hints and they started asking questions. The head of the Office of Management and Budget said if I got three board members to advocate for it he'd put it on the agenda. The Chief Administrative Officer said he'd go for it if OMB went for it. But if I ever did an end run like this again he'd have me fired. Board members would go for it if other board members went for it. One board member had a slime ball Chief of Staff who fingered my necklaces and tried to go for my breasts. I couldn't slap him because I needed his boss's approval on my action item. (Although what I said did make him back off to the secretaries' laughter. I only wish I could remember what I said.) The Board member who hired this slime ball eventually went on to higher office from which he was removed due to questionable actions with campaign contributions. Like gravitates to like I guess.

With all my ducks in a row my director had to let it go to the Board where it passed. The Agency male admins were totally pissed that the stupid, inexperienced female got through the only exception that year to the hiring freeze. Especially the next year when the Sheriff was transferred from the judge's son-in-law to me.

Another of my departments, the Treasurer, hired the actuary who reported each year on the retirement fund. The report included recommendations on the contributions to be made from the county's General Fund and by county employees to keep the fund out of the red. This particular year the recommended contributions were high and the Board of Supervisors wanted a better explanation of the actuarial study. I was assigned the task.

As I talked to the involved parties I learned one thing and made note of in my report. No one understood how the retirement system worked. The report was so long the director gave up on his editing after half of the second page. (One of the admins said he never realized length was the key to keeping the director at bay. If he couldn't get through the whole document he wouldn't do any of it.) As per usual at the board meeting the director tried to explain what was in the paper but had to give up and let me take over. At the conclusion of my summary one of the supervisors exclaimed, "I've been on this Board for fifteen years and this is the first time I've understood the retirement system." They changed how the system worked at an estimated $1.8 million savings a years. (Unfortunately later developments wiped out those savings but they were there for a while.)

I still had Purchasing and one of Purchasing's sub-groups was Duplication. The year Duplication sought an extra employee the Board wanted more of a reason than copy volume. Again I looked for the root of the problem. Needing an extra employee wasn't the problem. The problem was the volume of copies being made by every department. And how the procurement of copy equipment led to a copy costing from one cent to twenty-one cents dependent on where it was made. As a result of my study the copy process and requirements for copies was significantly changed as was the policy of leasing equipment. The CAO estimated my recommendations would save the County over $1 million a year. And Purchasing didn't get the extra employee.

Unfortunately all good things come to an end. The Agencies were dissolved. All the admins had to find positions back in the departments. By this time I had gotten bored with working for the government. All my working life I've looked at a job as how can we do it efficiently and effectively. Why should I work overtime because other people couldn't get their act together? Unfortunately that attitude did not always hold in many government operations. Or in many corporate operations as I later learned.

While I had been at the County Engineer a county-wide zero-based budget system was implemented. The directions for preparing the budget were so obtuse budget documents were continually returned from OMB for revision. I re-wrote the manual. Using my manual the next year we completed budget preparation in half the usual time. Other admins who used my manual were still using it years later. Some admins didn't want to use it because their work was so important there was never enough time to get it done. Making it efficient would lower their value in their director's eyes. Because I knew so many departments with that mentality when it came time to bump back I decided to bump out. The next step was real estate.

HUSBAND NUMBER TWO
San Diego, 1974 to 1980

During the time I started working for the County I had found an apartment complex that had been built for Native-American women who needed job training and a daycare center. The Native-Americans had not shown up in the numbers expected so the complex was opened to any renters. It was perfect for me, daycare for Josh and a place for John when he was out of school. The woman who ran the center was a gem and I could go to work safe in the knowledge that someone would be there when John got home. The clincher was that she would help in potty-training Josh.

In February of 1974 I had her take pictures of me in a bikini sitting next to the pool. I sent a few copies back to my co-teachers in Michigan so someone could claim the bet money.

The daycare lady was close to my age and more than willing to go out on weekends to the bars. We met guys, we danced, we drank, we had fun and my second husband, Ray, appeared in my life. He was married. I rebuffed him, he pursued. Soon we were living together and he had filed for divorce. I realized that I was the exact opposite of his retiring, subservient, poorly educated wife. That alone should have warned me that this was not to be a marriage made in heaven but he was gorgeous, sexy and had a good job so I gave in to his charms. As Mom had often told me, a woman was nothing without a man and the boys needed a father. (After my experience with Ray I never dated a married man again.)

About the same time I had been assigned to the Traffic Department working for Powell Harrison. The relationship with Ray developed halfway through my assignment. After being with him for a few months some of the men in the department started telling me to back off from Ray. The more entangled our relationship became the more abrasive and argumentative I grew. I shoulda listened. Ray had a well-developed ability to manipulate and control people to his line of thought. Under the impression, per Mom, that I was nothing without a man, I gave in to his manipulations. However, the more pressure I was under at home, the more I acted out at work. I learned to fight back but not before it affected John and Josh.

He moved in. John got waylaid by some kids who stole his bike and roughed him up so it was time to change locations. We got an apartment for a few months then his wife moved out of their house in University City, a neighborhood with middle and upper class residential areas. We soon moved in. His wife was easily manipulated and against her attorney's advice she took a property settlement far below what she was owed. Ray saw nothing wrong in lowering his children's standard of living while maintaining his own. He expected her to get a well-paying job to make up the difference knowing full well she was not capable of anything more than minimum wage labor. Convinced of this worth I stupidly went along with it.

Ray had three daughters. Sherrie was about 18 months older than John, Holly about four months older and Erica about three years older than Josh. We went to his sister's house to visit and while in their pool her husband accidently hit me in the face. My black eye was pretty prominent when I went back to work after the holiday so I told everyone that Gerrie had been upset about the divorce and punched me out. It took a lot of convincing to get the believers to accept the accident as the truth. (At least I hope it was an accident. Gerrie's husband, Wayne, was such a great guy it would have been pretty difficult for the accident to have not been an accident.)

The house was small so we added a bedroom with a walk-in closet, bath and fireplace. The contractor thought he was dealing with the local yokels. Footings had been dug, the inspector signed off and the cement poured. I came home after they had left for the day. When Ray came home he saw me outside taking pictures.

"What's up?"

"I think they filled in part of the footings to save on cement. That pile of dirt is a lot lower than it was this morning. I just want evidence in case we need it later."

"Shouldn't we have them redone?"

"I wouldn't worry. They're only off by about three or four inches and in this climate they don't need to be that deep anyway."

Time went on, the contractor didn't get things done and we still owed about 20% of the contract. He wanted the money to finish the project but we wanted the project finished before he got the money. It looked like a stalemate until we hired other tradesmen to finish the work. We actually paid less than if we'd paid him the 20%. Then the contractor served us with papers for small claims court action. I sent him the pictures that included a ruler showing the actual depth of the footings. We never heard from him again.

Ray's mother came to visit. His dad had been a wife beater and his beatings had caused a miscarriage as well as addling his mom's mind and hearing. One day John came into the kitchen.

"Mom, mom, I didn't know Grandma knew Spanish."

Wondering about this new-found skill I walked to the living room where she was watching and nodding her head in unison with the dialogue to Bonanza on a Spanish-speaking station.

On the other hand, at times her hearing seemed very acute. One day she took the kids into the canyon for a hike. Within a few minutes John was at the front door.

"Grandma wants a shovel."

"A shovel? What does she want with a shovel?"

"I don't know. She just wants a shovel."

An hour later Grandma and the kids arrived at the front door. In the shovel Grandma held was an extremely long rattle snake its ends hanging over the scoop. I managed not to scream when she offered it to me suggesting it made a really fine stew. I guess she wasn't too happy when we chose to send the snake to the bottom of the garbage can.

John was elated. "You should have seen it Mom. She just raised that shovel and whacked the snake right in the head. Wow I didn't know Grandma could do that."

I thanked my lucky stars the rattler hadn't struck before she connected with its skull.

During lunch and breaks Powell and I got into some interesting conversations. One day while discussing his ex-wife and some of her issues he asked if I had ever seen a porno film in a theater. I answered "No," adding that Ray had never seen one either. So he gave me two free tickets. Ray and I got to the theater a little late and walked into a dark auditorium. I was behind Ray. Suddenly he stopped. I bumped into him as I heard him gasp, "My God."

Looking over his shoulder I saw the entire screen filled with an erect penis. Stunned all I could say was, "Wow." While Ray could hold his own in the size department I'd never seen one so magnified.

We only stayed about ten minutes because the place was filthy and the sounds even worse. The next Monday I told Powell it was very interesting for the time we were there. We laughed and went on to other topics.

Ray and I married and our first anniversary rolled round. Powell presented me with a one night pass to a motel with porno movies, a water bed and mirrors on the ceiling. The place wasn't bad but after two or three movies the exploitive nature of the films got to me and we turned off the television. Later we did buy a water bed.

That Monday at work I sat in the office I shared with a man who was a deacon of his church. I think it might have been Lutheran. Powell, true to his nature, had surreptitiously let slip to some of the guys in the office that he had given me the free pass. One walked in with a Board of Supervisors document for me to review. While I was looking at the letter he bent down and quietly whispered, "So, Powell told us about it. How was it?"

I whispered back, "The first film or so was kind of interesting but it got old fast. But the water bed and mirrors were great."

He stood up taking back his document and left. Within two minutes another guy was at the door with another document for review with the same questions that got the same answers.

By the fifth guy and seeing the same document more than once I was trying very hard not to burst out laughing. Finally I whispered, "You guys can stop coming in here. I am not going to give anyone more of a description then the first." A little chagrined he left.

At that point the church deacon looked at me and asked, "What's going on? Why are all those guys coming in here?"

"Don't worry he was the last. They were just trying to get me to describe my weekend in more detail and it isn't going to happen."

"Your weekend? What would they want to know about your weekend?"

Looking at him I felt a little embarrassed. Not about the weekend but the shock to him that might come from my revelation.

"Well, ummmm, it's not something I'd usually discuss with someone of deep religious faith."

"That's fine. Even with my deep faith little shocks me."

"OK. My husband and I celebrated our first wedding anniversary at a motel that shows porno movies. The reason the guys were coming in is that Powell gave me the free pass and told them what was going on."

The deacon's mouth fell open. "You were right it isn't something to discuss in a work situation."

Smiling I agreed and went back to my budget.

A few minutes later I heard, "So what was it like?"

I started howling with laughter. He got red in the face. I closed the office door to give him the same information the others had gotten. I closed the door because I didn't want others to hear him gasping in shock. Which he did. But it did prompt an interesting discussion on porn, the treatment of women and equality in the home and workplace.

The following memories are out of sequence because while funny I can't remember exactly when they happened.

On a trip to the zoo Josh, then age six, had to be found three times. Except the third return included Ray's hand firmly entwined in Josh's hair. My mother, who had moved to California after my Dad died, looked at Josh sympathetically.

"Joshua, do you always get into so much trouble?"

"No," sighed Joshua, "but my hair does."

In the trained bird show, a raven untied shoelaces. John's elation at being chosen for this trick soon turned to dismay. After numerous attempts the raven finally returned to its trainer in frustration. Out of the silence came John's small voice, "Double knots.

After a day on new skates that involved banging his head into the open garage door, running into a tree, falling over a wall and performing a half-flip over an open car door, eleven-year old John proudly proclaimed, "At least I've learned how to fall down right."

Josh, age six and the unwilling participant in some of John's mishaps, dryly commented, "That's the only thing he's learned."

After Ray and I separated I worked in real estate and money was often in short supply. (I'm not the sales type.) I hadn't realized how short until Josh lost a tooth. The next morning he sadly said, "I put my tooth under the pillow and what did I get?" Holding out his hand, he continued, "A tooth."

Trying to recover the situation, I said, "You must have a tooth fairy who's forgetful."

"No," he sighed, "I think I have a tooth fairy who's broke." The fairy visited that night.

In 1977, my Mom had taken ten-year-old John and five-year-old Josh to Torrey Pines Beach. The beach ended at a rocky outcrop that during low tide could be walked around to get to another beach beyond. The beach beyond was Black's Beach, the retreat for nudists. That day a couple had walked around the outcrop carrying their clothes. John took one look then turned to my Mom and loudly proclaimed, "Grandma she's not a natural blonde." While the woman laughed my mother later asked me how he would have known that but I feigned total ignorance.

When the movie, *Airplane*, came out in 1980 my Mom and I took Josh to the movie at a drive-in. I don't remember if John was with us but at that point Josh was eight. We had arrived maybe fifteen minutes late into the movie. After the second feature Josh wanted to see the beginning of *Airplane* so we stayed. The point where we had arrived came and went. Josh still wanted to see more. Then the scene appeared where Julie

Hagerty activated the plane's autopilot, an inflatable doll named 'Otto,' by blowing up the doll in a position that suggests fellatio. The doll and Julie lean back in the pilot seats both smoking cigarettes as if at the end of a sexual encounter. At that point Josh announced, "OK, we can go now." My Mom asked many questions but I was never able to provide a logical answer.

THE FIRST BOTHE HOUSE
San Diego, 1974 to 1980

In 1976, within a year of the remodel, Ray and I purchased another house. Just felt like looking at houses one day and there it was. The house was on Bothe Avenue in the west end of University City where all the big, expensive houses were located. I think we paid about $150,000. Even after the 2008 housing crash that house is still worth close to $700,000.

The house was a bargain because the woman was a heavy smoker (the walls were yellow), had lots of cats with no litter boxes and had left the yard and pool go to weed. We saw the repairs but also the potential. The layout was fantastic making a 2,200 square foot house look like 2,600 or more. We did have some good times while getting the house in shape. Maybe he figured he better be nice or he'd have to hire the help.

For months Ray's old house was on the market. Every day we thought we were going to lose the Bothe house so finally my mother loaned us the down payment. After escrow closed the agent told us that the owner had received and rejected five other offers, two of which were higher than ours. She just knew we were ordained to be in that house.

The ordination included pulling waist-high weeds, building cement block retaining walls (for which I wheel-barrowed the block), installing sprinkler systems, landscaping front and back, washing walls two and three times to get the cigarette stains out, painting, replacing carpeting, replacing bathroom fixtures and toilets.

Ray had blamed John for breaking one of the toilets. He refused to replace it so he could continue to blame John. That there was no way John could have broken it was not something Ray would consider. The toilet was on the second floor. I replaced that sucker all by myself plus hauled it down the stairs and out to the driveway for disposal. I was so proud. Ray was not pleased.

In 1978 Ray and I went to Hawaii. Ray hated to go to the beach; sand was not his landscape of choice. Finally near the last day we went to a beach on the Big Island. I walked to waist deep water, put on a snorkel and just sat to watch a whirling mass of angelfish representing probably fifteen different species, swirls of fluorescent minnows, an absolute wonderland.

Still under the influence of *Jaws* (plus I'd read the book) the shadows in the distant depths made me nervous so after an hour I went back to shore. A short way up the beach I noticed big waves coming into a small cove. Body surfing was also a favorite sport so I ran into the water and hopped a wave. The force of the water pushed me straight to the shore. Then the force of the retreating water dragged me away from shore parting me from my bikini.

I couldn't stand up because I was still somewhat modest in those days. Ray being insanely jealous was also a consideration. I sat in the water and waited. Finally Ray came up. He was bored and wanted to leave. He found the bottoms but not the top and was laughing uproariously as I skittered out of the water to the waiting towel.

It's weird that Ray and I were so diametrically opposed at times and so close at others. When we went to counseling the therapist told us that he had never had a couple quite like us; that you could feel the electricity and bond between us. Only later did I think that you could also feel the electricity from an electric chair but that doesn't necessarily mean it's good.

Not to go into detail but Ray was not the husband of the year. The marriage went from bad to worse when he punched me out one night coming home from a party. He had disappeared into a bedroom with another woman for about 15 to 20 minutes to 'talk.' The woman was one of his boss's ex-girlfriends and I knew her type was not inclined to just 'talk.' When I made a number of remarks about the situation he said he wanted to go home. While driving he decided to shut me up. Unfortunately for him I don't shut up and if someone hits me I hit back. So he got as good as he gave something he definitely had not been expecting.

We went to counseling over Ray's objections that it would interfere with quarter closing at work. The therapist impressed on Ray that I could have him arrested and he most certainly would lose his CPA certification. That kept him under control for a few more years. He'd scream me into corners but didn't raise a hand. (Although the walls and doors didn't come out too intact.)

That I still thought there was something to salvage demonstrated how blinded I was to his charismatic personality. John and Josh were into competitive swimming and one night before a meet Ray 'demonstrated' how he could bend his arm behind his back and touch his neck. John could not bend his arm in the same manner so Ray bent it for him, straining the muscles and causing him to do poorly the next day at the meet. That I didn't walk out then was a further indication of my inability to see reality. (And the lack of flexibility is genetic. Even with 29 years of working out I still can't bend my arm further than the middle of my back.)

We separated and filed for divorce. I bought a two-story four bedroom on Cather Avenue on the east side of University City not too far from the old house Ray had owned in his first marriage. That house had been long sold. He had wanted to keep it as a rental and become a real estate mogul while not paying my mother back for the loan but I had put my foot down and the house was sold.

Cather, as usual, was a fixer but because I was a realtor I could claim a commission on the buying end so had money to do some of the fixing. I had a pool installed (my kids were not going to get less than his kids) but within a few months Ray and I decided to try again. Of course the day I was supposed to move back into the Bothe house he decided he wasn't going to try again but I was not to be deterred. I had rented the Cather house, I had the furniture loaded and he was getting me, like it or not.

(I rented the house to four bachelors who did not believe in yard work. At one point I had to weed the back area around the pool. A renter who had a big belly and a small pecker came out stark naked while I was weeding. Talking about nothing in particular he paraded what he assumed was his godsend in front of me. Finally tired of having to see this mockery of manhood I said, "Why don't you go back inside and get dressed. You have nothing that interests me." Chagrined he went back in the house and I never saw him again.)

Of course the attempt at reconciliation was a bust. (His catting around didn't help particularly when I figured out the name of one of the kitties and showed up at her door when he was inside.) I think he only half-heartedly protested because Sherri, a first class gymnast, needed ankle surgery and he would have had to take off work or hire someone to take care of her during her recovery. Going back also was the final straw with John. He was so depressed my Mom took him to a psychiatrist. Ray had spent our whole time together convincing me I was a bad parent and both of us had been way harder on John than was necessary. (John's snail-like pace at his chores that resulted in others having to finish his work might have had some influence on the family dynamics.)

We finally reactivated the divorce. While we were dividing our possessions Ray had been taking books and records I had had years before we got together. His premise was that what was mine was his, his was his and ours was his. My protests were not well received so he punched me out one more time.

As part of the settlement I had given him the house for my share of the equity. He called the police to have me thrown out of 'his' house. The police took one look at me, one at him then told him to pack a bag and get a room for the night. He was not happy as he left particularly since the door had a deadbolt to which he did not have a key.

While living with him the second time around, knowing it wasn't going to work, I had bought another house on Bothe but a few blocks up. After his night out he came back, cleaned up and went to work. I packed up and left. With me went all the furniture that didn't belong to his girls and, of course, all that I had brought to the marriage.

In the past few years he had gotten into photography as had I. However, according to him my pictures were inferior to his so he had taken a number of his shots, had them enlarged and placed in very expensive frames. He got home just as the rental truck was leaving for the other Bothe house. Of course he was livid.

"What right did you have to take all the furniture? It's supposed to be divided evenly."

"But Ray it was divided evenly. You have a picture here that cost $250 to enlarge and frame. That one over there cost $225 to enlarge and frame. You must have about ten of those scattered around the house. Add it up. The furniture was cheap or mine, the pictures weren't. You got your share. Enjoy it."

Months later we were still wrangling about the pay-off to me on the property settlement. In his mind after I moved back the money he had given to me for household expenses like food (for him, me and the four kids) should be deducted from the equity he owed me. When that ploy didn't work he pleaded poverty and wanted to stretch out payment of my equity over two years. I agreed just to get it settled.

For some inexplicable reason while the lawyers were drawing up the papers I went to the County Recorder's office to see what had been recorded the past few days. I was in real estate at the time but had no deals pending recording. No one I knew had any deals pending recording. I just seemed to be drawn to the office.

Low and behold, two documents *had* been recorded. One for a hundred-thousand loan on the Bothe house plus a Grant Deed for the most expensive house in University City. The new owner of record was the realtor he intended to marry. After further investigation I determined that the hundred thousand had been used for the down payment but was not being listed as a second against the house due to a side-agreement. His name was on that money. The realtor was involved in a multi-million dollar lawsuit against some company that made headgear for pilots. Her husband had been killed supposedly due to the unsafe design and manufacture of the helmet. She stood to make a large sum of money when the case was settled. This later proved to have been the major reason Ray married her.

I called my attorney and told him to drop the agreement. We were going back to court with a vengeance. At the next hearing my attorney was fire and brimstone. It was as if he was arguing the Equity Funding fraud. I had my hand over my mouth most of the time because I was trying not to burst out laughing. Particularly as I kept sneaking looks at Ray and his attorney with Ray getting greener around the gills and his attorney's eyes getting bigger and bigger at each accusation.

When my lawyer finally ran down, the judge looked over his glasses at Ray and in a quiet voice said, "Did you do that?"

Ray nodded.

"I can't let you do that. You pay her the equity in 30 days."

"But, but," Ray stuttered, "I don't have any liquidity. I'll have to sell my stock."

The judge quietly replied, "Then you better get busy."

Ray turned to his lawyer who up to this point had not had a clue about Ray's financial shenanigans. "What about the furniture? What about the community property?"

"Shut up," his lawyer replied, "you've caused enough problems already."

My smile was broad as I turned to him then sauntered down the aisle and out the door.

Ray married the realtor and I was told by other realtors that his temper tantrums were exacerbated by her tendency to get drunk on very little alcohol then pass out. He so antagonized her son that he was sent to military school to prevent his trying to off Ray. Her daughter hated him. Most of this came from fellow realtors whose kids were friends with hers. Upon learning Ray was going to marry her one realtor looked at me and said, "My god, why? She's dumb as a fence post and not half as pretty as you."

"Ah yes," I replied, "but she does have the thing most important to Ray. Money and the prospect for more."

She got her settlement, over a million dollars, and refused to let him touch a penny. The note that supported she owed him the hundred thousand disappeared. They divorced and she basically took him for the hundred grand.

I shouldn't have. I should have been above it all. But I wasn't. I wrote him a letter asking how it felt for someone to screw him like he tried to screw me. For some reason, he didn't respond.

His third marriage was the reason my last name is Samuels. Upon hearing my name at a school function a parent said, "Oh you must be Marie." (The wife he had just married.)

I replied, "No, I was his second wife."

"Oh, I'm sorry PRil." (His first wife's nickname.)

"No, I'm Flo."

"Flo! Oh, Flo. So sorry, it's hard to keep them straight."

The next day I changed my name to Samuels. My maiden name was Jharmark but it was constantly being misspelled so I chose my Dad's first name and added an 's.' While I have been told many times you have to go to court to change your last name, at that time (and maybe still now) you didn't. Once you had documentation such as utility bills in your hand you could get your name changed via Social Security and use that to change your driver's license. Social Security did give me an argument that without a court order they couldn't make the change but when they couldn't show me the statute requiring that, they gave in.

During the reconciliation fiasco I had my first major back problem. In prior years I would have muscle spasms and an intense dull pain. I could walk but slowly. Crawling made it easier when I needed to use the bathroom but in all the pain was bearable. The spasms generally cleared up in a few days and the dull pain in a few weeks.

This time I could not walk more than 20 feet. The pain was intense like having a knife jammed into my spine then moved up and down. Shots of lightening went through my hips and down both legs. Going up and down stairs was agony. I was not up to having sex. This was not acceptable to Ray because he could not sleep without sex. He therefore proceeded to twist and turn my body to help eliminate whatever problem was causing the pain. Picking me up and shaking me up and down and right and left was his chiropractic method. He didn't know what was causing the problem but he was going to get rid of it no matter what.

One day I took Sherri to a follow-up appointment with the orthopedic surgeon who had done her ankle surgery. When the kids helped me in and out of a chair in the examination room the doctor asked why. I told him about the pain and that I must have sciatica or arthritis. "Nonsense you're too young for either. I'm getting you x-rayed right now."

I had a herniated disc. His options were surgery or exercise. I chose the exercise and within about three months the pain dissipated. When the doctor heard about Ray's ministrations he just shook his head in disbelief. When told that his manipulations had not been medically sound Ray dismissed the doctor's findings. Nothing he did had had any effect on the problem. Over the years the back issues came back to haunt me and pop up later in this narrative. Suffice it to say that in later years the first move anyone made to 'help' me was rebuffed immediately.

Based on local gossip Ray moved to the mid-west as vice-president of a company that went out of business. Now on his fourth wife, he continued his fist-control marriage model eventually putting her in the hospital. I learned about this when she asked me to testify about his abuse in her divorce action. I was willing but never heard from her again.

Wife number five may or may not be with him because in doing my internet research, often called snooping, I have seen a sixth name pop up on property records. When discussing wife five with one of the daughters, she noted that Dad had mellowed. Or, I silently amended, had just found someone who knew to keep her mouth shut.

But Ray did attain what he had always wanted, lots of money and a house in Rancho Santa Fe, the most exclusive enclave in San Diego County. Coming from a background where he used an outhouse until he joined the Army, he did advance in the world. Oddly enough, when we lived together any request on my part for money to purchase new clothes for my sons or new carpet or a decent car was met with accusations of being materialistic. Maybe he couldn't see himself so had to substitute me for what he was.

Even after the divorce I was still besotted with him so I went to our former marriage counselor and asked what I had done wrong. His response was interesting. "You stayed. He's a sociopath. Nothing you did less than total obedience would have helped. When you first started to dating him you gave into his demands and set a false impression of who you really are. He can't handle someone he can't use as a doormat."

From that I developed my relationship philosophies.

No one is totally responsible for all the problems in a marriage. If you pick someone who is seriously out of whack because you have blinded yourself to their issues, you are responsible for the results even if you do nothing.

Married men are off-limits no matter how 'bad' their marriage unless the wife is seriously ill and wants the man to find someone else. If it isn't bad enough to struggle through the pain of living alone then it isn't bad enough to justify adultery, Why get involved with a coward?

And last, what happens in the aftermath? If my ex goes on to a happy, lasting relationship then I probably caused most of the problems. If he continues to screw up and I go on to a happy, lasting relationship then probably he caused most of the problems. If, as has happened in my life, we both continue to screw up we probably had equal input to causing the problems. It doesn't resolve the emotional or psychological issues we had but it certainly puts a different perspective on finger-pointing.

Before we leave Ray we have to talk about Don, his boss. Don was in his 30's with bottle-bleached, blonde hair, a wicked smile, a fancy sports car, a house in the hills overlooking the ocean and a string of women in a variety of states. He liked airline hostesses because unless he gauged it really bad they were generally passing each other in the air and not on land. We never went out with Don that he didn't end up with a woman. Each time a different woman.

When he had parties he invited all his ex-girlfriends and they would outwait each other to see who got to stay with him that night. At his birthday party one year one of his girlfriends had presented a frosted cake made like the body of a woman with breasts, curves, pudenda hair and all. Don plunged his face into the hair. However, as he once confessed to me, not a lot was accomplished most nights because drinking made him a little, ummm, unable to perform. One night was really his comeuppance.

On Friday nights Ray and I, along with people from his and my current jobs and friends from former jobs, would meet at the Rueben E. Lee Riverboat Restaurant in the lounge area. The place was always packed particularly with pretty ladies. Of course Don was always there. We generally had twenty to thirty people in our party.

One night Don made the circuit then came back with two women who he had met before. They talked and Don laid on the charm. I laid on the sarcasm. My comments included reminding him to get the names and phone numbers plus brief descriptions to keep them straight in his mind. Everyone at our table was laughing. (I think others were as unimpressed with his womanizing as I was.) The ladies left. Don made scathing but humorous remarks to me about keeping my mouth shut. Even with the humor I'm sure he was ready to kill.

He made a second circuit this time picking up two new ladies. They talked and Don laid on the charm. I laid on the sarcasm. The ladies agreed to walk out with us to the cars as we were going elsewhere to eat and maybe join us. Then....they left. I hooted about Don's luck thus far, he made a few remarks and we piled in the cars to the new restaurant.

Don picked up another woman who joined us for dinner. She left the restaurant with us then…she left. Don looked at me, a glower in his eye, as I raised my hand. "Not saying a thing Don the night is still young."

We went to a bar with a band whose singer was a very pretty lady. Don picked up a girl in the bar, danced, talked then… she left. He got the singer to join us for breakfast after the club closed. He was getting cozy and I decided to let him off the hook. His luck had been so bad so far maybe he deserved a break. Or maybe I was just getting tired. At any rate, the lady agreed to leave with us to see Don's car, got to the car, walked around it then…left.

At this point, tired or not, I couldn't stop myself. I was laughing so hard I had to lean against our car to keep myself from sliding to the ground. At this point a little perturbed Don turned to me. "Don't say it bitch, just don't say anything."

I waved my hand in the 'No' signal then burst into another round of laughter. Even Ray was laughing.

Finally Don got over his feelings of desertion and said, "This was the worse night of my life. What was it Flo? Six? Seven? And I couldn't score with one? In fact I think they all gave me fake phone numbers. What's happening?"

Trying to talk and laugh at the same time is problematic but I was able to get out something about the futility of using really old lines on really smart women. Maybe he needed to ratchet down the intelligence level of the women he was trying to make. Reluctantly he agreed. I think that was the last time he went out with the gang if I was along.

BOTHE HOUSE TWO AND SOCCER
San Diego, 1980 to 1987

I bought the second Bothe house because I was going to enjoy the old lifestyle whether I was with Ray or not. Plus I wanted John and Josh to stay in the same schools. However to enjoy the old lifestyle I needed more money. I had found employment at NASSCO (National Steel and Shipbuilding) but the lure of extra money from having renters was too much. I started renting rooms in 1980 and have not stopped since. Around 2008 a couple who were trying to buy a house but could not afford the payments snobbily noted they would never give up their privacy. I replied, "Yes you have your privacy but I have a house." That stopped the conversation cold.

Moving into that house, again a fixer, I decided to install shelving in the garage. I was going to prove to Ray I wasn't as stupid as he had liked to point out to me in front of the kids. I got my materials from the local FedMart (the precursor to Home Depot) and started to work. After carefully measuring, sawing and checking for studs, I nailed up my first cross piece. Unfortunately one of the points I had marked as a stud was my water line. Back to FedMart. After the salesman saw my face drop with each sentence on how to cut and solder pipe he suggested the hose used for dishwashers. Fit it over the area with the hole, clamp it good and voila, no leaks.

Four hours later with a repaired water line and the framework complete I stepped back to admire my work. One of my renters, a quiet man who worked with me at NASSCO, stood in the doorway to the garage as I proudly pointed at my achievement. The quiet man quietly said, "Good job. But what are you going to do with the ladder?"

Following his gaze I realized the horizontal shelf supports neatly ran through the rungs of my six-foot stepladder. I sat on the step that led from the garage into the house and laughed. The renter said, "How can you laugh? I'd be mad as hell?"

"But what good would it do? They'd still be running through the ladder."

He, John and Josh promised to never tell a living soul how Mom built shelving.

Josh wanted to play soccer so I signed him up for the local soccer league. One day while going home from work I noticed kids in the soccer fields playing soccer. "Hmmm," I thought, "why hasn't Josh been called?" At home I called the league director to learn they had more kids than coaches. Within two days, soccer instruction book in one hand and whistle in the other, I was coaching a boys' soccer team. Being that my lack of coordination resulted in more laughs than learning I had the better players demonstrate the moves then everyone follow them.

We started with eight kids, three less than a full team, but I told the boys better to try and lose then to quit and never know. At one game a coach who had been coaching for years told me I should give up and disband the team to save them from further humiliation (such as the drubbing his team had given us). But by the middle of the season we had a team. We also had an assistant coach whose boy was on the team and who had been a soccer player overseas. He had realized I was over my head and lent assistance as much as he could.

At the season's mid-point the teams were ranked. Those at the bottom of the heap (Hey, that's us!) were grouped into one sub-league and the ones at the top into a second. At the end of the season the winner of each sub-league would be in the play-offs. Playoffs rolled around and we were at the top of our sub-group. Game day the coach with the advice to quit looked at me and said, "Hey, haven't seen you in a while. What are you doing here?"

"Getting ready to play in the play-offs."

"Oh yeah," he noted as he looked around for whatever team he assumed I had attached myself to. "What team? Are you the soccer mom or an assistant?"

"No, I'm the coach. Same team as last time."

His eyes bulged. "You're the team we're playing?"

"Guess so."

Shaking his head he walked away.

We did lose though.

By one point.

1 to 0.

At the awards ceremony we got trophies for most improved. The other coach said to everyone that he was impressed with our 'can do' attitude although I was more inclined to call it our 'don't quit even in the face of total failure' attitude.

Josh went on to play another five or six years. The last team had some of the best players in the recreational league and the biggest egos. No matter what I did I could not get them to play as a team. One game we lost because the backfield was arguing instead of playing. However that game also had Josh's greatest soccer achievement.

Playing fullback he was debating with the goalie when I screamed, "The ball damn it." Turning towards the other side he saw the ball come barreling toward our net. Still inside the penalty area he kicked it away. Way away. As in over the head of the other team's goalie and into the net. Totally awesome. At that point I should have gotten him into football because field goals would have been a snap. Definitely a lost opportunity.

Halloween rolled round and I set the stage for all the kids who would come up the stairs to the front door. The record player had music with moans and groans. A black light outlined the door frame from inside. I ratted out my hair and wore a thick robe that made me look like Sasquatch. When I heard the knock I would douse the lights, turn on the black light, go to my knees, open the door and moan.

Two little girls screamed and ran back down the stairs. At the sidewalk I could hear their parents urging them to go back; the person at the door wouldn't hurt them. I heard them coming back up the stairs so turned on the light and shut off the music. As I opened the door one trembling little girl looked up at me in tears.

"We're s'posed to scare you, you're not s'posed to scare us."

Later that night I heard footsteps on the stairs. Turning off the light, turning on the music, I knelt and opened the door to look at a pair of nylon-clad knees. Looking up I saw a woman's face with a big smile.

"Wow, I've never served process like this before."

She handed me the subpoena (I think Ray was still trying to get his furniture back) and walked down the steps laughing. I've never been served process like that either.

I can't remember exactly when I met the guy from SAIC or his name (this was 30 years ago) but he was highly placed, pretty wealthy and very overweight. I'll call him Neil. I've never been into overweight, out-of-shape men but being treated like a queen altered my eyesight. We went together for about a month or so and I finally broke up with him. I wrote him a letter telling him that he was a really nice guy but he was 55, I was 37, he was very sedate, I liked to hike and bike, he didn't care what he looked like while I made certain to keep my weight down and look my best, I was sorry but... This letter has ramifications later in my tale.

The most memorable occurrence while I was going with him was the dinner for the Major.

Neil had at one time served with NATO in some high position and had become friends with a guy who was being promoted to Major. The Major was based in Monterey so Neil took me to Monterey for the celebration dinner he planned for the Major. We stayed in some posh hotel in Carmel with fireplaces in all the rooms and fancy tile floors and walls. He bought me upscale luggage that included a suitcase, garment bag and briefcase plus a silk blouse and skirt and a filmy summer dress. As I noted, being treated like a queen can help blind you to negative characteristics. And the luggage, like the letter, had later ramifications.

Anyway we took the Major and his wife to dinner at one of the more expensive restaurants in Carmel. Just entering the restaurant the Major was impressed because on Army pay he, his wife and their two kids were barely making it. Neil ordered a hundred-dollar bottle of wine. The waiter uncorked the bottle and poured each of us a glass. Neil held up his glass then motioned to the Major to take the first drink. Knowing what I know now the host always tastes the wine first but maybe Neil had had too many other drinks beforehand to remember. He waved to the Major.

"What do you think of the wine?"

The Major drank, smiled then said, "Wonderful. I've never tasted wine like this."

Neil waved to the Major's wife who dutifully took a sip and responded in kind.

Neil gestured to me, "What do you think of it Flo?"

I took a good mouthful and immediately spit it out. Coughing I sputtered, "It tastes like vinegar. It's gone bad."

Neil took a sip, spit it out and bellowed for the waiter. At that point the Major leaned towards me and whispered, "I've never had a hundred-dollar bottle of wine. I thought that was how it was supposed to taste."

The second Bothe house was a two-story with the main living area on the top floor accessed by stairs from the street. A large rec room with a full bath was on the bottom level behind the garage. That area became the boys' bedroom and left me two bedrooms on the main level to rent. My bedroom was at the front of the house with a balcony that overlooked the driveway.

Some of my renters were really cool people and others were losers of the year.

One guy moved in and got drunk the third night he was there. Sitting on the family room couch with me watching television he started talking about the rotten prosecutors who worked for the San Diego District Attorney's office. This got my attention because when I'd worked for the Fiscal and Justice Agency one of my assignments was the District Attorney. I knew a lot of the Assistant DAs. I prompted him for a reason.

"They're prosecuting me for molesting my daughter. That bastard in El Cajon won't let me see my daughter without a chaperon. I can't even have her overnight. Bastard. He's working with my ex-wife to keep me away from my kid."

I quietly replied, "Well the courts are pretty reluctant to sever all contact between children and their parents so there must be something they know that is making the DA do what he's doing."

"Nah," he drunkenly declared, "that bastard," and here he mentioned the bastard's name "has got a thing going with my wife so he's doing whatever she wants."

I happened to know the bastard in question and the bastard's wife so at that point it was pretty clear I had a probable child molester living in my house with my eight-year-old son. John was 13 by then and could take care of himself but I wasn't too sure about Josh. Even if I hadn't had kids I wouldn't want a child molester in my house.

Looking him straight in the eye I said, "First, I know the guy. And he's happily married. He isn't the type to lie for anyone. Second, I don't want someone in my house who has been accused of child molestation so you've got exactly 20 minutes to get your ass out of here. And I'll give you 48 hours to move your stuff out."

He started protesting then saw my look. Within ten minutes he was history.

Three days later he still hadn't picked up his stuff. I called him. "If you aren't here by noon tomorrow your stuff is going out the balcony and into the driveway."

His argument was cut off by the click of my phone.

By two p.m. the next day I had his mattress, box spring and clothes in the driveway. As he drove up to the house in a truck he could see me balancing his television on the balcony railing. Jumping from his truck he raced to the driveway screaming, "Don't, don't, I'm moving now." He was out in an hour.

A young woman renter had a Jensen-Healey convertible and wanted to install a stereo. I will always remember her lying on the trunk of her car with her hands full of wires leading from the dashboard. While most will say this only happens in movies, turning on her radio really did start her window shield wipers and starting the car started the heater but not the car. Finally her father came over and straightened out the mess but watching her try to figure out how to get the car started for the few days before he came was a sight.

Another renter, a pretty Asian female, went to Baja to drive a truck as back-up for the Baja 1000 Dirt Bike Race. John went with her. He was about 14 at the time and when they returned, his eyes were wide with wonder.

"San Felipe was so weird Mom. The streets were filled with dogs and huge holes. One was so big it swallowed a Volkswagen. Someone driving a road scraper came up to the hole and the driver in the VW was screaming at the scraper driver not to run over him. But the operator just ran the scraper into the hole and pushed the VW out. The VW guy was screaming the whole time but I guess for the people who live there that was just the usual way to get the cars out of the holes. I never saw anything like it."

At Josh's elementary school parent-teacher conference one day I noticed a sign in the cafeteria next to a pile of lost items:

Clayton's Believe It or Not.

> The jackets, hats, lunchboxes, underwear, shoes, etc. to the right of this sign belongs to some of your kids.
>
> Your kids claim they've never seen this stuff before.
>
> Either aliens from outer space are leaving these things here each evening or your kids are hoping you'll buy 'New' jackets, hats, etc.

During the week when student pictures, semester class changes and the eighth-grade magazine sale were scheduled I called John's junior high school and asked if the following Monday was a school holiday. Came the tired reply, "No, unfortunately."

John's fourteen-year old friend Mark was having problems in school. He tried to justify his poor grades. "Shawn got an A on the test and I got an F. I have to point out it was a hard test. Of course if he got a B I still would have gotten an F. I guess I would have gotten an F no matter what he got. I really have problems with that class."

Real estate had been interesting but not financially rewarding. I do remember two listings that caught my eye. One came up in the MLS as 'Large dog in back yard.' Two days later it was changed to 'DOG BITES.' After being on the market for six months another house was re-listed as follows:

> *'JUST REDUCED! Rustic run down ranch house in bad need of paint. Winding path through sparse lawn. Carpets in spacious living room need help. Broken window accents 5th bedroom. Completely fenced rear yard, but no lawn.'*

The house sold within the week.

During this time I did have some loyal clients. The latch for my driver side door had broken. The estimates in the $800 range were money I did not have at the time so I had to wire the door shut. This necessitated either crawling through the driver side window or entering via the passenger side then over the stick shift floor console. Most clients would have gotten another agent. But mine believed and I sold two houses with my car in that state of disrepair.

NASSCO

San Diego, 1980 to 1984

My job at National Steel and Shipbuilding where they built and repaired oil tankers and military destroyers was as Office Administrator in the Safety Department. The company had 7,000 employees and every day brought something new. One of the new things was a secretary who knew people in Tijuana who would fix my car door for $50 and a six-pack.

Which they did.

Being the Safety Department we got all the accident reports. Some descriptions occasionally caused second readings:

> *'While welder was welding, I felt something in my left eye, so I sent him to First Aid.'*

> (Report for a burn from a piece of welding slag that had slipped into a female employee's coveralls and fell to her groin area.) *'Employee apparently got a piece of slag while welding flat as she sometimes drops the top of his coveralls.'*

The annual holiday schedule signed by the Vice President of Industrial Relations was published showing that the yard would be open for all three shifts on New Year's Eve. The schedule was sent to the Safety Manager with this notation:

"Dear Frank. Does (VP's name) know what the yard is going to look like if we work New Year's Eve?" If I remember correctly the last shift ended around 10 p.m.

> *'Man was walking down the high table* (a large open area)*, lost his footing and fell. This is done all the time*

*and is standard practice for all workers on the high
table.'*

The Pipe Shop had a problem with cats. Actually the
problem was with the maintenance guys who had to clean up
after the cats who were being fed by the pipefitters. The Safety
Department was brought in because of the potential diseases the
cat droppings might bring along with the cats possibly getting in
the way of operations. Our Industrial Hygienist made three
recommendations one of which was hooking up a radio, tuning
in a station that played, as he put it, 'obnoxious rock and roll'
and turning up the volume.

A Safety Specialist replied to his recommendations that the
pipefitters had agreed not to feed the cats in the template shed
and would gradually lure them away by moving their food dishes
from the template area. At this point the cats would probably
veer towards the foundry where, as the specialist put it, "The
foundry at least has a steady supply of sand." And she wasn't too
impressed with the rock and roll torture.

"Let's not be foolish. Any cat that can survive 12-pound
wharf rats, flying wedges, paint overspray and dried kibble –
well, I just don't see where rock and roll would hold any terror at
all."

*'The employee was exiting from a unit and slipped
and hurt his left arm. He performs this task all the time.'*

One of the union guys decided I was going to be his main
squeeze and invented numerous minor and non-existent
problems to justify his coming to the office every day to leer. On
one trip he stood next to a large ring binder hanging on the wall.
In an attempt to flirt with me he tried a slow, sideways glance.
Unfortunately his glance was executed too quickly and he caught
his nose on the binder. The laceration and reaction of other
people in the office considerably reduced his visits.

When a worker dropped a piece of metal on another
worker's foot, *'Workers should always warn fellow*

> *employees when they are going to accidently drop something.'*

Each month 16-foot safety banners were hung throughout the shipyard. One such banner that hung from a building was weighted down with scrap wood and metal. The banner's constant flapping created a storm of falling debris. This prompted an employee's safety suggestion recommending the banner be removed. The banner's slogan? A CLEAN WORKPLACE IS EVERYBODY'S BUSINESS.

> *'While walking on the deck of the ship, I tripped over a welding line. I put out my hand to break my fall and hit a loose board. The board hit me in the mouth, knocking my dentures over the side of the ship into the bay. Injuries sustained--a sprained ankle and wrist, lacerated mouth and no teeth.'* Probably made up? This one had witnesses.

Jack, a safety officer, was critical of women who were not '9s' or better notwithstanding he wasn't a winner himself. This was pointed out when the office staff discussed how smoking might catch his ample mustache on fire. One woman, a target of his disparaging remarks, commented, "We could always put out the fire with a track shoe. Of course with your face no one would know that we used a track shoe."

> *'While moving a portable toilet from the ship's deck to the pier, crane operator discovered that toilet was occupied. Employee in toilet was somewhat disoriented when he came out. Operator now understands importance of checking toilets before moving.'*

As an energy-saving measure time switches, designed to turn off the lights after fifteen minutes, were installed in company bathrooms by Maintenance. Unfortunately no one thought to inform the employees and many found themselves unexpectedly 'in the dark' when using the facilities. The problem prompted a letter from the Safety Manager with suggestions on how to make the situation safer. The Maintenance Department response indicated how other employees had reacted. "Thank you for your response. It was one of the few that were printable."

> *'Employee was getting a drink of water. When he bent down, his tooth collided with the drinking fountain and broke. I have advised him to be more careful and to consider investing in some SuperGlue in case this happens again.'*

During a virulent outbreak of the flu I overheard the following conversation about a manager:

"He yelled 'Stay out of my office.'"

"Was he kidding?"

"No, he's probably got the door locked. You should have gone around and coughed in his window or put a straw through his keyhole. Did you give him the report?"

"Yes but he asked Rose to make a copy first."

"Maybe you should have rinsed it in Lysol before giving it to him."

"I didn't need to. I autoclaved it at Medical."

Although the shipyard had many hazards Ozzie was not known for being careful. He was on light-duty in our office when he left one day on a short delivery taking the department bicycle. Two hours later he returned in another set of clothing. When asked about the change he explained:

"I was riding my bike in the storage area, caught the back of my pants on some metal and ripped the whole backside off. I had to borrow someone's welding jacket while they found me some clothes."

Jack said, "You're lucky you weren't riding backwards. I bet everyone got a good look at your underpants."

Ozzie replied, "No they didn't. I don't wear underpants."

Someone else piped up, "Maybe that was why it took them so long to find you some clothes."

The day I thought I was intoxicated at work was the crowning touch.

I'd been out the night before a tad too late and had been drinking up to the time the bar closed. Dancing most of the night made me feel fairly sober. However, since I had to be at work by 7:30 a.m. the time between the last drink and the first hour at work was limited. Sick to my stomach and at the other end I went to the bathroom to sit for a few minutes and contemplate not doing that again.

As I got up the room swayed. 'Shit,' I thought, 'I'm still drunk. What am I going to do? I can't be in the Safety Office and drunk. Oh God, I am really screwed. How can I go back to the office?'

Screwing up my courage, straightening my back, ensuring I was walking normally, I returned to the office. At that a dozen heads turned towards me. My only thought was, 'Busted!'

"Hey Flo," called a few voices, "did you feel that earthquake? Man, it rocked the ships pretty good."

With a smile plastered on my face and relief in my heart I acknowledged that yes I too had felt the earthquake. That was the last time I stayed out late on a work night.

One of the Safety Reps was working on a Masters in Occupational Safety. Unfortunately his grasp of the English language was limited. Knowing I had written much of the documentation and manuals coming out of the Safety Department he asked if I would edit the paper required for one of his courses. Of course he would pay.

One glance made it clear that his lack of writing skills was surpassed by his lack of research skills. I returned the paper telling him this was not an edit job but a total re-write. He offered more and since I was financially short I accepted the assignment.

Two things happened. First, the professor evidently hadn't seen this guy's previous work so he accepted the paper as being from him. Second, the professor entered the paper in a national contest where it won second place. And some significant cash.

When the guy told me I said I should get a share. He laughed. I dropped the subject. The next semester he again asked me to write the paper for another class. I told him the price had gone up and quoted an amount that would give me part of his previous winnings. He refused. I shrugged my shoulders and returned to my work.

I don't know who he got to do the paper or if he did it but he flunked the class. (If it was the same professor there was no way he wouldn't have flunked.) Revenge works in mysterious ways.

We had Management Dinners once a month with booze provided and I vividly remember two meetings.

The NASSCO executive group had decided that the only way to compete with Japanese shipbuilders was to adopt their practices. To do so we brought their production people to our shipyard to tell us what we were doing wrong. The price tag for this was $5 million dollars a hefty consultant fee in the early 1980s. The Japanese came, they saw and they reported. As one consultant said to my boss, the Safety Manager, "This yard is so dirty. How can anyone work in a yard so dirty?" As we surveyed the spilled oil, tools and parts littered across the yard along with haphazardly stacked materials we could but agree.

At the Management Dinner after their departure for home the company President droned on about all the great things the Japanese had done, all the great recommendations they had made that the company was going to begin implementing immediately. One of the superintendents, an exceptionally sharp man who had been with the company for years, drunkenly rose to his feet.

"We've been telling you that stuff for five years. For five fucking years. And you wouldn't listen to us because we didn't know anything. We weren't smart. You threw away five million because you wouldn't trust your own employees." As he crashed to his chair he got a standing ovation from most of the yard people and especially the Safety office.

The second incident was when the company hired a hypnotist. The stage was set with maybe thirty or forty tables in front of it. Executives sat among managers who sat among secretaries. My boss, Jim P., and a number of safety officers were at our table.

Five people from the audience were brought onstage to be hypnotized. The hypnotist went to work and more than the stage group came under his spell. I was the only one at our table who didn't go under. Jim denied it vehemently but was unable to recount anything that happened on stage from the time the show started to the time he was awakened.

The hypnotist suggested to a supervisor to do various things like doff a non-existent hat, etc. Then he told him he was naked. The supervisor clutched at his private parts crossing his legs. The hypnotist then suggested everyone in the audience was naked. The supervisor gazed around the room and his eyes rested on the president of the company, Richard V. Pointing at the president he laughed, "Wow, now I know why they call him Big Dick."

Two months later the supervisor was still hearing about that one.

While working at NASSCO I started dating Jack. He had an apartment in Ocean Beach but most of the time he was at my place. At one point he moved in but within three days moved back out because he couldn't take the commitment and confinement implied by living with me. But I continued to date him because he was pretty funny.

One day he was coming up the walk to the front door when I heard a scream. As I pulled open the door I noticed a tarantula on the top step. Ah, one of John's tarantulas had gotten out of its terrarium (he had two, each in a separate enclosure). I yelled at John to get his pet back where it belonged then had to walk Jack up the stairs into the house. I didn't know he was that freaked by spiders.

The guy who held the mortgage on my house wanted it inspected for termites. They were there and the house had to be tented. We moved all the plants and animals including the two tarantula terrariums to Jack's apartment. That night we went to dinner and when we came back Mr. Escape Artist was on top of the other tarantula's enclosure trying to move aside the glass top. Jack screamed. John jumped out of a sound sleep and swept the escapee back to its home. As I turned away I noticed Jack piling the last of five large books on top of the glass cover then repeat his barricade for the other terrarium.

That night we went to bed and I lay back waiting for some tender nothings in my ear. When I didn't receive any I looked over to see Jack stiffly on his back with a can of Raid in his hand, his finger on the trigger.

Running was Jack's love but he had never run a marathon. San Diego County was going to be the site of an International Marathon that started in Chula Vista and ended in Rosarito Beach, Baja California. Jack decided this would be his test. While he was in training running the ten miles between his place and mine I also started training but only for a 10K that was being run the day after the marathon. This was before I joined a gym. Though I always needed exercise I hated running.

Marathon day Jack had it calculated out to the minutes. Based on his times running the ten miles plus a few fifteen and twenty milers he figured to be done in two hours, forty-five minutes. His daughter and I waited at the finish line in Rosarito. And waited. And waited. He staggered in four hours and forty-five minutes later. The one thing he had forgotten was to pre-drive the route, a route that had a number of very steep grades in the Mexican portion.

That night he continued to run in bed to the point that I gave up and slept on the couch. The next day we went to the 10K but it was obvious Jack was physically shot. His daughter finished before me but I was close, something that surprised both of them when I walked up behind them and said, "Boo!"

On Monday the marathon was the chief subject. As Jack walked about the yard with a less than springy step he heard from participants that it was the hardest marathon they had ever run. Some with twenty marathons under their belts said they thought they weren't going to make it. Jack shook his head. "My first marathon and I had to do Mt. Everest."

After we broke up I continued to run but not as much and decided to try a ten-miler. About four or five miles in I started walking then running then walking. By nine miles I and a teenager were the only ones left. I considered just quitting but someone ran back and told me that word had spread and they were holding the finish line open for me. As it came in sight the teenager said, "I'm not going to finish with someone your age. I'd be too embarrassed." He sped ahead but when I got there I got all the applause. I may have been two hours behind the pack but I finished. That night I ran in my sleep.

Jim P. told me two stories about previous Halloweens.

One night he had taken a beer glass and gone trick-or-treating in a neighborhood near his. At his first stop the woman invited him in, got him a beer and they talked. Soon her husband joined them. At one point he said to his wife, "Honey, aren't you going to introduce us?" to which his wife replied, "Introduce you? I thought he was your friend." At that, Jim related, he got up, thanked them for the beer then left.

Jim had an assistant I'll call him Bruce who consistently wore clothes that looked like he was coming back from a long hike. No admonitions could get him into business dress. In addition he was shy, finding it difficult to talk to or even date young ladies.

Halloween night he showed up at Jim's door wearing a nicely tailored suit and white shirt but no tie. Jim's wife, I think her name was Sherrie, answered the door. Bruce told her he was attending a party but didn't have a tie. Would Jim have a spare?

Sherrie invited him in but he declined. She left to find a tie. Upon return she helped knot the tie and stepped back very proud of how he looked. He thanked her profusely then turned to walk away revealing that the suit front did not have a suit back. At all. Evidently he wore something like a man's thong, the shirt collar and a few strategically placed straps to hold the suit on.

Bruce later told Jim about his evening. He had made a number of acquaintances with young ladies who were intrigued by someone so bold. His method of introduction was to invite a pat on the fanny in exchange for patting theirs. Unfortunately, one of the pattees had a very large boyfriend who proceeded to ring Bruce's clock. Bruce noted he had had a great time despite the shiner.

My boss had hired a friend as the Assistant Safety Manager or some such title. The guy knew a lot about safety procedures but very little about managing. More than once he would issue an arbitrary or unrealistic order or make a sexist or racist comment that shocked even hardcore shipyard workers. When this happened and the boss wasn't available I would object and he would proceed to tell me to go to hell. I would speak up even more. His solution to every issue was to outshout the objector particularly if that person was a woman. Didn't faze me and our conversations usually ended with him screaming and me calmly telling him the screaming didn't work. More than once he was reprimanded by the boss and counseled by Human Resources because they all knew he was dead wrong. But he was my boss's good friend and my boss hated to fire anyone.

Finally the breaking point was reached. The Assistant was in the yard reviewing some rigging on a crane. If something was wrong all he had to do was point out the error and describe how it was supposed to be done. Simple. But not for King of the Yard.

"Who the fuck nigger-rigged this cable?" he bellowed to the nearly all-black rigging crew. Walking around the crane he further declared, "Looks like a bunch of wetbacks set this up," to the nearly all-Latino crane operator group. Within 30 minutes four grievances were filed with more promised in the immediate future. Within a few days he was gone. Wonder why.

PERSONAL ADS AND SURVIVING MY SONS

San Diego, 1980 to 1983

My Aunt Joy lived in Tucson, Arizona with my Uncle Floyd and cousin Sheila. Aunt Joy had always had a bad heart from a bout with scarlet fever when she was young and finally her heart gave out. With the boys my mother and I were on our way from San Diego to Tucson for the funeral when we stopped in Yuma, Arizona for lunch.

John looked at me and said, "Mom, how do you feel?"

"How do I feel?" I replied. "Well how do you think I feel? We're going to Aunt Joy's funeral."

"Well I mean besides that. Are you in a good mood?"

Warning bells went off. Turning to look at him full on, I asked, "Just what has happened that I need to be in a good mood about?"

"Well," he mumbled, "you know the black snake I've been keeping in the aquarium?"

"Been keeping? As in past tense?"

"Uh, well, yeah. Past tense."

"So where is it now?"

"Umm, we don't know. It got out of the cage and we haven't found it yet."

"Yet. So how long has it been out of the cage?"

John looked down at Josh then looked up. "Ummm, two weeks?"

My mother almost inhaled her forkful of food. I stared first at John then at Josh both of whom had the look of 'this is our last day' on their faces.

Of course I laughed. "If it hasn't attacked anyone in two weeks it's probably gone or dead in the walls. So don't worry, I won't." Two very relieved boys set to their lunch.

John wanted to go deep sea fishing for his birthday (the end of April) so my mother arranged the trip. He called me at work to tell me we had to be at the dock at four. I replied, "Well that's OK I can just get off work a little early."

"Umm, no, it's not in the afternoon."

"Four in the morning? You've got to be kidding me. I might as well just stay at the bars until they close then come home."

"Grandma can't go, she said she gets seasick and…"

"John I didn't say I wouldn't go. I just need to adjust my mind to the departure hour."

I didn't close down the bars and we did get to the dock on time but Josh was a zombie while John was totally awake. On the boat the first thing Josh did was head for the berths. However to get a berth you had to pay extra and I didn't have extra so we went into the galley and he lay on the bench with his head in my lap. One of the fishermen took pity and gave Josh his berth. We didn't see him again until shortly before we started back to shore.

John was in seventh heaven. Josh finally staggered out and we baited his hook only to catch a barracuda. We'd been fishing for tuna and suddenly we had five or six men trying to trade their tuna for our barracuda. We figured if those guys wanted it so bad it must taste good so we kept it. On the way back the early hour finally hit John. He had been sitting on one of the bar stools and had just gotten a piping hot cup of hot chocolate when he instantly fell asleep. Luckily he had on thick jeans or that cocoa might have permanently affected his equipment. What a way to wake up.

The Rolling Stones rolled into San Diego in October 1981 and I wanted to go with John. Josh swears he wanted to go too but he must not have been that enthused at the time because he wasn't with us. John wanted to take a girl he'd met at school so I bought an extra ticket. Her father was up in arms. We needed some strong, brave man to protect us from all the rock and roll hippies and drunks. I assured him that John and I were capable (particularly since we were both taller than the father) and finally he relented. At the concert I was taking pictures and told John that his girlfriend could show her Dad that everything had been A-OK.

"Yeah he'll probably be real reassured when he sees the bong behind me."

Later we waited for someone from NASSCO who had worked the concert to take us home (my mother had dropped us off). John and the girl were sitting on a wall, a cup of soda next to them. John was thirsty and decided that the germs he might get were less important than slaking his thirst. Grabbing the cup he took a couple of good chugs before he started spitting and hacking. The soda had been liberally laced with rum.

Within a few minutes a stoner wandered up.

"Man that was a good concert wasn't it."

John agreed.

The stoner swayed a little then repeated himself.

John agreed again.

The stoner said, "Man I think I was at the concert. I'm really stoned."

John agreed again.

The stoner held out a peanut bag. "Want some peanuts?"

John looked in the bag. "There's only one."

"Wow," the stoner mumbled. Looking up at John with unfocused eyes he added, "wanna share?"

We went on a ten-day camping trip in early June of 1982. Our first stop was Mammoth Mountain and it was so cold that water on the tables froze overnight. Josh slept in the tent with me but John had opted for his sleeping bag outdoors and basically shook the whole night. His friend Mark, who joined us the next morning, was to add a few interesting moments to the trip.

No matter what the weather when camping I keep clean by wearing a bathing suit and taking a sponge bath. At Mammoth they had sinks and flush toilets so that morning I stood in front of the sink in my bikini washing and sluicing the water over my body. Women in thick warm-ups were incredulous that I would do such a thing in 40 degree weather. As I sluiced with my teeth chattering I stammered, "When you're cold, you're cold for 15 minutes but when you stink, you stink all day." The next morning two women joined me for our morning shower.

Next stop was Yosemite where I noticed John and Mark wandering around the campground then every once in a while making a beeline to our tent area. They'd slowly saunter out again then rush back. Later that evening I realized they'd been stealing firewood from other tent sites.

We hiked to the top of Nevada Falls and met an Asian girl from San Diego who was there with her boyfriend. A few months later we met again – at the US Festival among 365,000 people. If that isn't an example of a small world what is?

Near San Francisco we stayed at a seaside camping area where John and Mark drew a laughing audience when they tried to get dressed standing up in a small pup tent. One guy said I should have charged admission. Later we checked out San Francisco. At a candy store where you scooped bags of candy out of bins I noticed John and Mark going to the cash register with tiny bags of candy. After about the fifth trip I sidled over to John and asked him what the deal was.

"The guy at the cash register is gay Mom. We've never heard a gay guy talk before." Said gay guy was trying very hard not to laugh.

As we wandered through Chinatown John looked up the street and announced, "I think we just left Chinatown." I followed his gaze to see billboards advertising sex clubs with nothing left to the imagination. Not being the Puritan type we discussed what else might be in the clubs since so little was hidden on the billboard.

The final 'incident' was in Golden Gate Park. I think it was the Academy of Sciences but whatever it was (remember this is 1982) there was a large movie theater about half the size of an IMAX. We went into the building with John and Mark saying they wanted to explore by themselves. Certainly I should have caught on that something was up but by this time I was getting a little tourist dazed. So Josh and I went through the exhibits and within maybe an hour I heard John and Mark walking up to me very rapidly with John whispering, "We gotta leave."

I looked at him, puzzled. "Why? We've only been here an hour."

Mark chimed in, whispering, "Yeah, but we gotta leave."

At this point I noticed some security guys looking around, luckily not in our direction, and I got the drift.

We left.

Out on the grass I turned around. "OK you two, what did you do?"

Mark looked at John, John looked at Mark then it appeared Mark was elected for the confession.

"Well we were wandering around and we saw these doors that said **Staff Only** and we wondered if we could get in. But we realized we couldn't just go straight in so we kind of looked around and saw some doors behind the movie screen and we thought maybe those doors would get us in so we tried them." At that point he stopped and looked at John.

Folding my arms I prompted, "OK, go on. You went through the doors?"

To make a long story short they not only got into the staff area but had fooled a security guard into thinking they were visiting someone whose name they had picked up from a sign on a door. They had wandered around the area for fifteen to twenty minutes until someone realized the person they were visiting wasn't even there that day and the chase was on. Hence the fast walk because running would have given them away. I think somewhere in there was mentioned something about wearing some staff jackets but I never did get the whole story. Suffice it to say we decided to go to other places the rest of the day.

I met Charlie I think sometime in 1981 or 1982. He was funny, irreverent, but not boyfriend material. Recently divorced he was out to develop a personal harem. I wasn't of the merry-go-round mentality but I remained in his inner circle as a friend without benefits just to see what would happen with all his potentials. It came down to his having one woman cook his meals, another clean his apartment, a third do his shopping and a fourth his laundry. A couple of others were there for personal duties. I think Charlie kept me in his circle just for the pure differentness I offered. I wouldn't do anything for him. Except one.

In those days men and women met through personal columns in the papers where the interested party had to write to a P.O. box and hope for a response to his/her letter. I had suggested to Charlie that this was a better way (and considerably cheaper) to meet women than the bars. Despite his overwhelming personality Charlie was a little shy in proclaiming his virtues so he declared this method was not for him.

But never being one to listen to someone else's 'No' I helped Charlie out. The Sunday his personal ad went in the paper

I was to join him at his place for lunch. As I walked in he was holding a newspaper and laughing. Looking at me through his shock of brown hair his eyes were dancing.

"You put a personal ad in the paper for me didn't you?"

"An ad?" I asked. "Why would I put in an ad? You said you didn't believe in that stuff."

"Yeah," he answered, "but when you see an ad that describes you to a T you kind of figure someone may have put it in for you."

He stood for moment pondering. "What gets me is how accurate it is. You know me better than I know myself."

I smiled. "Maybe that's why I'm your friend and not a girlfriend. I know you too well."

The next weekend he invited me over to tell me about some of the results. His bed was buried in letters and pictures, some revealing and some downright nude. Laughing he pointed at the letters.

"Look what you did. I am buried in so many possibilities I don't know where to start."

"So you haven't responded to any of them?"

"No, I responded. And what a group. One woman asked to meet me here and when she walked in she was already undressing."

"Well that must have thrilled your heart."

"Come on Flo I like sex but I want it to be what I initiate not with someone I've just met for five minutes. Although that wasn't even five minutes more like two." Shaking his head, he laughed again. "I almost had to physically carry her out of here to get rid of her."

"So what else has shown up?"

Searching through the pile he pulled out one letter. "Here's one you'll really enjoy."

The writer had extolled her charms. She was <u>very</u> beautiful, <u>very</u> well-off, <u>very</u> intelligent, had a <u>very</u> good sense of humor, etc. (She had underlined every 'very.') Her credentials included being a La Jolla real estate broker (the rich of the rich in San Diego) and half owner of a car dealership in El Cajon. Sounded like a match made in bank heaven. Gesturing at Charlie with the letter I said, "Well?"

"God Flo you should have seen her. Your two thighs would have made less than one of hers. She was so fat she waddled. And she looked like someone had hit her in the nose and didn't stop. Plus it was like talking to a door. No brains, no humor. I couldn't wait to get away."

We discussed some of his other responses and I left.

A few days later I had a personal ad date of my own. While I still hadn't joined a gym, I exercised and watched my diet. As a result I was a size 8. (Today I'm a 12 and planning to get back to an 8 but have not implemented my plans as of yet. In other words I've gotten lazy.) Because I made an effort to look good I expected it of the men I dated and was very explicit about this in the ad.

The guy who showed up had a stomach that would have shamed Santa Claus. Extremely overweight his clothes fit him like they were ready to spring for freedom. After a half hour of conversation I determined that even if not grossly overweight he was so limited in intelligence and humor that an hour would be torture.

As I tried to make my quick escape he demanded to know why I wasn't interested. So I told him. To which he replied, "Well I don't need someone like you. I met a woman yesterday and she thinks I'm great. She's very beautiful, very intelligent, very funny. What's more she's a La Jolla real estate broker and owns half of a car dealership in El Cajon. I have a second date with her tomorrow."

To which I silently responded, 'Hmmm, where have I heard that description before?'

I had a couple of other personal ad dates that were a little beyond normal. One guy who had sent funny cards with even funnier comments written in them met me with both arms in casts. I agreed to return him to his house and on the way he admitted his arms had been broken in a drug deal gone bad.

Another guy kept ordering water with celery then finally admitted he hadn't eaten in a day or two because he was staying at a friend's house and there was no food. This was during the time when personal ads were answered by calling a number and leaving a message at two dollars a minute. I asked how many ads he had responded to on his friend's phone and he estimated in the high fifties. Then I asked how he expected to pay for them. With a worried look he asked, "You have to pay?"

But by far the best was the lawyer who sent an 8 by 12 picture and a three page letter filled with witty stories, poems and a self-description with interesting tidbits. By the picture he was very good-looking and in his mid-thirties so I was intrigued. After three letters and no response to my request for a phone number or meeting I decided to find out just who this dude was. Despite giving a partially phony name I was able to track him down. He did not have a secretary so when I entered his office he asked when I had made an appointment. I said, "When you sent the first letter with the picture that is obviously about 30 years out-of-date." While the conversation was short I derived satisfaction from the pure astonishment on his face.

The Steve Wozniak *US Festival* was scheduled for Labor Day weekend in 1982 and I wanted to go with John and Josh. (After I got there I realized I was probably one out of 10,000 people over 40 but with 365,000 people it probably didn't matter.) The tickets were steep so I had entered a radio contest.

One afternoon I got a call at work. My scream of excitement notified everyone that I was going to the *US Festival*!

As I was getting ready to leave early that Friday Jim P. walked in. Now Jim and I were the same age (actually I was maybe half a year older) but he looked like he was in his fifties and I looked like I was in my early thirties. When he discovered where I was going he said, "You're going to some rock and roll festival and you're camping out on blankets? You're in your forties, why don't you grow up?"

To which I replied, "What and look like you?" The entire office broke up.

Luckily he and I had been trading quips ever since he had been hired to manage the Safety office so I could hear him laughing as I left.

That was one hell of a three day concert. To understand why I went I have to give you a little background on my love of rock and roll, heavy metal and the various music forms that most people my age don't generally like.

My first introduction to this music genre was the group *Talk-Talk*. I heard the song on the radio only I didn't realize the song 'Talk-Talk' was by the group *Talk-Talk*. You can imagine the conversation with my kids (and John's friend Mark of course) when I'd say, "Who sings that song 'Talk-Talk'?" and they'd answer, "*Talk-Talk*," and I'd respond, "Yes I know that's the song but who sings it." In desperation they finally bought me the album.

But it still didn't help me connect the names of groups to the songs they sang and I was constantly asking who the group was. At a *Police* concert that included one of *Motley Crue's* first live appearances, John, Josh, Mark and I were walking down the stadium steps to get to the field area.

Hearing a song over the loudspeaker, I called loudly to John. "That song, John, I really love that song. Who sings it?"

With a resigned shake of his head, he replied, "The group we're here to see tonight Mom, *Police*." Mark just tried to hide from all the people around us who were laughing.

At any rate Friday night at the *US Festival* included *Talking Heads*, *Police* and *Oingo Boingo*. That night we slept in the car and John had to cram his 6 foot frame into the front seat. The next morning we all showered in the overhead sprinklers that had been erected to keep people clean and cool. (The temperature was over the 100 mark all three days.) Even though they sprayed everyone with water cannons between acts the heat enervating. By Saturday night Josh and I were whipped and actually slept through *Pat Benatar* and *Tom Petty and the Heartbreakers*. John was fascinated. More than once he came back to tell me all the drugs he'd been offered on his wanderings particularly the guys who were holding signs advertising their wares. (I think a number of girls also offered other things but John wasn't buying.)

When John went to school on Monday (he would have been a sophomore in high school) the *US Festival* was the main topic of conversation. Telling his classmates his mother took him to it was met with hoots of derision. I had to get duplicates of the pictures so he could prove to his classmates that his mom really was 'hip.' At the time Josh was still in elementary school so they didn't care.

The strain of paying the mortgage and other bills on two houses finally came to a head. The strain was exacerbated by the in-ground fiberglass Jacuzzi gas line breaking and having to drain the Jacuzzi. During the winter storms we learned the flotation abilities of fiberglass Jacuzzis as it eased itself out of its concrete framework. The carpet had been shot when I bought the house. I never had the money to replace it. Of the two houses my payments were lower on the Cather house and that one had a pool. A concrete pool.

The Bothe house had to go. I put it on the market in the fall of 1982 (it could have been a year before or after that, can't remember). From that point the sale became a comedy of errors (assuming comedy was the correct noun).

I got a call at work from a realtor. This was close to Halloween.

"I tried to show your house today but we didn't want to disturb the occupants."

'Occupants,' I thought, 'what occupants? The only occupants are John, Josh, me and two renters all of whom are at work or school.' "What do you mean? There shouldn't have been anyone at home."

"Well, uh," the agent stammered, "they were in the living room. We could see it when we walked up the steps."

"Yeah I know you can see the living room but no one was at home."

"I know that is on the listing but there was someone there and we, uh, didn't want to disturb them."

Totally confused by this I assured the agent I would check, ensure the 'occupants' were not there and she could show the house the next day.

That night when I arrived home I parked in the garage then climbed the stairs to the front door so I could see these 'occupants.' Sure enough there was someone in the living room. On the couch that had been turned to make it visible from the front window were two figures. One looked female and the other looked male. They were in the 'prone' position with the male on top and the pants pulled down to reveal what looked like a butt. The 'female's' legs were spread and her pants were askew. Another 'occupant' was in the chair facing the couch with the cat curled in its lap. Even knowing where these 'occupants' had come from (John, Mark, old clothes and some realistic stuffing) it was hard to yell at them because I was laughing so hard.

Another showing was classic vaudeville.

The agent came in the front door with a man who was carrying a briefcase. He had a very stern look and charged into each room as if searching for spore representing malignant growths that might rise to smite him down. The agent mentioned he had allergies that had significantly reduced the houses she could show.

He charged into the bedroom areas as Josh sidled up to me and whispered, "The oven's on fire."

Smiling at the agent as she followed her client into the bedrooms I looked down and, sotto voice, said, "What?"

"The oven's on fire," Josh repeated. "John put something in and it caught fire."

I casually rushed to the kitchen to see John leaning against the breakfast bar cabinets with his foot holding the oven door closed. Large plates covered the stove burners.

"What does Josh mean, the oven's on fire," I barked as low as I could.

He removed his foot, the oven door opened slightly and a sheet of flame blew out. Quickly putting his foot back on the door he replied, "That's what he means. The stuff in the oven is on fire."

Knowing that a full scale conflagration would be a sure deal killer I whispered, "Can you keep it under control while that agent is here?"

John pushed harder on the door. "I think so. I'm trying to eliminate the oxygen so it might die out." John was studying chemistry in preparation for college so I figured he knew what he was talking about.

I searched around the kitchen for the fire extinguisher. Just as I was pulling it out of the cabinet the agent and her client came swinging back to the family room on the other side of the kitchen breakfast bar.

Hiding the extinguisher behind my back I smiled at the agent. "How're things going?"

"Well, OK I guess but he keeps saying he smells smoke. You haven't had a fire here recently have you."

Clutching the extinguisher that due to its weight was sliding to the floor I replied, "No, not that I know of. Why don't you show him the lower level."

She ushered her client to the stairs and as they descended I whispered to John, "You think it's out by now?"

He let off the pressure on the door and a flame once again shot out. Pushing the door back tight he mumbled, "Don't think so."

By this time Josh had gone back to the couch on the other side of the breakfast bar and was eating something while watching television. In those days not a lot bothered Josh and the crisis in the kitchen was one of those things.

The agent and client came back up. The client took a quick look at the kitchen and family room then stormed out of the house with the agent trailing negatively shaking her head at me to indicate it was a no-go.

As the front door closed I pulled the extinguisher up and got it ready to shoot.

"Ready?" I asked John.

"Ready," he replied.

He let the door flop open and I blasted the inside of the stove with the extinguisher.

This was one of those powder-based extinguishers and the kitchen and family room were soon filled with a cloud that hit the ceiling then slowly sifted downward. By the time we got the fire out the cloud, along with the ashes from the fire, had settled about shoulder level where Josh was sitting on the couch. He continued to eat and watch television. As John and I waved away the cloud coughing and choking I turned to Josh on the couch.

"Jesus Christ Josh how can you just sit there? You're sitting in a cloud of extinguisher stuff and ashes. What's wrong with you?"

Looking up at me he said, "Is that from the fire? I thought I was just going blind."

The house never did sell so I just gave it back to the previous owner. He had my initial ten-thousand down-payment yet screamed about how he was going to sue me for backing out on the deal. He later sold it for a lot more than the ten thousand down so I never heard from him again. When I added up the rent I had received over the two years we were in the house I still came out ahead. But it was time to move so I evicted my tenants at the Cather house and sometime late 1982 or early 1983 we moved to the place that became our home for the next sixteen years.

SKIING IN SOUTHERN CALIFORNIA
San Diego, 1980 to 1984

After the move to the second Bothe house I decided it was time the boys learned to ski. While I was still with Ray we had gone water skiing once at Lake Tahoe in May and I was the one in the water getting people up on the skis. So the boys knew how to water ski but at least with snow skiing I wouldn't be freezing my butt off in 54-degree water.

After the little hills in Michigan, Bear Mountain and Snow Summit in the San Bernardino Mountains were impressive. A vertical drop of 1,665 feet beats 485 feet any day. The slopes were a little scary, at least to me. The first time I didn't ski. I got the guys up and taught them the basics then let them go. They loved it. My mother was incensed. I had all these bills and I was spending money on skiing? "They won't remember the bills Mom but they will remember the skiing." They do to this day.

After the first two times I also rented skis and got my ski legs back. John was the more daring often coming back to the lift line base with wide-eyes and reports of hills with moguls as big as Volkswagens. He quickly advanced to the low expert runs. Josh was more cautious but he still was hitting the intermediate slopes.

One day I was on a lift and I looked down to see a figure in a sled being taken down the hill. A figure with the same jacket Josh had been wearing. As soon as the lift stopped I raced to the point where I had last seen the sled. John came up. Josh had been in an accident and was at First Aid.

We both skied to the First Aid station and found Josh sitting in a bed eating ice cream and watching cartoons on television.

"What happened, what's wrong?" I asked anxiously.

"Some woman had a kid with her and the kid skied right into me. I hurt my knee." He pointed to his knee that was packed in ice.

"Does it hurt?" I asked.

"No it feels OK. I just can't ski anymore."

I looked at John. John looked at me. We still had about two more hours on our tickets. "Welllll," I said, "if you aren't in pain then you could probably stay here for a little while longer and we could finish out the day."

By that time the nurse was by his side and she nodded her assent. "No problem. We don't have anyone else needing a bed and he's getting along just fine. He'll probably need to see a doctor when you get back home but there's not a lot you can do about it now unless you take him to a hospital emergency room. We don't think that's necessary."

To this day Josh tells people how I abandoned him in pain and misery at the First Aid station while John and I finished out the day. Like he wouldn't have been eating ice cream and watching cartoons if he'd been at home. On Monday Grandma took him to the doctor where a cast was applied just to be safe. He said it was strained tendons but not anything that would be permanent. At least we got full value for our tickets that day.

I joined a family-oriented ski club that had a chalet at Mammoth Mountain. Our one weekend at the chalet was a trip to remember.

I had a car that did not always work well. At one point I parked it at the dealership and left this note. 'It broke again. Engine turns over but won't catch. It threw up green and yellow fluid on freeway after it quit. Could it be morning sickness? If real expensive, just shoot it. Call when fixed or destroyed, whichever is most merciful. P.S. I'd like a decent car.' The service manager said the note was so funny they were only going to charge me half the labor. However it was still giving me problems the weekend of our trip to Mammoth.

By this time we were in the Cather house on a street at the top of a steep grade. That Friday afternoon I limped my car up the hill, the clutch or something telling me it was not going to make it to Mammoth. Someone, I can't remember who, offered to lend me his van. It needed some work but would probably get me to the mountain and back. Unfortunately it only got me to the end of the street. Desperate (I had paid for the chalet, lift tickets and the equipment rental and I was NOT going to lose that money) I called my mother. Could I use her car? Well yes but it had been giving her problems starting so I should be careful. I figured I could handle it so another renter drove me to her house and we piled our stuff in the car. (The car was a white TransAm that had a 'Go Granny Go' rear bumper sticker. My mom liked to get the jump on other cars at the stop lights.)

We took off, stopped in Victorville for gas and the car wouldn't start. Of course no one at the gas station had jumper cables. So I'm waving people down (the road at that time was two-lane and not very crowded) trying to find some jumper cables. Finally someone stopped and we got the car started. By this time John was wondering if we shouldn't maybe go back home but I said, "No, we are going skiing and we are going to have fun. The chalet is on a hill so if the car won't start we can either find jumper cables or roll down the hill and jump start it." I think this was when John got interested in cars because he had so much to do in keeping that one running that weekend.

We got on the stretch of 365 between Victorville and Mammoth that was relatively straight and relatively empty even during ski season. I pulled over, hopped out of the car then told John to get in the driver's seat because he was driving for the next few hours. Now John was fifteen, had not had driver training and had never, to my knowledge, driven a car. At least he told me he'd never driven a car. As in with very wide eyes and a quivering voice, "You want me to drive Grandma's car? I've never driven a car."

"Well John, you gotta learn sometime. The road is straight. Keep it a few miles below the speed limit. When people flash their lights, move a little to the right to let them pass and keep both hands on the steering wheel. I've had a rough week and I want to rest."

I can't remember how many hours he drove. I do remember he recounted to everyone there and everyone when we got back home how long he'd driven, how far and how everyone was going so much faster than he was. (I think he described every car that passed us.) At any rate I took over near Mammoth and he sat in the passenger seat still jazzed.

To get to Mammoth from the chalet you had to drive or take a shuttle bus. We took the shuttle bus early Saturday morning bringing the skis, boots and poles we'd rented in San Diego. Our day long skiing was only interrupted once when Josh and John told me to follow them down a slope that was really easy and it was one massive mogul. By the time I was at the bottom both skis had released and I had snow in every available crevice. I slung the skis over my shoulder and started swinging them at John as I chased him to the ski lodge. Of course, being a much better skier than I, he was still on skis.

To avoid the hassle of carting the equipment back and forth on the bus we left it in a locker at the lodge and took the shuttle back. That night it started to snow and by morning it was close to a white-out. People started leaving but we couldn't because our ski stuff was still at the lodge. We started up in the car but something happened, either it stalled or we didn't have chains or something so we had to go back.

We didn't want to go back to the chalet. Aside from the hill it was on the other club members had become a little snooty when the kids started having fun and John and Josh were the instigators. (One kid said it was the first time he'd actually laughed at the chalet.) Plus I had met a man who had brought his daughter and proceeded to clarify his relationships with women. A woman who was his daughter's friend would be his friend. A woman who was not his daughter's friend was 'a snack for Daddy.' I asked if the friends of his daughter knew about this restriction. Evidently they found out when they made an overture to him on their status.

I parked the car in front of a restaurant and Josh elected to stay in the car because he was tired and wanted to sleep. The restaurant guys said he could come in but he preferred the quiet of the car. Since the shuttle run was about fifteen minutes we figured we'd be gone maybe a half hour, forty-five minutes at the most. Off we went to rescue our ski equipment.

Between the bus that ended up on its side and the cars that spun out and the drifts, the half hour turned into close to four hours. By the time we got back the car was buried under at least two inches of snow. The side windows had maybe an inch at the bottom that was not covered. Opening the back door I saw Josh wide-eyed.

"I gotta pee," were the first words out of his mouth, his voice seeming to float.

"Pee?" I asked as I pulled him out of the car and started him towards the restaurant door. "Why didn't you go to the restaurant?"

"I was afraid to open the door. I thought I'd been buried alive."

"Josh, you could see out the bottom of the side window."

"Well I've never been buried alive so I didn't know what it would look like."

At least he didn't pee his pants.

My last memorable ski adventure (until I moved to Oregon) was with Leon.

Leon was a tall, black man I had met at the Family Fitness Center and as such he was really in shape. In his late forties he'd always been in the top five or ten for bicycle or running races. He worked as the Produce Manager for a national grocery chain and had many friends, all of whom skied. But in the fifteen years of their friendship they had never gotten him skiing. That was going to change.

We went to Bear Mountain and he wore a one piece ski outfit that was either orange or yellow, I can't remember. (Although my mind's eye sees yellow). He wanted people to see him coming down the slopes as the black Jean-Claude Killy a famous French alpine ski racer who dominated the sport in the 1960s. Being over 6'2", in that bright outfit, he would not be missed.

For the better part of the morning he took lessons and practiced on the bunny slopes. By lunch he was bored with the bunny slopes. I said I'd take him to some of the really easy intermediate slopes. I knew all of them as I never was an expert skier except once for two hours but more on that later. I got him in the chair for the lift and we took off his eyes getting bigger as we went higher.

"How high is this going to go?" he said as he looked to where the lift ended way at the top of the mountain.

"Don't worry. This has three drop-off points. We're getting off at the first one where all the slopes are easy intermediate."

We hit the first drop-off and Leon panicked. He got tangled up in the chair, couldn't get off.

Pulling him back into the chair I told him to calm down we'd get off at the next drop-off. It was where the harder intermediate slopes were but we could take our time getting down. I rehearsed with him how he was going to get out of the lift chair at the next drop-off.

Which for some reason was closed.

Now we had a problem. We were going to the top and the few intermediate slopes were close to single diamond, the lowest of the expert. We had the option of staying in the chair and going back down to the bottom because we couldn't get off the lift on the way down. Going back on the lift? Where all his friends would see that he panicked? Not an option. He'd get off at the top and make it down somehow.

We got off and of course the minute he got off the chair he fell. I told him this was totally normal that no one stood up and skied away the first time they used a chair lift. He felt a little better. I found the easiest expert run and we started down. And he fell. He got up, went maybe fifteen yards and fell.

Now I have to tell you this about Leon. He was a true gentleman. He did not believe that women should swear and more emphatically he did not believe that men should swear in front of women. But by his fourth fall the f-bomb was falling all over the mountain.

After about fifteen minutes he told me to ski down to the bottom and come back up because it was going to take him some time to make it down. I protested, he insisted so I skied down to the bottom of the hill and took the lift back up. I got off the lift and wondered where he was. I cupped my hand to my ear.

"FUCK!"

There he was!

When I got to him it was frustration city. I suggested we could get one of the ski rangers to take him down in a sled but that was a worse alternative then riding back on the lift line. During this conversation he was trying to ski and of course f-bombing all over the place. Mothers went by with their hands over their children's ears. Even the wolves slunk away.

It took him about an hour and a half to get down a ten minute run. I had gone up and down maybe three or four times each time stopping to show him how to do a traverse or side step or snow plow down to the next level where I would meet him on the next run. At the bottom he said he was going to practice some more on the bunny slopes and would meet us back at the bottom of the lift line at closing time. At 4:30 we gathered near the bottom of the lift line to watch Leon, his skis over his shoulders, trudging towards us with a marked limp. He had sprained his ankle on the bunny slopes.

What was really ironic was that I ran into him a number of years later and he had become an expert skier. He no longer took lessons because the instructors told him they had no more to teach him. He had skied throughout the United States, Canada, Europe and I think South America. I said, "You mean I was the one who got you skiing, you've been all over and I've gone maybe ten times since the first time? There's something wrong with this picture."

At least he learned how to ski the expert slopes. I don't know about the f-bombs.

CATHER AND DATAGRAPHIX
San Diego, 1982 to 1984

When we moved back to the Cather Avenue house, one of my renters from the Bothe house moved with us. He, along with some of the other renters I had while living at Cather, is mentioned in the skunk story that started this book. He's also mentioned here for a quick intro to the power of concentration.

As a Big Brother he mentored two or three boys in the 9 to 11 age group. As such they were at the house more than once for sleep-overs. Add in Penny the fox-terrier who had to be confined to the kitchen with a gate due to her inability to understand house breaking plus two cats who liked to tease her plus my two sons plus their friends and weekends were not very quiet. But I had learned to cope.

One night a date picked me up at the house. The date was a man who had been married but the most his wife had brought to the marriage was a small cat that left with her. Consequently his lifestyle was a little more sedate than mine.

I was in the kitchen reading the newspaper when I heard the doorbell. The kitchen opened to the front entrance. My renter, his overnighters, Josh and John were using the stairs to chase each other, stairs that ended at the front door. As Josh swung by he opened the door. My date stared in as three more boys raced down the stairs chasing my renter, the cats tried to escape to the outdoors and Penny tried to catch the cats as they flew past.

Stumbling in, he spied me at the kitchen table.

"How can you stand this?" he cried.

"Stand what?" I asked as I looked up from my paper.

"This noise! This confusion!"

I wrinkled my brow. "What noise? What confusion?" Needless to say it was a one-date relationship.

The first Christmas in the Cather house Josh wanted a bicycle. It would be his first none-hand-me-down bicycle so it had to be special. He vacillated between a road and a mountain bike but finally settled on a road bike. I bought one after work and took it to a guy who worked in the Safety Office and was going to assemble it for me. He carried it up the stairs to his second-floor apartment.

The next morning Josh said, "I looked at the bikes the other kids have and I like the mountain bikes better. You can ride them on the hills and stuff and I think I'll be riding in the hills more than on the street." I asked twice to verify that he was sure. He was sure.

That evening my colleague carried the bike back downstairs. I bought a yellow mountain bike and he carried the new bike upstairs. Keep in mind all this up and down was with a bulky box, something a lot harder to maneuver then an assembled bike.

The next morning Josh approached me before I left for work. "You know yesterday I said I wanted a mountain bike?" Seeing my left eye starting to squint, a sure sign I was not pleased, he hastened to add, "No, no, I still want the mountain bike. I just don't want it to be yellow. I don't like yellow. I mean, if I am getting a bike I wouldn't want it to be yellow."

At work I asked my co-worker if he had started to assemble the bike. He gave me a suspicious look. "What if I have?"

"Ummm, if you have is it to a stage where you can't disassemble it?"

One eyebrow inched up. "Why?"

"Ummmm, well, Josh never did designate a color but this morning he kind of did designate a color. Anything but yellow."

He sighed, looked at the ceiling then said in a resigned tone, "I'll have it downstairs by the time you get there."

The day he was to assemble it I came bearing gifts of appreciation. When he opened the door I looked at him with a pained expression. "Ummmm…"

"No," he babbled, "I am not packing that thing up again. No, no!"

Took me a couple of minutes to convince him I was kidding.

We went to the second *US Festival* on Memorial Day weekend in 1983 but it wasn't as much fun as the first one. Only this time I had to make triplicate copies of the pictures so both John and Josh could prove to their classmates that their mother had taken them to the *US Festival*.

By mid-1984 I had nothing to do at NASSCO. Originally I had been hired to get the Safety and Industrial Hygiene departments organized, i.e. ensure that the clerical staff did their jobs and that paperwork flowed efficiently particularly responses to OSHA and the press when there were major injuries or deaths.

Within a month or so I was reviewing safety specialist paperwork for logic, responsiveness to the issues and citing the correct OSHA regulations. Then I designed the software system for reporting injuries to OSHA and CalOSHA. I wrote the shipyard Safety and Repair manuals including Industrial Hygiene, Fire and OSHA requirements plus citing appropriate electrical, plumbing, painting, and enclosed space codes. I developed the budget, picked up the budget and capital equipment work for Security and the Fire Department and performed a host of other duties not in my job description. By 1984 I had performed a study and designed a software system to link medical and workers' compensation costs to supervisors so the company could target those supervisors creating problems. One analysis illustrated what we'd been telling the unions for years. The highest incidence of eye injuries requiring the employee to leave work was always opening day at the Del Mar Race Track.

I've always documented how work was done. As a result I had documented repetitive activities like the monthly statistical reports and budget monitoring to the point that the clerical staff could do them. They could also prepare the annual budget. I started working for other departments preparing a Shipbuilding Cost Accounting Manual for the new accounting system they were implementing. Following up on Workers Comp cases. Got a project, give it to Flo.

But it didn't get me any farther up the promotional ladder and the projects weren't challenging. A Management Trainee program opened to prepare those with degrees for supervisory positions in the yard. I applied but was told that no women would be allowed in the program. As the Director of Human Resources put it, "You could sue us for sex discrimination and win. And we'd have to pay. But you'd never get another job in San Diego." Such was the power of a key corporation in a Navy town.

I left NASSCO for DatagraphiX, a company that made microfiche output equipment and high speed printers. As such the company had sales offices throughout the United States. That became important the day the San Diego Padres won the National League Pennant and were on their way to play the Detroit Tigers. Within minutes our switchboard received over a thousand calls from sales people in Detroit trying to snag playoff tickets from Padres season ticketholders.

I had scheduled a trip to Mackinaw Island, Michigan with a guy I had met in San Diego. Bret (not his real name) was working for General Dynamics in Detroit. He came to San Diego maybe six to nine times a year to coordinate with the local GD plant and we connected when he was here. His home base was

Washington, D.C. but he was on loan to Detroit. I call him Bret because based on what happened using his real name would be kind of embarrassing.

To him.

The trip happened to fall on the very weekend the Padres would be in Detroit. I thought, 'Wow, serendipity. Wouldn't it be great to get some tickets to the games? I could sell them and basically pay for my trip plus make a profit.' Low and behold one of the managers had season tickets and was willing to sell the playoff tickets for face value. I was on my way to riches.

The flight to Detroit had one stop in Dallas and the plane I had to catch was at the other end of the concourse from where the San Diego plane landed. I had to hustle big time to make my connection. As I ran down the walkways I heard someone call my name.

It was Neil from Monterey fame but not the Neil I had rejected. This Neil was totally buff. All the weight had been replaced by nicely toned muscle. He asked where I was headed and said he had to catch a flight in the same area so he'd help me out.

"Wow," I exclaimed as he grabbed my bag, "you have really changed and all for the good."

"Yeah," he replied, "and it was all because of you."

At my questioning look he went on. "When I got that letter from you I was pissed as hell. I tore it up and threw it in the waste basket. Then I decided to look at myself in a full-length mirror to prove how wrong you were. After one look I got the pieces out of the waste basket, taped them back together, put the letter on my refrigerator and joined a gym."

"That's wonderful. I'm really happy for you. You look great."

"So where are you going?" Keep in mind he's asking this while carrying the luggage and garment bag that he had bought me for the Monterey trip.

"To Detroit for a trip to Mackinac Island with my boyfriend."

He stopped and looked at me. "Wait a minute. I'm carrying the luggage I bought for you so you can take a weekend trip with another man?"

With a big smile I shrugged my shoulders and offered to take it back. Letting bygones be bygones he carried it to my gate. I told him to call me when he was in San Diego again and his only reply was, "Something like this could only happen with you."

(As an aside I have been in a number of airports. The Oakland airport is the only one that announces, along with keeping an eye on your baggage and telling security about suspicious people, that illegally parked cars will be ticketed and towed. When is the last time you saw an illegally parked car in the gate section of an airport? Strange.)

I had advertised the tickets for Saturday and Sunday in the Detroit papers. We were keeping the Friday tickets because Bret had never been to a baseball game. Bret picked me up at the Detroit airport Thursday evening and installed me in his apartment. I called those who had responded to the ticket ads and made arrangements for the pick-up on Friday at Bret's place. At $200 a ticket I stood to make a $500 profit on my trip. Bret was working Friday but we planned that he would call me from work, I'd pick him up and we would go to the game from there.

I was waiting in the apartment for him to call and the phone rang. I answered with a happy 'Hello Babe' and got a dead silence.

"Hello?" I repeated. "Is someone there?"

I heard, "Who is this?" from a decidedly angry female.

"This is Flo. Who is this?"

"This is JoAnn, Bret's girlfriend. What are you doing in his apartment?"

"Well since he invited me to visit him I guess you could call me his girlfriend too."

A dead silence for about ten seconds then, "Where is the bastard?"

"At work. He's supposed to call me to pick him up. In fact he might be trying to call me now so we better make this short."

"You tell that son-of-a-bitch to call me the minute he gets home." This last sentence was in a somewhat shrill voice. The bang of the receiver was loud.

Finally Bret called me to pick him up. I mentioned the lady(?) caller. His first reaction with panic in his voice was, "You answered the phone? Why the hell did you answer the phone?"

"You said you were going to call me to pick you up. Wouldn't it be kind of hard to know it was you calling me if I didn't answer the phone?" (He had not told me to monitor the calls through his answer machine.)

"Damn it, I didn't want you to answer the phone!" This was in a much louder tone of voice.

"So how would I have known to pick you up? Were you going to shoot an arrow through the window with a message?"

"Just pick me up and I'll try to figure out what to do."

"Not having two girlfriends at the same time might be a start."

He hung up not too gently. I went to the car that was parked in a car port where the roof was held up by metal poles. Against one of which I kind of creamed the car's right front fender.

Being slightly pissed off does tend to make one a little less alert to possible car crunching protuberances.

Driving up to his place of work the crumpled fender was away from him. As I made a U-turn and pulled up to the curb it was now proudly displayed. His face crumpled like his fender.

"What happened?"

"I was a little upset about your hidden girlfriend and being upset when I was backing out meant I didn't pay close enough attention to the pole holding up the carport."

Shaking his head he mumbled, "I don't believe it. I just got the car out of the shop two days ago. It was there for two weeks for body work after a woman hit me in the condo parking lot. Two days."

"You want me to continue driving?"

"Yeah the damage has been done."

We had a brief discussion about the girlfriend. The ten-year-relationship girlfriend who lived in D.C. We decided that since I was already there and the reservations already made we'd do the baseball and Mackinac Island things then never see each other again.

That night at the game I learned the seats were behind a post. Bret said, "Wow those guys you sold the tickets to will be pretty upset when they see where the seats are."

I replied, "I'm not worried they have your telephone number and address." His smile indicated he didn't quite get it.

Can't remember who won but I do remember they did the Wave and Bret was like a little robot when he got up and down. He also was very robotic during the whole game never once cheering or razzing or saying much at all. Now that I could see him in his home environment it was pretty easy to say adios.

We went to Mackinac. It was foggy both days. The atmosphere (in the bedroom) was on high frost level. When we got back to his apartment Sunday night he went into hyper-drive about how he couldn't have me there one more day as he was too used to being alone. I had to leave. Since my plane didn't depart until Monday I asked where he expected me to go. He didn't care just as long as it wasn't in his apartment.

Luckily I knew a woman, I think her name was Sandy or Sharon, who lived nearby with her husband and kids. We'd become friends years back when I was still living in Michigan and helping people who were having child visitation or other divorce problems. We hadn't kept in touch but she welcomed me just the same. They could drop me off at the airport the next morning no problem.

Bret left me at the door after a nearly soundless ride and laid rubber in his haste to leave. We had agreed that his duplicity had caused part of the problem with the crumpled fender so I only had to shell out $200. At Sandy's I told her and her teenage kids about the money I'd made on the tickets. The teenagers left and about two minutes later we could hear one of them on the phone.

"Come over, come over, we've got a real live ticket scalper staying at our house. Come over and see her."

While at DatagraphiX I took John and Josh to the Del Mar horse races. Del Mar is probably the third or fourth most important race track in California and pretty large. We entered, I purchased racing form booklets for both boys and we headed to the standing room only section of the track. The Grandstand loomed above us.

John studied his booklets intently. Josh took a look then said, "I want to see the horses."

I took him to the paddock area for the first race where he studied each horse as it was promenaded along the paddock area. He was twelve at the time. He made a few marks on his booklet then told me which horses to bet and in what order, win, place or show. We returned to the standup area, I placed the bets and the race began.

All of Josh's horses came in as he had predicted. I screamed. Now understand that I am very loud when excited. Or laughing. John told his friends that he never worried about getting lost in a crowded venue. All he had to do was stand back, wait a few minutes then listen for my laugh. Homed him in every time.

I raced to the betting windows to collect the winnings. Josh and I went to the paddock area for the second race. He looked at the horses, made his little marks in his booklet. We returned to the standing area, I made his bets as directed, he won again.

By the fifth race (out of the eleven scheduled) I had a little parade following me to the betting windows. No matter what the race Josh was scoring about 75% wins on his bets. By the tenth race I was totally out of control, screaming as every horse came in as Josh had predicted.

On the eleventh race Josh gave me instructions on the betting, putting down everything. Being the adult in the group, I decided he was going to lose all his winnings based on his bets so I bet the horse to place instead of win. The horse won. Even to this day Josh has never let me forget that I screwed him out of over $150.

As we left the track a guy came up and handed me a $100 with an invitation to join him the next evening for dinner. Josh had won him over $2,500 and he wanted to show his appreciation. I did the dinner, he was not an interesting person but at least our family was ahead $100.

The next day various people dropped by my office to congratulate me on my winnings. When I asked how they knew one lady responded, "We were in the Grandstands and we could hear you. All the way up there. You are really loud when you're excited."

Josh was never able to repeat his success in subsequent trips to the track. Maybe it was just luck but we all concluded it was his innocence. As he understood the mechanics of statistical analysis it killed his instincts. But that was one hell of a day for all of us. John came out negative that day and subsequent days so he was not impressed with his brother's abilities.

I had been hired as a Senior Department Administrator to share duties with a male SDA. However the woman I was replacing had been responsible for much of the data processing functions performed in and for the department. Because the other SDA was more accounting oriented I would be lead for implementation of a personal-computer-based connection to the main frame. This included assembling the PCs, learning the software and teaching the software to users. At the time the DEC PCs we were using were pretty clunky relative to RAM, hard drives and the software developed for them. I can remember many times when I was still working at one or two o'clock in the morning trying to get something to work or salvaging something that had crashed due to software and hardware limitations.

Another duty of my position was to listen to my boss, the Vice President of Operations, pontificate on problems within his span of control. After I got to know the managers I realized some of the problems were the Vice President and his concept of span of control.

Basically he liked to stir things up. When hired I had given NASSCO two weeks' notice. I met many of the managers when I interviewed. When I started at DatagraphiX most of the departments had been reorganized, managers now reported to someone else and their responsibilities had changed. Within about six weeks of starting the VP wanted to discuss with me another reorganization. He was not pleased when I suggested maybe giving everyone a chance to adjust to the previous reorganization before moving walls again. I soon learned he reorganized about every three months. It wasn't hard to see why things didn't work as smoothly as they should.

Within nine months I had completed the PC implementation and organized my duties to the point that I had little to do. I started working with the divisions to trouble-shoot problems where they didn't have the staff to do the research and analysis.

One issue was the cost accounting reports that were designed to highlight areas where defects were occurring. Trouble was no one understood the reports. I had worked in accounting and budgeting for years and I didn't understand the reports. The Accounting Manager contended there was nothing wrong with the reports. The supervisors were resisting using them. After my butting heads with him for a month the VP ordered him to change the reports. They were now understandable and defects decreased. The Accounting Manager, understandably, was pissed.

Unfortunately in 1985 the company had to cut back 10% in all departments. Since my position had become superfluous I had to go. But I did have an option of transferring to another department. Accounting. Wasn't much of a choice so I set out to be a consultant.

Before I leave DatagraphiX I have to mention Joanie and Mark. Joanie was a black woman who had married a white man. Mark was gay and had a live-in companion who he called his husband. A few days before the company Christmas party, Mark asked Joanie if she was going to the party and perhaps bringing her husband. Joanie said yes to both questions then asked why Mark needed to know.

"Well if you bring your husband it won't look so strange when I bring mine."

Joanie stuttered, "Ummm, well, Mark, it's not quite the same."

NEIGHBORS
San Diego, 1984 to 1986

After the layoff I worked in software training, often developing the programs I was going to teach. One job involved my teaching software to men on Workers Comp who suffered back injuries at work and were being retrained for other professions. The training company was a scam, keeping the students in classes until it was time for them to graduate and the company had to find them employment. Since they were not college trained nor had any real experience there would be no jobs or low-wage jobs. If no jobs were available or the student balked at minimum wage the company would ask the trainers to fail the students so they could be dropped with cause. Of course the state would never get the money back but the company would have fulfilled their training obligation. Too bad the students were too dumb to learn. I didn't last long because I refused to go along with the scam. But while there I did have an interesting experience.

My herniated disk had gone bad again. By the weekend I was having trouble walking but I was still up enough to go to a football game. I made it into the stadium and through the game (I think the Chargers won) but at the end my date had to half carry me to my car. On Monday I came to work bent over to the point that I was looking directly at the floor.

Keep in mind these students had suffered back injuries. Not a day went by that one or the other didn't complain about their back, how hard it was to sit for more than an hour, how they couldn't walk and on and on. Then I walked in doubled over. I conducted the lesson plus walked around the room helping individuals. They were awed. More important they were cowed.

173

If a woman could suffer that much pain and not whine plus still do her job what did that say about men? Never heard another complaint.

At another software training job at the Navy Supply Depot in San Diego I made a big splash on my first day by spilling a cup of coffee into our printer. One of the Depot higher ups was a mental case from the Viet Nam war. From the first day he was showing up at our training office or following me into the lunch room or waiting for me outside the training rooms. He loved to tell me how he killed people during the war or saw women raped or other gross incidents to intimidate me. I think he had some kind of power over my company being there because they weren't doing too much to stop him. Finally I told my manager and co-contractor I was going to higher authorities and I could care less if we lost the contract. The guy was either canned or sent elsewhere because I never saw him again.

When I moved back to Cather Avenue the house next door was occupied by an older woman and her much older mother. The older woman was a little strange and, as mentioned in the skunk story, had built a brick wall during the winter between her house and mine. She claimed she had seen rats around our garbage cans although these would have been the first rats to occupy the area in probably twenty years. The wall extended from the back of my garage to about six feet from the front sidewalk. Since most of University City was occupied by white collar types, rats and dumpy yards just weren't part of the picture.

Spring hit and we turned on the pool pump and other filtration systems. But they worked erratically and the electrician I hired concluded something was wrong with the electrical line. I had John do a little exploratory digging on our side of the wall. Sure enough her workmen's picks had done a number on the conduit containing the electrical line.

I wrote her a letter noting the problem and stated that it would cost $167 to repair the conduit and line. Her response was that my conduit was on her property and therefore she had no legal responsibility for the damage. Well thems were fighting words to me. No matter where the conduit was her workmen had broken it and she was going to pay for it.

Based on the survey marker in the sidewalk her wall was on my property so I informed her that she was liable for the repair and if push came to shove additional monies for her encroachment on my property.

She responded by hiring a surveyor for $250 to prove the wall and my conduit were on her side of the property line. Basically they were but they were inside my fence line so the mistake was due to the fence location that lined up with the survey marker. It was an encroachment based on adverse possession and she bought it with the house. Being a real estate broker had its advantages.

Next she hired an attorney for $250 who presented me with an agreement wherein she would grant me an easement for the conduit revocable at her discretion with a ninety day notice. I remember looking at the attorney and asking, "Are you serious? Would you expect anyone to sign this?" Shaking his head with a woebegone expression he admitted his client was not too sharp in understanding the law.

After two more futile letters to her I filed in small claims court for $800. On the day of the trial I entered the courtroom with pictures and pierced conduit in hand. By this time the conduit had been encased in dirt and water that had caused most of it to rust. When my case was called I presented both the pictures and the conduit to the judge. His look of consternation at seeing this dirty, rusty six foot section of conduit lying on his desk set the courtroom to hysterics. The lady protested but the judge agreed with me on the cost of the repair as he delicately lifted the conduit and motioned to his clerk to remove the evidence.

She paid the $167 plus some other costs but never recouped the $500 spent to prove I was wrong. Within a few months the house had changed hands. Her 24-year-old nephew, Steve, moved in. If she was weird he was totally off the chain.

When Steve moved in he promptly set himself as the person who would police the neighborhood to ensure its pristine sanctity. Going to each person's house on our street he told them where to keep their garbage cans, how to stack wood to avoid termites in the fences, proper lawn care, etc. Considering that most of the houses were owner-occupied and people bought houses in the area because our street looked so nice his comments were not graciously taken. One time the lack of grace was very evident.

Steve had a brother staying with him and his brother had a car. A beat-up-piece-of-junk car. Rather than park in Steve's driveway or in front of Steve's house the brother parked across the street taking up the parking space in front of someone else's house. This someone else got a little tired of visitors not being able to use the space in front of his house so one day he marched over to Steve's house to request the car be parked where it belonged in front of Steve's property. Now Steve was about 5'10" and the other guy about 5'5". Steve stood behind his screen door and informed the neighbor that the car was being parked at its location because he, Steve, did not want a piece of junk parked on or near his property. After the little guy almost tore Steve's screen door off the car was parked in front of Steve's.

Steve never quit. He did not like noise and called the police when the boys had friends over to splash in the pool. He complained about John working on his car in the garage. He yelled at them constantly if they played their music above hearing level (his not theirs). He threatened me repeatedly with reporting me to the neighborhood association that I and no one else on the street had ever heard of. (Evidently one was named in our grant deeds but had never been organized.)

One day he had been berating Josh about our wire-haired terrier Gil's barking at him. Josh picked up Gil and said, "Wow, are you afraid of this ferocious attack dog?" Steve reached over the fence and punched Josh in the nose. I called the UC police division. The officer who answered said, "God is he at it again?"

I asked what he meant.

"I'm on temporary assignment from the Pacific Beach division and I know exactly who you're talking about. That guy is a legend in the San Diego Police Department."

"So why don't you do something about him."

"We wish we could but we have no other option then to investigate his rants and just fail to follow up." In this case he was told if he punched Josh again he would be facing jail time so we had no more incidents.

The boys retaliated with pranks. One involved a renter who joined the boys, including John's friend Mark, in infiltrating Steve's back yard and peppering his sliding glass doors with water balloons. I was asleep upstairs when I heard a loud 'whump' then the doorbell. Getting out of bed I went to the head of the stairs that led directly up from the front door. At the door were two police and my renter. Glancing up he saw me and waved his hand behind his back for me to stay out of sight. I stepped back and listened as he explained to the officers that he was a renter, the next door neighbor was a liar and the boys had been watching television with him the whole time. The next door neighbor had made a lot of enemies on the street. No telling where the balloons came from.

After the police left I went downstairs and noticed the renter had a large knob on his forehead.

"So how did you get that knob? It wasn't there earlier tonight."

The boys were laying on the floor laughing as the renter explained that when he saw the police car pull up he had run to the back sliding glass door to warn the boys and the door had been closed. The 'whump' I had heard was him bouncing off the glass onto his butt. Luckily the whump was loud enough that the boys had heard it and were able to assemble in the living room innocent as lambs.

Other renters during this period included the man with the gun in the skunk story starting this book. Joe had other attributes including a New Jersey accent. Some kids had been harassing Josh and one night he came home a little bedraggled. They had jumped him in the canyon and roughed up him and his bike. Josh knew the kid's name so Joe got the number and called the father.

"You know Josh's mother is my lady and I'm not happy about your kid roughing him up. I just got back from a meeting on the East Coast with the Teamsters and coming home to this makes me mad."

On the other end of the line you could hear the father yelling at his son, "God damn you, you really got me in trouble this time." Josh had no more problems.

(Josh sealed his safety the day he called John when two kids two years older than him were waiting for him outside the store. John made it clear that if Josh ever was attacked, they would bear the consequences no matter who did the attacking. Josh was not harassed again. Shades of my days at the inner city school in Pontiac.)

Another renter didn't have the money to pay the rent. One day I came home to find the house had been robbed. Since the only room that had been hit was mine it was pretty obvious who the robber was. Who else would know about the antique gun and platinum and diamond ring setting? (But didn't know about the diamond rings in another renter's room. Ha Ha!) However without proof I could only be angry that the 'robber' had taken costume jewelry that John and Josh had given me over the years.

One thing that crossed my mind was people's reactions to robberies. I had read how those who were robbed felt 'raped' or 'violated' as if the sanctity of their home and body would never be the same. What rubbish. Something was lost. Maybe it couldn't be replaced but no one had died or been hurt or actually raped. Deal with it.

John's high school graduation party really demonstrated where the UC police stood relative to Steve.

University City High School had a 1985 graduating class of about 465 students. John wanted to have a party at the house. Now keep in mind this was a 1700 square foot house with maybe 1200 of those square feet on the first floor. The pool landscaping was being replaced so at that point it was mostly dirt around the pool. But I figured 25 maybe 30 kids, we could handle it. Illegal though it was we would be supplying beer and no other alcohol would be allowed. No drugs, no smoking in the house, no pot. Strict rules. Be a breeze.

Two days before the party I was sitting at the kitchen table reading the newspaper when I heard John and Mark, also sitting at the table, discussing the party.

"Did you get the flyers made?" asked John.

Mark's answer was affirmative with the addition that they had been mostly distributed.

"When's the band going to show up?"

Mark mentioned a time when my head popped up.

"What flyers? What band?"

John looked at me but not *directly* at me. "Well, we ran off a few flyers to tell people about the party."

"And what is a few?"

"Umm, just a few."

"Try a number on me."

A soft voice with kind of a questioning tone. "Four hundred?"

I think my eyes went a little wide at this. "And a band? What kind of band?"

"Well you know a band. It's just some of the guys at school have a band they play around with."

"So how many people are in this band? Like what instruments do they play?"

"Umm, well you know. A couple of guitars."

"And?"

"Well I think one guy plays the drums."

"And?"

"Umm maybe a saxophone. Or so."

Leaning back in my chair I kind of huffed out a breath then took one slowly back in.

"Let me get this straight. You have invited 400 people to a party at this house with a band that has, at the minimum, five players?"

At this Mark piped up, "I think it's seven" to which John waved at him to basically shut up.

But Mark wasn't through. "We're charging admission though, five dollars a head. So we can pay for the beer and food. And everyone has to give us their car keys when they come in so no one will drive home drunk."

Shaking my head I laughed, "Small comfort when we get thrown in jail for a riot. I guess we need to call in the other renters for crowd control and beer runs because I sure can't handle it. And I bet this band has sound equipment which means most of the living room will be taken up with them."

"Don't worry Mom we'll handle it."

That night the only other graduation party had 35 kids and was under total control. Ours had over 125. Pictures I took show a wall of kids in every room downstairs, in the back yard around the pool, in the pool, on the patio and in the front yard. (Luckily it was a large front yard.) Cars and limousines were parked for four blocks around my house, in some cases blocking off streets. Luckily all the neighbors had been warned and many had left the area for the night. At one point I was taking fees at the door when the police drove by. They looked at me, I looked at them. I shrugged my shoulders, they shrugged theirs and I never saw them again. Of course Steve was livid and kept shouting across the fence that we had to quiet down or he would call the police. Obviously his calls didn't have much impact.

The next morning my house was a disaster with kids all over the floors and back yard. They finally dragged out in the early afternoon and the boys took up mops and pails to clean the floors that were now caked with mud from the back yard. They even rented a carpet cleaner. For blocks around the road and sidewalks were strewn with bottles and cans. It took two days to clean up the streets.

About four years later I was writing out a check at the local Safeway when the clerk looked down. "Wow are you John's mother?" When I concurred she exclaimed, "I was at his graduation party. That was the greatest party of my life."

It certainly was the biggest.

Right before the Fourth of July that year we went to Tijuana ostensibly to buy some Kahlua but for John and Mark to buy fireworks. Now buying fireworks in TJ and transporting them back to San Diego County is a big no-no but it's done all the time. Since they like to pull cars out of line at the border I wouldn't drive across. If they got fireworks they had to figure out how to get them back through Customs on their own.

We were passing back to the United States through the gates and the agents were checking everyone out. I had to show my bottles of Kahlua, open my purse, turn out my pockets. The boys were walking through trying to look nonchalant. A woman agent was looking long and hard at John and Mark's respective crotches. She asked them to turn around. They did. She looked again. They were starting to sweat. She thought about it then waved them through.

As we exited the door Mark ran to a pillar holding up the crossover, got behind it and pulled down his pants. I heard, "Ohh, oww, ooohhh." Seemed the fireworks he had hid in his briefs had started to leak with all the nervous sweat and his private parts were now somewhat burned. He did not appreciate my burst of laughter nor my sly looks and guffaws into my hand as we walked to the car. John came through it fine.

Years later when Josh tried to smuggle some across he got busted. No fine but he did lose the fireworks and the money he spent on them. From that point he bought from those who had already smuggled them across the border.

HUSBAND NUMBER THREE
San Diego, 1986 to 1990

In 1986 I met Rob who was to become my third and last husband. The marriage was a mistake from the beginning. I listened to my mother who thought companionship was more important than really being in love. Consequently I gave in to Rob's entreaties to marry. While we had some interesting experiences Rob's real contribution was that he and his Yamaha Venture tour bike introduced me to motorcycling. That shaped my life for many years to come.

When I lived at the second Bothe house I had bought a wire-haired fox terrier. She was introduced in the skunk story. As I noted earlier the breeder had given us a 'deal' if we agreed to breed Penny and we ended up with two puppies the breeder was going to put down because they did not conform to show requirements. We sold one and kept the other who, like Penny, was totally untrainable. Gil escaped more than once and was often returned by Rob with Gil proudly balanced on the tank of the motorcycle.

One Monday I returned home to find this note on the kitchen table.

> took josh to school. ran out of gas at bottom of hill. lots of traffic. lots of rain. couldn't push car, uphill both ways. tried to commit hari-kiri. only had a pen knife.
>
> walked home, drenched. wanted to put dogs out so i could get motorcycle out of garage. put gil in backyard without leash. penny doesn't want to get out of bed. poor dog, arthritis acting up because of weather. good dog, she

won't run off if i open garage door. caught up with her in clairemont.

got car home. stopped raining. thought I'd put another coat of paint on the bookshelf. put both dogs in backyard. painted bookshelf. let dogs back in. gil wants to sniff bookshelf. i yell. gil runs behind bookshelf. i chase. gil makes circle around bookshelf, keeping in constant contact with wet paint.

it's eleven o'clock. this is not a good way to start the week.

However, it was Rob's relationship with Steve that brought real excitement into the house.

Rob was a retiring person who rarely stood up for his rights. His method of dealing with problems was to either go into his workroom for hours or sit in front of the television and sulk. So when Steve started in on Rob, Rob slunk away. On the other hand Rob did have a tendency to fight back when he had had enough.

One day we were using a compressor to blow the water lines in the pool. Gil liked to dig trenches and the dirt often ended in the pool then into the filtration lines. Rob was running the compressor when Steve came out and shouted at him over the fence to turn off the compressor because he, Steve, was having a party and the noise was disturbing his guests. Rob turned off the compressor and explained it would probably take about a half hour more. Steve insisted it be turned off now. Rob explained again it would take a half hour more and we had the compressor rented for only a half day. Steve again insisted. Rob turned around and restarted the compressor.

Within fifteen minutes the police were at the door. A complaint had been lodged that Rob was threatening Steve with the compressor. How I can't imagine but it must have been worded that Rob was aiming the compressor at Steve. The police checked the backyard, realized what was going on and just suggested we get done as soon as possible. Rob finished up the pool lines then brought the compressor to the deck that faced Steve's kitchen sliding doors. We could see the gaggle of people crowded into the kitchen. Rob turned the compressor on then walked into our house, picked up a book and went upstairs saying, "Call me when it runs out of gas." I think it took an hour.

The real flare up was when Rob bought a NC machine with the idea of doing work from home (he was a machinist by trade). He set up the machine in the garage and the next day Steve was at our front door. At the time I was using a broom to sweep the kitchen floor.

"I want to see your garage."

I looked at him, aghast. "You want to what?"

"I want to see your garage. I know you've put some machinery in there and I want to see if it's legal."

I laughed at him. "Get off my porch you asshole. I wouldn't let you in the house if you were bleeding to death."

At that he tried to force his way into the house. I hit him with the broom and he started to smile as if I were so silly to try and stop him with a broom. When I raised it higher to aim at his head he laughed and walked back down the sidewalk.

Rob got home from work and I told him what Steve had done. Within a second he was on his way to Steve's house. Josh and John chased after him. They had never seen Rob take a stand. This was going to be the fight of the century.

Well it wasn't much of a fight because Steve kept his screen door locked but the door did look a little damaged after Rob tried to rip it off its hinges. He also made it clear that if Steve ever stepped a foot on our property again he *would* rip it off its hinges.

Within two days we were visited by men from zoning, the building department, the health department and one other I can't remember now. The third guy going in met the second guy coming out and they both expressed the opinion that they were not pleased to being used for a neighbor's vendetta. One official later told me that they had threatened to fine Steve for filing false reports or something like that. At any rate Steve did not complain about the NC machine again.

A few things I have in my notes from back then.

While a high school senior John had received a solicitation letter from a credit card company that read "I'm sure it's no news to you that your present financial status places you far above the average in terms of means, influence, and credit resources." Considering the $1.67 in his bank account he asked, "Am I missing something? Do I have a job I forgot to go to?"

A friend of Rob's liked to brag about his fast car and daring escapades on the freeways. The bragging ended when he complained about being unable to get more than three stations on his radio and Rob asked, "Why don't you slow down to let the radio waves catch up?"

Our trip to Las Vegas did have an interesting finale.

Rob wasn't real big on planning so we had embarked on our trip without rain gear. This didn't matter a lot on the way there but on the way back when a rainstorm dropped the temperature to forty degrees not having rain gear took on new meaning. By the time we got back home I was bordering on hypothermia. We stripped in the garage, ran upstairs, showered then came downstairs to get some food.

I walked into the kitchen and thought, 'Something's not right.' The kitchen, about twenty feet by fifteen, was country-style with a breakfast area. It had a white and black tile floor with two-inch molding along the bottom of the walls. About an inch above this molding was a dirty streak that wound its way all around the kitchen and breakfast area.

Looking at the streak I turned to John who was 20 at the time and said, "Why is there a dirt streak above the molding?"

John looked at it and said, "I don't know. We cleaned up and maybe I pushed the mop too far up the sides."

To which Josh piped up, "No he had a party while you were gone and they needed to use the hose to clear everything out to the deck."

"The hose?" I asked.

"Yeah," Josh responded, "they brought in the hose from the back yard and sprayed the floor then tried to sweep everything out with the big brooms."

I turned back to John seeing him look at his brother with an 'I'm going to kill him' stare then burst out laughing. "The hose?"

John went to work immediately and had the dirt streak cleared off in record time. Twenty years later Josh informed me that John and his friend Mark had been on the roof (remember, two-story house, pool in back). They had been alternately diving off the roof into the pool and pulling a keg out of the pool up to the roof so they could have a drink between dives. Incredibly enough my hair did not start turning really gray until years after John moved out.

We were on the freeway one day when the back end of the car swerved and Rob had to fight to get the car under control. We later learned it was an earthquake. With that experience still in mind one night our water bed began to slosh dramatically and a loud roar filled the bedroom. Rob and I jumped from the bed clutching each other for the end of the world. Hearing the roar grow louder we looked out the window to see a gigantic tanker plane flying past our window. It was close enough to make out the call letters on the side.

Seemed that the Navy was having touch and go practice on the aircraft carriers out to sea along with inflight refueling. Fog had socked in the coast. Rather than cancel the practice or re-route the tanker used to re-fuel the jets in the air they had sent it on its original path over University City. Only thousands of feet lower than the required cruising altitude. With the number of phone calls the Navy had to field I think that was the last time that happened.

For years I had had sinus headaches that went from my sinuses all the way to the back of my head down to the top of my neck. These headaches were real Harvey Wallbangers and required double doses of sinus pain medication to relieve.

One night our waterbed broke and I had to sleep on the hard base. Something else happened because I dimly remember Rob was on some kind of cushion. Maybe the waterbed was the kind that had a baffle running down the middle and only half of it deflated. In any case by the next morning my neck was cocked at such an angle my head was almost laying on my shoulder.

Even though I don't believe in chiropractors I knew one who would give me a deal. He managed to get my head sitting correctly on my neck but I didn't like his recommendation of repeat visits to deal with the problem. I've never believed in the practice anyway because it is so illogical. If the problem is misalignment of vertebrae and manipulation aligns them correctly how can that correct alignment continue without something keeping the vertebrae in alignment? If the alignment failed once what stops it from failing again the minute you walk out of the chiropractor's office? Makes no sense.

My next stop was the orthopedic surgeon who had diagnosed my herniated disc. The diagnosis this time was cervical arthritis. I didn't have sinus problems I had nerve problems. I was given an anti-inflammatory, neck exercises and a neck harness to use with a water bag thrown over a door to relieve the pressure and help the nerves calm down. The harness was too boring to use so I got a cervical collar that produced the same results.

While this condition has given me massive headaches over the years it never stopped me from doing fun things that might aggravate it. The fun things lasted a lot longer than the aggravation. The collar helped along with exercise. Sit-ups made it flare- up but the flare-ups were shorter lived due to building up the muscles in my neck and maintaining flexibility. Just a note to those who suffer from this condition – it didn't stop me, don't let it stop you.

From the start I should have listened more closely to the conversations between Rob and his mother. He had had an appointment to one of the military academies that he had not acted on because his female high school counselor had been the one to urge his to complete the application forms. He did not do anything if the person urging him was a woman. His mom told me about his father tearing up her kitchen to install new cupboards and sink then walking away from it leaving her to wash her dishes in the bathroom for months. I think she finally had to hire a contractor to complete the project.

Rob's refusal to complete projects if the completion did not affect him was manifested in 1989 when John graduated from college. John wanted a college graduation party at the house although he did promise it would not be on the same magnitude as his high school party. (Looking up, I mentally voiced 'Thank God.')

Rob decided that the deck was too rotted out for a party so needed to be replaced and the pool was too discolored and needed to be painted. So the deck was torn out, the cross studs laid and at that construction stopped. The pool was drained, the sides washed with acid, the neutralizer applied prior to the paint and that project stopped. No questions concerning when either project would re-start were answered.

At the time Rob was in Akido and the other participants had become his defense against the ogre, Flo. No matter what issues we had he would run to his friends, tell them how I never liked anything he did and always criticized him. They would pat his head and coo that they were there for him. When this was brought up once in my presence I got out the pictures of the tile he had installed in the kitchen, hallway and bathroom. I noted that the pictures were on my corkboard at work to show people how talented my husband was. I also had pictures of other things he had made and how I had praised him for the work. When the discussion appeared to not support the picture he had painted of me the conversation was dropped.

A week before John's party Rob told me he would be at Akido practice the next few nights including Friday the day before the party. I think he also mentioned he would be out of town at an Akido competition that weekend. I nodded my head, picked up the phone book and started going through the yellow pages.

"What are you doing?"

"Finding a carpenter or handyman to finish the deck."

"Why do you need someone to finish the deck? I can finish the deck."

"I'm sure you can but not in time for John's party and it is getting finished in time for his party. I can finish the pool or the deck but not both. So I'll do the pool and I'll hire someone to do the deck."

"I can finish the deck."

"Well you have until Wednesday morning. Otherwise Wednesday afternoon I'll have someone out here working on the deck."

Knowing that I would tell one and all why a contractor had been hired to complete the deck he completed it himself. Only he did get back at me. All the decking was laid out wide enough that a woman's stiletto heels would go through the gap between the boards. Therefore women would have to use the deck in their bare feet or walk very carefully across it.

But I did get the pool done myself.

About four months later I filed for divorce.

THE HOUSING COMMISSION
San Diego, 1986 to 1990

Before and during my Rob time I had been trying to make it as a software programming consultant. While I had contracts they were languages I had to learn so the time to complete was a lot longer than it should have been. This affected the old profit margin. On the other hand I did a really good job. Using Lotus 1-2-3 and macros I developed an invoicing system for an engineering firm that they were still using ten years later. An inventory system for a school district's food services, developed in dBase III+, was also used for ten years. I had the ability to structure systems just not enough knowledge to get them done fast. Or to get more contracts.

I also worked Tech Support for a company that produced HVAC scheduling and maintenance software. That job was short term when I learned that the accounting portion of the program required the most support because it was so messed up. For example, to close out each month the users had to change the internal date on the servers to the last day of the month, shut down the servers, re-boot, close out the month, then change the date to the current date, shut down and reboot. Any data that would have been input automatically during the closeout had to be input manually to get the database up-to-date. When I suggested that I could help the programmer set up the system so it worked correctly I was fired.

After spending an hour on the telephone in the lobby of the bank that held my mortgage, with young Josh crying as he witnessed me begging them not to start foreclosure I decided the consultant life was not for me. I went to work for the San Diego Housing Commission.

As far as the Budget Analyst was concerned the job was supposed to be clerical. As far as the Finance Director was concerned the job was to smooth out the budgeting process. Since he was the one doing the hiring I was picked. One of the interview tests was to analyze a pie chart reflecting how Commission monies were spent. I noted the chart data was confusing in what it was trying to convey and redid the chart to better tell the story. This was right before it was supposed to be published so that made an impression.

I took the lead in areas where my County zero-based budgeting expertise came in handy. The budget was developed in Lotus 1-2-3 so I developed an overhead spread calculation that eliminated the time-consuming task of inputting the spread by hand every time the budget changed. To keep me busy I was given the Fixed Asset inventory since nothing had been done for over ten years. That required matching 10,000 items to the records and writing procedures. Nor had the HUD Administrative report been done in ten years so I was assigned to figure out the calculations and write the procedures. (Both were supposed to be every two years.)

At one point I was appointed the Acting Purchasing Agent and Risk Manager. I was not made permanent because I didn't have experience as a Housing Assistant. A friend of the Director did have this experience and she was selected. Another factor might have been my uncovering issues in the purchase of services for the public housing units that others wanted to stay hidden. A year later the PA told me she had no idea what she was doing and was leaving. By that time I had another job so I couldn't help her.

But there were some fun times.

When a staff member received a threatening phone call the downstairs lobby was closed. Seeing the receptionist reading a newspaper in the break room I commented, "Great way to spend a day."

Her reply, "I usually don't believe in horoscopes but today's said to adjust willingly to unusual changes in schedule."

I had two outfits for Halloween. One was a gypsy dress with gypsy makeup and a light bulb I carried to tell people's fortunes. The other was to wear normal clothing (business wear during the day or an evening gown for Halloween parties at night) and make up my face to look like a zombie.

This Halloween I had gone with the zombie routine. I was talking to some co-workers when someone came up behind me and said my name. I turned, he gasped and the papers he was carrying became airborne.

Later that morning I was sitting in the office I shared with the Sue, the Budget Analyst. I said, "Oh shit, I forgot I have an appointment with the dermatologist today at noon." (It was for a growth on my wrist).

Sue said, "What's wrong with that?"

"My car is in the shop so I'm going to have to take the bus looking like this. At lunchtime no less."

Sue started laughing and suggested I wash the makeup off. But I responded that the day was still young and my face had far to go before the evening was over.

A little before noon I trudged to the bus stop enduring the many remarks from people passing by in cars. The bus driver and passengers looked a little askance at me and most sidled away when I sat down. At the dermatologist's office I was ushered into an examination room and waited. She walked in, took one look and uttered, "I certainly hope you're not here to see me about your face."

Later that night at a party a guy said, "I hate to tell you this but your chin is falling off."

THE SMC AND GARY
San Diego, 1990-1992

Rob and I divorced in 1990 and finalized the property settlement in 1991. While I had not been overly impressed with the marriage I had been very impressed with motorcycling. Sitting in the passenger seat of his Venture, feeling the wind in my face with nothing between me and the road was almost like being a part of the land. At 46 I had fallen in love. With bikes. The most important point though was not the riding but where the rides took me, places I never would have gone in a car.

Trying to find potential boyfriends who rode bikes was not easy. Bars with bikes outside, particularly Harleys, generally had occupants who smelled bad and looked worse. I put ads in the personal columns and met a few men but they were not my type (remember, in-shape, intelligent and with a sense of humor). After a few months of this I sat down one day and thought it through. What is the best way for a single woman to meet a single man who is interested in the same things she is? Skiers had singles clubs. Arts aficionados had singles clubs. Hikers had singles clubs. But there weren't any singles clubs for motorcyclists.

So I started one, the Singles Motorcycle Club. Throughout this narrative I describe some of our rides but the ones described are probably 10% of the ones actually taken. I can't think of any ride (and I have the trip reports to prove it) where there weren't a lot of laughs based on a lot of screw-ups. However I write only about those where the screw-ups were worse than usual. For that same reason some of my white-water rafting trips have been skipped. Lots of laughs but not unique enough to make the grade for inclusion.

Through the club I met many male bikers, some female bikers and a number of women who had the same aims that I did. Meeting men who rode. But of all the men I met while in San Diego most of my memories revolved around Gary, Dave and Mike.

Gary was a tall, rangy, blonde, incredibly good-looking Navy man stationed at Miramar Naval Station just east of University City. He was also shy with a limited education and 11 years younger. (But that was a step up since Rob had been 12 years younger.) A few weeks after I started the club, which involved advertising in the paper for volunteers to help out, I had a party at my house. Probably 25 to 30 people showed but when Gary walked in the door I was smitten. We talked a little throughout the night but since I was hostess the conversation was pretty limited.

A few days after he called to invite me for drinks near the base. While drinking we discussed the kind of lady he was looking for and, surprise, he said, "Like you." When I asked why he hadn't said that right away he noted that he thought the age and education difference would make me totally uninterested. But I wasn't. When under my mother's thrall I had rejected anyone without a college degree (I had two). But as I got older and went through husbands I realized a degree wasn't the only thing of value. Particularly with Ray. Look what I got with his college degree. Gary had an old Gold Wing tour bike and we went together for six months only breaking up due to his drinking. But those six months had some pretty funny incidents.

A week before Memorial Day weekend, having just returned from a week at sea, Gary had four days off and wanted to go camping. We had planned to camp Memorial Day weekend at either Death Valley or Kings Canyon but he thought a short trip would be nice before our long journey.

"Keep it within 125 miles of home."

"Sure," I replied, "no problem."

The plan was to ride to the Big Bear area using scenic local roads, camp at Silverwood Lake for two days while exploring the San Bernardino Forest then come home, refreshed and relaxed.

That was the plan.

However, as Gary had learned with me, plans do not always come off as anticipated. After group rides where I had set up the route, led the ride and gotten us lost every time he opted to only ride with me if someone else did the route. And led the ride. On our first date we meant to take a short 120 mile round trip ride from San Diego to Julian. However, based on my directions, we ended up in El Centro 120 miles *one* way. On the way back to my house we had encountered wind, cold and rain clouds so low that as we rode down Interstate 8 our heads were obscured by the fog layer. Trying to make things right I had said, "But it's an adventure." I heard that from him a lot when we took trips.

We started out Thursday morning and took Interstate 15 north. I had picked the camp ground, Mojave River Forks, from a book on camping and made sure it had the important items – showers for me and a fire-pit for Gary. (He had this thing about campfires.)

At our first gas stop in Temecula we explored some side streets trying to get to State Route 79 heading north because I was too busy talking to check street signs. According to the map 79 turned towards San Bernardino at Yucaipa. However, after making the turnoff that we guessed at because there weren't any signs, the area became distinctly residential. At a gas station we learned the turnoff was a few miles back and signed only for those heading west, not east. No one was able to explain the logic.

This was in late May so the whole ride was from one gorgeous flower strewn vista to another. Not only were there spring flowers but huge, multi-colored blooms covered the cacti. The scenery included heavily wooded mountain sides with steep cliffs giving way to meadows full of wild flowers. On the third day we passed acres of lilac in bloom with colors ranging from white to deep purple. The vista stretched to the horizon.

But enough of the travelogue. On to the screw-ups.

We picked up State 38 near Yucaipa to take the back way into Big Bear then continued on State 18 towards Lake Arrowhead. Past the lake we turned off 18 onto State 173 which would lead to our intended stay near Silverwood Lake. We noticed a sign, 'Pavement ends, one mile.' Within a hundred feet we saw another sign pointing to the left with the notation, 'Silverwood Lake, 14 miles.' By now, with all our meandering, we had gone close to 160 miles. The road led alongside a sanitation plant.

"Want to see where the highway ends?" Gary asked.

"Sure," I replied comfortable with the idea that we only had fourteen miles to go before we could make camp and relax. (As a note to non-motorcyclists, even though the rider is doing most of the work the passenger still has to maintain vigilance to ensure she leans the right way on turns, doesn't slam her helmet into her rider's head, stays balanced on the seat, checks the route, etc. Although to be truthful, if the road is pretty straight I and other passengers have been known to catch a few winks on the way.)

We rode to the end of the road. Looking at the stretch of sand-covered dirt Gary commented, "Boy, I'd sure hate to go down there on a bike."

Turning around we retraced our trail and turned down the road to Silverwood. Within 100 yards the pavement disappeared to be replaced by a graveled, rutted trail. Gary stopped the bike.

"Whoa this can't be the way to Silverwood."

After a few minutes discussion I asked Gary if he ever told the guys on base about some of the situations I had gotten him into. "Hell no," he replied, "they'd send me to a shrink for staying with you." At that he decided to walk up the trail a bit to see if it got better and I decided to go to the sanitation plant to ask where we were.

Walking into the station past dozens of signs with warnings not to step a foot on the property without authorization I cautiously entered a building.

"Hello," I called, my voice echoing down some stairs, "is anybody here?"

A young dog came out and greeted me, luckily without growls or fangs, and I proceeded to explore. After about five minutes of hearing my voice echo I went back outside to see Gary returning from the trail.

"It goes on and on. I do not want to take the bike on that trail. What did you find out?"

"No one's home. There are bicycles, clothes, a radio playing and a half-empty lunch pail on a table but no people. It's spooky."

We looked around and saw someone at a large pond area. Someone did work there! As we approached the ripe smell of raw sewage wafted into our noses.

"How do we get to Silverwood Lake?" Gary asked.

"What," the man answered.

"The road seems to end here. How do we get to Silverwood Lake?"

After three tries, it dawned on us that the man was hard of hearing. Either the noise of the equipment had deafened him or the sewage had damaged more than his sense of smell.

"Well," he said, "you can take the road that's gravel. It's a county road but it's not maintained. Or you can double back forty miles to get back on 18. Or you can take 173 around the mountain."

"But the pavement ends within a mile." Gary protested.

"That's right," said the man, "it's the only unpaved state highway in California."

"Great," said Gary, looking at me pointedly, "the only unpaved state highway and we'd find it."

"Well, it is maintained," said the man, "the state keeps it graded. It's about ten miles long. So you can backtrack 40 miles or try the road."

Gary sighed. "I really don't want to go back, so I guess we'll try it."

"Just keep to the mountainside and you won't have any problem."

That ten miles was very interesting. From smooth to ruts to sand, for every 100 yards we went we hit every combination. I learned some new swear words (I guess the Navy teaches you more than a skill) and that Gary is a very good rider under adverse conditions.

"Well, look at it this way, honey," I said while he wrestled the bike through another sand trap, "this road is so deserted we won't have to worry about other cars."

I didn't have the words out of my mouth when two Suzuki Samurais tore around a corner and almost ran us off the side of the mountain.

"The power of suggestion," Gary shouted, "maybe you better not say your thoughts out loud."

A little later while still wrestling the bike and turning the air blue he brightly said, "Wow, what a bargain I got with this bike. A tour bike and ATV rolled into one."

As we went around corner after corner, I wondered why the man had cautioned us to keep to the mountainside – there wasn't any place else to go.

After Gary had lost five pounds wrestling the bike, we finally made it to the bottom of the mountain.

"Watch," Gary laughed, "we'll finally make it and I'll dump the bike." Just then we hit a patch of sand and almost did dump the bike. The 'power of suggestion' briefly flitted through my mind.

Gary said goodbye to the mountain (it's the same gesture you see when you run someone off the road) and we prepared for a quick trip to the campground. Amid increasing gusts of wind we drove to the Mojave River Park. Set in a desolate stand of cactus it was not very inviting.

"Let's go all the way to Silverwood," I suggested, "the book shows three campgrounds there."

While there were three campgrounds the trees weren't very big and we wanted to be in the trees so we decided to take State 138 to Crestline and get back into the forest. The wind had picked up and I learned some new words since Gary didn't like cross winds any more than he liked sand.

At Crestline we stopped to get a drink at the Hayloft, a local bar, and asked the barmaid if she knew of any camping areas where we could have a fire. Unfortunately none of the campgrounds in Crestline had fire-pits. By then we were so tired we decided to take anything so she called a Camp Switzerland. The price was right, it was close and it had showers.

After getting lost once we made it to Switzerland, set up camp and took long showers to get 173's dust off. We returned to the bar to relax before going out to eat. The local restaurant was about to close but we didn't have the energy to get up so the barmaid nuked some frozen pizza and we ate there.

Playing pool I noticed a large stone fireplace. (It wasn't too hard to notice as we were the only people there.) I mentioned to the barmaid that Gary was really disappointed about not having a campfire.

When he went to the bathroom the barmaid brought me a large box. "There's scrap wood behind the bar. You can start a fire if you want to gather the wood."

About two minutes later, as I was dragging scrap wood out of a pile and slipping on the debris on the ground, Gary came out and asked me what I was doing.

"Getting your fire for you," I replied.

He motioned towards the back of the alleyway. "You better watch out. You don't know why they have those coffins out here."

Since it was very dark and very spooky, I finished my scrap wood gathering quickly and returned to the bar. (We learned the coffins are used for coffin races over the Fourth of July. Do not ask me why.)

At least we had our fire.

As we sat back and toasted the blaze, Gary said, "Someday we'll look back on all this and laugh. See, we're even laughing now."

He didn't know those words would come back to haunt him.

At Camp Switzerland we had no problem sleeping (probably because we were the only ones there) and left about 10:00 a.m. the next morning. Since we had been on about every road in Big Bear we decided to head for Idyllwild in the San Jacinto National Forest. Before leaving Crestline we stopped at the Crash Inn, the local locals bar, to see the shirts, socks, bras, underpants and other 'things' hanging from the ceiling and walls.

We took State 18 south to Interstate 10 south where we picked up State 243 into the mountains. At Idyllwild we camped at the Mount San Jacinto County Park that, thank you, had fire-pits. It also restricted motorcyclists to the camp sites near the front gate I guess to spare other guests from being aroused by those loud bikers. We went to the Chart House for dinner a rustic upscale restaurant that is no longer in Idyllwild sad to say. The restaurant had a huge fireplace but it was only lit when it was cold, which it was to us but not to the natives.

Returning to our campsite we lit the fire and enjoyed wine and beer until we were so covered with smoke we had to go to bed. The next morning some moron in the next site decided to chop wood at 6:00 a.m. I was too tired and the air too cold to go out and hit the idiot with one of his pieces of wood. Naturally Gary slept right through it. (Considering he could sleep through jet noise when he was on base at Miramar I guess this would be expected.) I did find it a little hypocritical that the county restricted motorcyclists due to the 'noise' but didn't have any rules about fellow campers playing Paul Bunyan at 6 a.m.

We now had more plans. Let's go to Palms Springs and take the tramway, something I had never done in the seventeen years I'd been in California. The tram ride was spectacular, ascending from 2,500 feet sea level to over 8,000 feet at the mountain top, traveling through five climate zones. At some points the tram appeared to be heading into a sheer cliff. When it passed a tower the tram went up and down like a small roller coaster. This caused some small consternation for those not expecting the dips, especially Gary. At the top we watched a movie detailing how the tram was built. I was amazed that some of the counterweights used to pull the tramway cables taunt weighed 83 tons.

We left the Tramway about 1:30 p.m. and decided to go all-interstate back to my house. About 130 miles of freeway, a nice three hour trip, we'd be back in time for a relaxing soak in my Jacuzzi.

We headed north on 111 to get to Interstate10. Up ahead we could see swirls of sand blowing across the highway. The wind picked up with heavy cross gusts. The bike became more and more difficult to control and sand pelted us. Gary turned around in the median and headed back to Palm Springs where the air was still. Checking the map he decided to go back on 111 and use a shorter route to 10. The shorter route worked, we got on 10 but it didn't do much good. The winds turned into a full-fledged 50 mph sandstorm. We pulled up at the top of an off ramp to see if the wind might die down after a while but it only got worse. I was standing next to the bike and a gust blew me into it so hard my shin was bruised. Cars slowed to 25 to 30 mph. A few motorcycles went by but they were riding single. Finally we realized we had to go back the way we had come over the mountains.

Gary got back on 10 heading east. Visibility was less than 150 feet only this was not fog or snow. It was stinging, cutting sand and pebbles. We stopped in Palm Springs to clean up as best we could. I bent over and shook my head burying the bathroom floor in a fine layer of sand. At the table Gary scratched his head and pebbles fell out. "I've heard of dandruff," he said, "but this is ridiculous."

I looked at him.

"I don't suppose this is the time to talk about our trip to Death Valley next weekend is it?"

"No," his replied eying me, "it isn't."

"And this also isn't the time to say someday we'll look back on all this and laugh."

"No, it's not the time for that either."

"Would you consider not going to Death Valley? The roads will probably be as windy and I'm not in the mood for weather like this for quite a while. In fact the only sand I want to see is at the beach."

"I don't even want to see that," he exclaimed with a relieved look.

'Golly,' I thought to myself, 'I must be psychic. For some unknown reason I knew he didn't want to go to Death Valley next weekend.'

On our trip home we fought crosswinds and cold for 100 miles. Keeping the bike upright was taking even more out of Gary than our unpaved state highway mountain adventure. I was thanking my lucky stars he was a good rider, big and strong because with a passenger he was basically wrestling over 1,000 pounds against heavy winds.

By the time we made it to Temecula Gary was beat and I was frozen. We stopped to gas up and I ran to the Swing Inn Cafe for coffee and heat. A man with a long mountain beard sat with his son at a table across from me.

As I removed my layers of jackets, sweatshirt and sweater, he commented, "Just came over the mountains on a bike, didn't you?"

"Yes," I replied, trying to talk through chattering teeth.

"Little windy and cold wasn't it?"

"You must be a local," I replied.

He was and went on to describe how bad the winds were at this time of year. I thought, 'Now I find out.'

Gary came in and we planned on how to get home.

"Now this is our last stop, right?"

"Right."

"No side trips to the grocery store?"

"No, no side trips."

"You don't have anything you need to pick up? No one you have to visit?"

"No, we can go straight home."

When we got there, I kissed the floor, the bike then Gary. Was I tired, was I nervous? You'd better believe it. Five hours of heavy cross winds and cold are not fun. We calculated our 125 mile campout had gone over 600 miles.

But the next morning as we enjoyed our coffee without moving a muscle, Gary said it all. "Yeah, we'll look back on all this and laugh. It was a great trip. It was one hell of a weekend."

The Wednesday following our odyssey he took me to a job interview on his motorcycle because my car was broken down. At the interview site I'd changed into a business suit with a narrow skirt but found that they were running late on the interviews. I returned to Gary who was relaxing on the lawn and asked what he wanted to do for an hour.

"Well I need to get gas and we could get a soda."

"Uhhh, Gary, I'm not exactly dressed to ride and I don't want to change back and forth before my interview."

"That's no problem. You won't be seen by a lot of people. There's a gas station right up the road and there were hardly any cars around when we got here."

I reluctantly agreed and straddled the passenger seat in my pencil-thin skirt. We got to the gas station and before the engine had stopped the bay door on the repair shop rolled up. Four guys came out to watch me get off the bike.

"Great Gary you had to pick the one gas station with every mechanic in town."

"Yeah," he replied with a grin, "pretty smart huh. Bet they're jealous as hell that I've got such a good-looking woman getting off the back of my bike." I made sure the guys got a good show.

Sometime early in 1990 Josh smashed up my car. Well actually he smashed up my car and two other cars, one of which had just been driven home from the new car dealership. Two of

Josh's friends woke me to tell me Josh had been in an accident. He was OK but the car(s) weren't.

It was just up the street and I found Josh sitting on the curb in tears muttering that it would take his whole life to pay off the bills. I knelt by him and tried to reassure him that the insurance would cover most of it and I would cover the rest. He said swerving to miss a cat had caused the crash but 20 years later he confessed he had been pissed off about something, drove too fast and couldn't make the curve.

At any rate, two police officers were there and one, probably in his middle fifties, started berating Josh for crying. "Stop your crying. Be a man. Stop that blubbering or I'll handcuff you and take you to the station."

After about five minutes of this I started rising from my kneeling position with my right hand in a fist and my arm cocked to punch. The other cop, probably in his early thirties, said, "Ummm, Bob, I think you better knock it off and let the lady handle her son." The older cop looked at me, my fist then walked away. Such power I had.

So I was without a car. Rob and I were still in the throes of finalizing our property settlement and I knew I was going to have to take out a second to pay him off. I didn't want a loan for a car on the records because it might raise the interest rate on the second so I figured I'd buy what was known in those days and probably today as a beater. Gary was going to help me find it.

I found a car in Ocean Beach, a station wagon with lots of miles but a low price. Gary took me there on his bike and when he saw it he pronounced it perfect. As he stated it gave him the warm fuzzies. We hopped in for a test drive and before we had gotten out of Ocean Beach the car died. I ran back to a phone booth and called the owner. Seems the car had been sitting for a while so the battery must be dead. They would be there in a few minutes. I ran back to the car and pulled up some daisies to present to Gary as a peace offering. Once again I had gotten him into a situation. Holding the daisies with the dirt from their roots falling in his lap he commented, "Remind me to never go sailing with you. The boat would probably sink."

Our rescuers arrived with an extra battery and as they ran around the car hooking up the battery and throwing it in the back seat I laid on the grass laughing. The Three Stooges had arrived. The test drive continued and the car appeared to work so I bought it as it did have the thing most important to me, a low price. We got the extra battery as part of the deal.

Other fun memories were going to Magic Mountain and the roller coaster ticket taker saying, after looking at Gary's flannel shirt, "Wow, somewhere a VW is missing its seat covers." I took him to a play at a small 80-seat playhouse in San Diego where I was the House Manager. Gary wasn't worldly and when the female lead bared her breasts, Gary blurted out, loudly, "My God, she's naked on stage."

Within a month Gary was history and I became more involved in club rides. One legacy Gary left me was my choice in riding gear. To this point I had been using heavy jackets and wearing long johns to keep warm in cold weather. Even though he didn't have a Harley Gary had once had a Harley and he still maintained the Harley mentality. That is everything you wear is black. Black leather jacket, black leather chaps, black shoes and black gloves. Even his helmets were black. When we rode he supplied me with a black leather jacket. But it was time to buy my own gear.

Brown leather jackets, one for cold weather, one for warm. Light brown suede finish chaps with fringe purchased at a rodeo supply store. Brown summer gloves (although I had to give in on winter gloves because the only ones available were black). Brown boots. To complete my ensemble I found a used brown helmet. When Gary saw me he immediately backed off. He was not going to ride with someone wearing leathers that color. I just dusted my jacket then said, "Love me, love my leathers." We were on the road within five minutes.

THE SMC AND DAVE
San Diego, 1990-1992

Around October 1990 Dave came into the club's life. Over six feet tall with a rangy build, eyes so dark they were almost black, long black hair held back by a headband, he looked like he should be carrying a rifle and wearing a feather and bead vest. Despite his looks he was incredibly shy and found it difficult to fan a woman's interest. That he rode his bike at supersonic speeds might have influenced this problem. Quirky as he was (and still is) I'd say I had more fun times with Dave then with any other person, male or female, that I've known. We've remained friends all these years. (Dave says it's because we're both weird.)

Every time I told a story about Dave he complained that I exaggerated. Those who knew Dave rolled their eyes at his protests. They had unintentionally participated in some of his misadventures aggravated by my ride planning. My routes were based on maps. Most ride leaders did the same but then they pre-rode the routes to ensure all the turns and roads were as depicted on the maps. Not me. I explained to one of the more adamant pre-riders, "If I pre-ride it, I'll know everything on it. There won't be any surprises. It'll be boring."

As a result, more than once we would come to a road that ended in a ten foot drop-off (in the suburbs no less) or was partly or mostly dirt or had a name different than that on the maps or could only be reached by a road not on the route. This resulted in numerous U-turns and backtracking, activities that caused many to call the 'Singles Motorcycle Club' the 'Where the Hell Are We Club.' Combine the routes with Dave's habit of leading a ride two miles in front of the next bike and screw-ups were bound to happen. Most important, since all rides started at my house I couldn't escape their comments when we finished.

On one ride I brought a video camera. My 'route' took us through a residential section that led to open range replete with marshes, hills, valleys, curves and lots of flowers. Because Dave insisted on drinking a 32-ounce cup of coffee before every ride we often had to stop at rather inconvenient places for him to get rid of the aftereffects. This time it was by the side of the freeway. I waved the rest of the group on. They had the route, we could catch up.

We arrived to find the group going in a circle. The street on the map ended at a six-foot drop-off and reappeared in a cul-de-sac at the bottom. AJ, one of my many detractors who oddly enough kept coming to the rides, decided he was going to take control and lead the rest of the way. That was OK by me as I could get much better video from the middle of the line of bikes.

We passed many beautiful scenes. A reedy pond with ducks and swans lazily plying the water, meandering curves through waist high brush and magnificent trees, quaint little villages with their small shops, a reedy pond with ducks and swans lazily plying the... I leaned forward to yell in Dave's ear. "Isn't this the third time we've been by this pond?"

Agreeing with my conclusion he raced ahead to notify AJ he was being usurped. From that point we led the ride but, alas, there was more to occur.

One of the roads was clearly and distinctly noted on the map as paved. It had been built as a cut out from a mountainside. However, the map's designation did not take into account that the road probably had not been maintained in the last ten years. The potholes and cracked pavement made going slow. About five miles in we realized it was going to take a while to get to the next town and Dave still had some coffee to get rid of. By now most of the other male riders had the same issue along with a few of the female passengers. I got a good video of maybe fifteen men facing the cliff face with their body parts hidden. The ladies found bushes. Few were pleased. Showing the video at the club Christmas party prompted a few guys to use the restroom.

In November we went on a weekend campout to Silverwood Lake. Brenda was the only woman rider among ten men and there were six passengers. One of these was the woman who had captured Dave's heart. Unfortunately she had captured most of the guys' hearts so he was having trouble scoring points.

As usual no one wanted to lead so Dave volunteered and I was his passenger. Halfway into the first part of the route we hit a construction area where we had to wait for a pilot truck to get us through about two miles of work. By this time breakfast coffee had started to work on the guys so there were a number of disappearances into the bushes. I tried to get pictures but Dave said I'd need a wide-angle lens for him and the other guys weren't being cooperative. I realized that women in cars had a better view than I did when I heard comments of appreciation.

We stopped to gas up. The rest of the riders had moved their bikes away from the pumps and stood around discussing the weather while we waited for Dave. Seeing him moving something in and out of the key hole on his gas cap a few of us wandered up to his bike.

"What's up? Why are you using a penknife in the lock?" asked Warren.

Dave kept wiggling his pocket knife in the key hole. "The key broke off in the lock and I can't get the gas cap off."

To a chorus of sympathetic comments he added, "Yeah it broke off a year ago and the pocket knife always worked before."

The chorus turned into a mob. "How could he be so stupid?"

"We'll be here all night."

"You didn't get it fixed and it's been a year?"

"This is just another example of his being inconsiderate." (This comment came from the girl of his dreams.)

Marge, one of the passengers, was standing next to me in the parking area. Well not exactly next to me because by this time I was sitting on the ground laughing. "Hmmm," she commented, "this will certainly separate the men from the boys."

They spent the next half-hour trying to turn, pry or hammer off the cap. Finally it came loose and Dave gassed up. Since the cap could no longer be screwed in Dave stuffed a rag into the tank opening. As we rode out of the gas station he turned to me and said, "You do know we're riding a 750-pound Molotov Cocktail."

At that I called to one of the other riders. "Here's the route. We'll meet you at the campground. We need to find a new gas cap so we don't end up as crispy critters."

After searching for an hour and learning that motorcycle shops do not routinely sell gas caps for bikes that are ten years old Dave decided to turn the cap over and tape it to the tank. (I dimly remember some kid making that suggestion but I don't want it thought that Dave couldn't figure out that kind of simple solution on his own.) From his saddlebag he hauled out a roll of two-inch wide masking tape at least six inches in diameter. Seeing this I said, "You know this is probably going to be a dumb question but why are you carrying around that huge roll of masking tape."

Deadly serious he replied, "Because I might cut my finger."

"Somehow," I commented, "with you that makes sense."

At the campground we caught up to the group as they were entering because they, who often made remarks about my navigating skills, had gotten lost. Later that night we went to the local bar where we slam danced. One such move bumped Brenda off the dance floor onto her butt so we had to dampen down everyone's enthusiasm. Back at the campground the ranger had asked us to quiet down. Within an hour an RV owner started his generator to our shouts that he should quiet down.

The rest of the ride was sweeping curves and beautiful vistas but not quite as funny as the beginning. Well maybe when Brenda showed us her lips tattoo on her buttock. That was kind of funny.

Gary's 'warm fuzzies' car soon suffered a cracked block. It had stopped on the freeway and only restarted after I had it towed to my house. As I noted to John it must have been tired and wanted a ride home. Because the repair was more than the car was worth I decided to take motorcycle riding lessons as a mode of transportation until that pesky property settlement was finalized. The lessons came to naught when I ran the instructor down during the final test. He shakily gave me my graduation certificate because, in his words, taking the class again wouldn't do me any good – I was great on balance but my coordination needed a lot of practice.

Dave and I both loved to dance so we went to a variety of bars over the years most of which tended towards dives. The band was important not the ambience and these dives had great rock bands. Even being 13 years older than Dave I could hold my own. On one ride I bet five of the guys I could outlast them on the dance floor and won all the bets.

One night he and I went to a goth-style bar and, at 46, I was the oldest one there. Some young man/woman (we never did figure out which) kept drinking beer, running up to the stage, yelling how great the band was and pointing us out to the crowd, telling everyone how great we danced. I figured he/she must have been blind drunk because Dave's dancing bordered on spastic. When we finally left at one in the morning someone drove by in a truck and dumped two lawn mower engines at our feet. Seemed to fit with the club's atmosphere.

The next night Dave and I went to the Ocean Beach Christmas Parade. The *Geriatric Precision Surfboard Team* laid down surf boards every ten feet and walked on them. They were upstaged by the *Gidget Brigade* that performed a synchronized dance to the accompaniment of the opening and closing of beach chairs. One float, built like a hamburger, was painted a color that unfortunately looked like rancid meat in the fluorescent glow of the street lights. The last float was a two story high toilet labeled *The Toilet That Stole Christmas*.

Getting to the parade was an adventure in itself. Dave lived in a small cottage behind another house. There was a double wooden gate leading into the property and a carport next to the front house. On the way through the double gate, Dave yelled, "Pull in your legs, this is a tight squeeze."

Going between the house and carport, he caught his pants leg (or so he said) on the bike's highway peg and slammed the bike into the house. By the time he got it stopped in front of his house my knees were tight against my chest with my feet on the seat and I was falling off the bike from laughing.

The next day was the Toy Run ride leaving from the Chula Vista Harley Davidson shop. The plan (which mistakenly did not take Dave into account) was to leave my house at 8:00 a.m., meet others at Mary Kay's Restaurant in Chula Vista at 8:30 then go from there to the Harley shop. We would go down with the run but veer off and continue down to Ensenada to take Highway 3 back to Tecate. Other participants were at my house by 7:30 a.m. By 8:10 still no Dave. I called his house. His answer machine came on. "Nag, nag, nag. I'm on my way already. If it's anyone else but Flo, leave a message." About five minutes later he came in waving a piece of paper with a big grin on his face.

"I knew you'd bitch at me so I rushed here and look what I got." At that he threw the piece of paper at me – a ticket for going 95 in a 55 zone.

For the ride the 400 or more bikes were sent to a park near the Otay border crossing. It looked to be at least an hour before we would even get into the park. Since we were to meet others at 4:30 p.m. in Mission Valley for the *San Diego Harbor Parade of Lights* we turned back. Unfortunately we lost two riders who later told me their sad tale.

Of the two routes into the park they took one that left about 30 Harley's in the mud. It took over an hour to get the Harley's back on the road. Then they got lost and some little kids kept asking for money to give them directions out of the park. They kept getting more lost and getting more directions (and paying more money) until the kids started looking alike. One rider said he was pretty sure they were the same ones. They didn't get back across the border much before four in the afternoon.

In the meantime we were on our Ensenada-Tecate route. South of Rosarito the highway goes into the mountains for about an hour. About twenty minutes into the road Dave said, "I hope we see a gas station soon, I'm on reserve." (For non-motorcyclists that is the equivalent of the fuel gauge light coming on.)

Naturally I wanted to ask why he hadn't gotten gas in Tijuana or Rosarito. But after being around him for three months I knew that any answer would have little basis in logic so I refrained. By the time we got to Ensenada (we figured/hoped it would not be further than going back to Rosarito) we were riding on fumes literally coasting the last 500 feet into the station. The other riders and passengers were shaking their heads at how dumb Dave was, as usual, but I was laughing. (Unfortunately for Dave the girl of his dreams was along and contributed to the 'dumb Dave' comments.)

That Christmas season included going dancing two more times, another club party, movies and dinners. But the culmination was spending New Year's Eve in Pasadena on Colorado Avenue, the route of the *Rose Bowl Parade*.

On the 30th Dave and I decided to see *Dances with Wolves* at 10:30 p.m. We intended to leave San Diego by 8:00 a.m. the next day for Pasadena. The weather had been rainy and cold all week with night-time temperatures in the 20s so we had had a massive, "Hell no I won't go" reaction from club members to camping out in Pasadena. We got back from the movie at 1:30 a.m.

Dave said, "I'll go home, get some sleep and be back here about 7:30 or 8:00 to pack your stuff on the bike." Right. I was well versed in Dave's ability to get up in the morning. He slept on the spare bedroom floor so I would be sure he was awake on time. (Actually he slept in the spare bedroom closet. He had a problem sleeping with any ambient light in the room and the closet was the darkest we could find.) We got out of my house by 7:30 after three hours sleep and out of his house at 9:30. He was not real fast in the morning.

The bike was a sight to behold. Aside from sleeping bags and pillows Dave had strapped a rolled four-foot by eight-foot piece of one-and-a-half-inch foam on the back of the bike. It stuck out both sides like the tail on a jumbo jet. He was so tired he lost his keys twice and if his roommate hadn't been there to recover the dropped and the lost we never would have gotten started. I had mixed his recipe for home-made Bailey's Irish Cream and accidentally used Kahlua instead of the Irish whiskey. So I had to use the whiskey to cut the Kahlua. It was definitely potent. Starting out the foam pad made the bike so unwieldy he had to repack it twice to compensate for our starboard list. Even with the repacking it was obvious that we'd be fighting wind shear for the 140 miles to Pasadena. I suggested we leave the mattress but he wouldn't hear of it.

In Pasadena by late afternoon we claimed a place on the curb where we could park the bike behind us and still have easy access to the street. Two couples with barbeques were to the left and about ten guys in their early twenties to the right. After setting up our gear, getting gas and feeding Dave the fun began.

So you understand how it went there were two objectives of the evening. Those on the sidewalk had to throw silly string, shaving cream, marshmallows, cheerios, water or whatever else was available into or onto anything that moved on the parade's main route. Those on the route had to 'cruise' the main street (Colorado Avenue) and throw things at or on anyone at the curbs. The motorcyclist's objective was to 'cruise' between, behind and in front of cars and pass as many cars as possible during their circuit.

Dave met and surpassed the objective more than once. We got so close to some cars we ticked rear-view mirrors (only four but enough). Dave would have one hand on the handlebars and the other would be throwing marshmallows in windows or spraying water at people on the sidelines. After each circuit we had to stop so I could get a cigarette and a drink to prepare for the next onslaught.

At one point we were both spraying people when we went by a group with cans of shaving cream. I lambasted them with water and as I laughingly turned to tell Dave of their reactions the bike stopped.

"Dave, don't stop the bike. I just sprayed those people."

"I can't help it, the light turned red."

"Dave, those people have shaving cream and they're walking toward us."

"Looks like you have a problem."

Two guys ambled over, cans of shaving cream in hand. One sprayed it in my face and the other in the back and on top of my head. I told Dave we needed to go someplace so I could wash it off.

"What's the matter," he replied, "little shaving cream causing you a problem?"

"Turn around and look you idiot."

He did and laughed so hard he almost dropped the bike. The shaving cream covering my head and face was dripping off my glasses. I looked like a snowwoman with a wig.

From then on I checked the lights before I sprayed people near intersections. By 11:30 p.m. we were busted so it didn't make much difference (our squirt bottles were confiscated). Dave was starting to feel the effects of the home-made booze so right after the New Year chimed in we piled in a truck (to cruise of course) and got bathed in champagne.

Later we walked down the street getting and giving hugs and finally we hit the sack. With all the people and barbeques the temperature was downright mild. We might have gotten some sleep except someone behind us was playing a boom box at top volume. Within a few hours the box was cutting in and out and driving everyone nuts. At 5:45 a.m. I got up and told the guy that about 14 people were going to kill him if he didn't shut off the radio.

"Wow, man," he replied, "you could have shut it off a long time ago. I was just too drunk to get up and do it myself." Dave swore he didn't sleep at all but I noticed he snores when he doesn't sleep.

The next morning we watched about 45 minutes of the parade then packed up and went to a sports bar to watch some of the Michigan game at the Gator Bowl. (I graduated from the University of Michigan but Dave was the real fan even hitchhiking to Bowl games where Michigan played.) I washed my hair in the bathroom and the black running from my head contained shaving, whipped and Irish Cream, cereal, marshmallows, champagne, silly string, cheerios, potato chips, confetti, ketchup and other oddments I would not want to know. It was the best New Year's I have ever spent, probably the most fun I've ever had.

In addition to being a House Manager at some of the smaller theaters I was also an Usher Captain at larger venues.

Club members were regularly dragged along to help. One event was a Variety Show at the Lyceum that was a benefit for the Fireman's Disability Fund. Dave missed it as he had a date with someone he had been working on for three weeks only to learn after the meal she had a boyfriend. I told him he was lucky.

The show included a song and dance troupe that consisted of kids from 11 to 16. Aside from the fact that they couldn't keep in step one of the star singers could not carry a tune nor could she keep time to the music. Every time she sang solo Warren, one of our group, kept looking back at the exits. I kept telling him there was no escape he had to stay for the duration. When she sang with the chorus she kept throwing everyone off key. It was one of the few times I considered having the theater pay me to usher. As a side note Warren was the rough-hued leather-clad biker type. He became so interested in the plays we ushered he started taking acting lessons.

In January we went to the Paintball Wars. As I look back on my life I realize there were some things I never would have done without Dave bringing up the idea. I made Dave stay at my house to ensure we would get started on time but, as usual, my plans were foiled when he had to go back to his house to get his Paintball shoes.

The wars were fun and tiring. The 'killing fields' covered many hilly acres and the camouflage clothes were heavy. For the uninitiated the wars are fought with two teams shooting at each other with paint balls. If the ball splats you anywhere considered lethal you're dead. The objective is to take the other team's flag and return it to your flagstaff.

I kept leaving my gun safety on so naturally I was killed a lot. One time I had a guy right in my sights, leaned over to line him up and watched all my balls slowly slide out of the ammunition tube and cutcly bounce down a hill. Splat I was dead again.

During another game I crawled on my stomach through the bush until I came to a small gorge. On the top of one side of the gorge sat a few of the enemy. As I studied the area I realized I was looking at the enemy's flagstaff and there was the flag! The fight was far away and soon the soldiers wandered. I snuck up, grabbed the flag then crawled back the way I came. No one would be dumb enough to crawl hundreds of yards on their stomach so no one looked for me there. Finally I saw the battle lines and ran to them waving the flag over my head.

Unfortunately I was behind *their* lines not ours. I quickly learned how painful paintballs are when shot at point-blank range. I carried the bruises for weeks. But I was congratulated. No one had gotten the opposite team's flag in the previous round. We didn't keep it but at least we had gotten it.

Dave really got into the games. In one game he imitated my belly moves and crawled all the way from our outpost to the enemy's. Grabbing the flag he ran 30 yards before being downed. When we were through he had a head full of paint that included up his nose and in his mouth. Our team consisted of Dave, me, a friend of Dave's from Ocean Beach and a group of guys on a bachelor party. (The bachelor party motif was a tad hard to figure out.) We didn't win any of the wars but it was a fun experience.

On the way back Dave said he would soon get his second wind and we'd go dancing. We decided to get a pizza, a movie, eat and rest then go to the ballrooms. By the time we got back to University City his second wind had come and gone. At the video shop we were looking at the rental movies and I asked if he wanted to get one or two.

"Well," he said, "if we get two we probably won't have time to go out dancing."

"Yeah, that's true," I replied.

He looked at me, I looked at him then he said, "I'll make you a deal. I won't say you wimped out if you don't say I wimped out and we'll get two movies."

By ten o'clock that night he was not moving too well. His knees were shot from the crawling and running, his back was hurting and he was a long way from getting any wind let alone his third. Luckily my years at the gym had done me well. I was tired but not sore (except where the paintballs had hit). After the last movie ran its credits he started, "Oh, I've got to get on that bike and it's so cold and my knees hurt and . . ."

It was the closet again. And my camera didn't have any film. He finally left about 12:30 a.m. Monday morning. As it was he spent most of the day discussing his knees and watching my movies on the VCR. We went for a short ride but his heart wasn't in it. His body was definitely out if it. These kids how out of shape.

In my newsletter I warned everyone about Bill. He'd invited me on a breakfast ride. We went to the desert via Ocotillo and as we returned via Julian I commented on how pretty the clouds looked as they drifted between the hills.

"That's rain," he'd replied, "Do you want to go on or go back through the desert?"

"It's your choice," I replied.

After nearly drowning on the bike and having my head and body pelted with very large hailstones Bill said, "Don't ever give me a choice. I'll usually make the wrong one."

We stopped in a bar and when I held my coat upside down the water literally ran like a river. We took our boots off and poured out the water. By that time the waitress had arrived with a bucket and mop. She handed them to Bill with the terse comment, "I'm not cleaning up that mess." Luckily it was a warm day.

At the beginning of September a woman from the city of Del Mar, a high-priced exclusive enclave, joined the group. This very rich, well-educated woman then met one of our riders who was 15 years younger and had a Harley. September 29 our ride ended at her house for a party. House was a misnomer. It was a literal mansion overlooking the ocean. We dined on the finest and wandered through the white on white modernistic rooms. The Harley man was definitely familiar with the house. A month later she met someone closer to her age and wealth and had to leave the group. Actually she said she didn't want the new boyfriend to know she was even *in* the group. That was our brief glimpse into the lives of the rich and famous.

On another ride mostly mapped by Dave we were lost three times and came to one point on the route by a different direction so knew where we were but not how we got there. We ate breakfast and one guy, Ray, told me he had asked the waitress the location of the next road we were to take. After explaining it to me I said, "Tell Dave, he's leading."

Ray replied, "Well I'll tell him but based on the day so far I don't know how much good it will do."

On the next leg of the trip Ray suggested we stop at the Mobil gas station for a bathroom break. Dave proceeded to pull into a parking lot that was right before the gas station and, of course, we did another 'circle the wagon train to get back on the road' trick. Ray commented, "Amazing. The sign for the gas station is big, red, blue and white and he takes us to a parking lot with a bus in it yet."

One night Dave and I went to the *Rocky Horror Picture Show* where a 'cast' duplicated each scene and line of dialogue. During this the audience shouted replies to the onscreen actors' comments and gyrated in the aisles imitating the movie's dance routines. Josh was a cast member and while Dave and I waited to get in Josh proceeded to run me up and down the line yelling, "My Mother the Virgin" (my first time there). They painted big red Vs on my face and Dave commented we were the only ones there over 20. During the movie one of the main instigators for shouting the replies and getting people up to act out the parts was Josh. Dave said it wasn't hard to see who had raised him.

A number of months later the Lyceum staged the *Rocky Horror Show*. Knowing Josh and his friends did the movie version the director asked that I bring them as ushers for the pre-opening so the actors on stage would have an idea of what they were in for on opening night. About halfway through the show the actor playing Dr. Frank-N-Furter leaned down from the stage, looked at Josh and said, "Listen you little fucker, I'm the actor here and I get all the laughs not you and your loudmouth friends." With a twinkle in his eyes Josh noted that the actor was in for a big surprise during the show's run.

Taking tickets on show days proved to be pretty funny. The older women clutched their purses as they nervously looked around at the men and women in mesh nylons, high heels, corsets and heavy makeup. "Myrtle, Myrtle, don't look but that man behind us is wearing a slip."

Dave's propensity for exploration did pan out at times. Once on a ride into the East County area of San Diego County we took a road off Interstate 8 called Shepherd Lane, a route that was dirt and ruts from the start. As we climbed the hill the sun came through dark rain-type cloud cover bathing the hill and jutting rocks with a green-tinged golden glow. The color saturation, along with the shadows and light from the clouds, made the scene almost, in Dave's words, surrealistic. As we climbed higher the valley that Highway 8 bisects and the mountains beyond were shrouded in clouds and mist lit by a red streaked sunset. Definitely a rarely experienced visual.

In 1991 the San Diego Singles Convention was held February 16 and 17. The SMC had a booth for Sunday and riders and passengers signed up for various time blocks. We needed fresh blood so to speak. Dave was coming over Saturday to help me put our promotional literature together. Friday night I made a banner and on Saturday we went to buy paint to make the sign more noticeable. Dave had once taken classes to be an artist so he was assigned to the crafts store while I did my other shopping. Forty-five minutes later he was still checking the paints. Opening a bottle he touched the paint then compared it to the other colors he'd chosen.

"I don't think this complements the other colors," he mused, "it has too much green in it." I didn't see any problem with it but went along with his musing. After a half-hour of this, which involved opening and testing about fifteen different paint combinations, my natural impatience emerged.

"For Christ sakes David, pick a color or we'll be up all night painting the damn thing."

By one-thirty in the morning on Sunday after trying to work on the living room floor, the kitchen floor and finally the kitchen table, we had the banner painted. As I tottered off to bed, my back a mass of aching muscles from leaning over the table, I admonished Dave, "Don't be late tomorrow."

Sunday morning I used iron-on letters on the front of a turtleneck to advertise the club. With my black leather skirt and knee high black boots I looked like a walking advertisement for the Singles Hooker Club but decided it would get attention. When Dave showed up, late, he was dressed in a long-sleeved blue shirt and jeans with his long black hair hanging down almost to his waist. Combined with his piercing black eyes and engaging smile I knew he would attract the ladies' attention.

At the Convention the women not only came to the table to sign up they hung around so much that other interested parties couldn't get near. Periodically Dave overcame his 'shyness' and went into the throng to return with three or four lovely ladies in tow. Then one of our ladies, a short, well-built blonde, walked in. Tight black leather pants and an even tighter black leather vest laced over her bosom with nothing underneath. A bulldozer couldn't have cleared the area of interested men.

By the end of the show, we'd given out close to 100 flyers and I'd received comments such as, "I think I'll buy a motorcycle" and "Hey, Pete, have this lady show you her chest." About 60 people left their addresses with 40 of those being women and most of them under 30. Dave was in his glory. Dozens of 'sweet young things' he could potentially date. When we got back to my house I practically had to break his fingers to get the names out of his hand.

The next weekend was a camp-out at Joshua Tree National Monument. After this campout a guy I'll call Repo had to bring Brenda to future rides to protect him from one of the women.

Repo rode a Harley and was a blonde, sweet-faced lad who could have doubled for a choir boy but worked as a repo man. In certain situations this included packing a gun. Definitely the 'bad boy' type, one of the ladies latched onto him as her rider.

At the campground everyone was hungry but it was too early for the planned dinner so I suggested we go to the Palm Springs Aerial Tramway. In the parking lot waiting for the tram Dave, Repo and I discussed the Harley legend of parts that didn't quite stay put. As Repo leaned against his bike laughing at the foolishness of this fable his side mirror fell off. When we returned from the tram ride Repo's passenger ran up to Dave and me and said, "Oh, I just think (Repo) is so cute, I'm going to fuck his brains out tonight. And if I can't get him tonight, I'll get him to my house tomorrow night and fuck his brains out there." That was probably one of the few times I saw Dave speechless.

Back at the campground we passed this bit of intelligence to Repo who, for some unknown reason, took off. His passenger ended up in some other guy's tent. Loudly in some other guy's tent. For the ride home the next day Repo convinced another rider to take her as a passenger. She complained that the rider got fresh. Why would he think she was that kind of woman? Beats me.

THE SMC AND MIKE
San Diego, 1991

During this time period I had met Mike, a Housing Commission employee at a bad period in his life. Broke, emotionally wired to a drug user who had married her probation officer, physically unwell due to an automobile accident, he was at the nadir of his life. His roommate and best friend, Paul, later told me that before we started seeing each other Mike spent many a night sleeping in the chair in front of the television, an empty bottle at his side.

We had met in December the previous year, talked a lot at work through February but didn't date until the first week in March. That I ran a motorcycle club had been the initial attraction even though his Harley was in pieces on his garage floor. As a second-job his nightly *New York Times* paper route provided an environment for intimate conversation. After dancing at our special sleazy bar, we'd spend hours in the car talking about life, why and how people mess it up and how to make it right again. Because so many things had gone wrong in the past year he had a lot of things he needed to talk about and I was good at listening. Within a few weeks he was spending most nights at my house.

In February I'd contacted the University of California – San Diego Medical School and found that I could get plastic surgery for a quarter of the normal rate if I went with their 'doctor-in-residence' training program. I had bags under my eyes and hanging skin under my chin from an operation when I had tuberculosis as a child. I didn't care how self-centered it was, I wanted them gone. The school had a cancellation and it was April 5, Mike's fortieth birthday. Not wanting to wait another three months, I'd taken the cancellation.

Surgery was at seven that morning. But I still could carry out my plans for his birthday that included hanging black-bordered posters announcing, 'Mike Laudermilt is 40 today' from the traffic poles and streetlights along the route from my house to his apartment. My 'co-conspirators' at his Housing Commission office were to hang the posters from the walls throughout the office. I'd ordered a black frosted cake that said 'Deepest Sympathies on your 40th' to be delivered to his office.

The night before the operation he came over after picking up his papers. We talked, made love then slept until around 2:00 a.m. when he left for the route. As soon as he left, I was out of the house hanging up posters. Per our routine, he came back after the route and stayed until 6:30 a.m. when he left for his apartment to get his work clothes. He would see the posters on the way. Soon after, I left for my operation.

Josh took me then picked me up late in the afternoon. I don't remember a lot except that Mike had called in the early afternoon then later in the evening to see how I was doing.

"You were real busy this morning weren't you?" he dryly remarked.

I laughed as well as I could with the stitches. "Yeah it was a real rush to get everything done before you came back."

"How are you feeling? I really wanted to go out dancing for my birthday."

"My face looks like Frankenstein's monster and I'm in no condition to go out anywhere, let alone dance. I'm sorry I had to do this on your birthday but it was now or wait three months. You probably wouldn't want to see me anyway, I look terrible."

"I thought I'd come over for a while anyway. You know, we can talk maybe."

He was over in about an hour and when he saw my face he grimaced. "That even looks painful."

"The doctor's going to remove some of the stitches tomorrow so it should look better. Not much but better. And I really don't feel bad. If you want to stay, I can put a sack over my head. You can pretend I'm someone else."

He looked uncomfortable, "No, I don't think you're in any condition for that."

He hugged and kissed me then left with a promise to be over the next night.

A birthday card I'd sent him was one of a dozen copies I'd purchased for such an occasion:

Happy ~~30th~~ 40th Birthday.

I have a feeling this is a birthday you're going to remember for years to come.

Inside:

It's funny the way those truly tragic moments have a way of staying with us.

Have a Great Day.

I wrote this section of my memoirs a month after Josh turned 40. I emailed him the verbiage from the card I had given Mike noting that I had wanted to send him the same card but couldn't find any more copies.

His response:

RE: Belated Birthday Card

I hate to point out your tragic case of Alzheimer's but you don't have a copy because you sent it to me on my 30th birthday.

Love Josh

(You remember, Josh! Your son!)

On Saturday the doctor removed most of the black stitches and my face looked a little better but not much. My skin was bruised from my eyes down to my cheekbones and my neck was mottled with black and blue marks down to my collarbone.

I asked the surgeon how long I'd have to wait before I could go back to my aerobics classes. He said two weeks. Then I asked about bedroom aerobics. He said one week then added, if I could wait that long. I assured him I probably couldn't. He chuckled and told me to try and avoid excessive movement or positions where my body was above my head. We both were laughing as I left.

Mike came over around eight that evening and said I didn't look that bad now that the stitches were gone. He helped me put together the club newsletter for mailing and made dinner. We watched a movie, made love, slept for a while and he left on the route. So much for doctor's orders.

He didn't appear to be that repulsed by my face and I was overwhelmed. How many men would not only visit but sleep with a woman whose face looked like she'd gone through a plate glass window? My ex-husbands did not want to be around me when I was ill. Their absence included my having to pick up my medications for the illness plus cook and clean as usual. Mike was different. When I'd felt my ugliest, he'd not only helped but had made me feel beautiful. How could anyone not care about someone like that? (I later learned he told Paul that I was very beautiful even with two black eyes.)

I was House Manager at the Bowery Theater and that night was a comedy. At the theater I wore dark glasses to hide my eyes and a scarf to hide the chin support I had wrapped around my head. Mike acted like I was the most beautiful woman there, turning to me at each funny line or action in the play, hugging me, kissing me. He held my hand as we left.

That night for the first time he used an endearing term. "Goodnight sweetheart, turn out the light." Under the same conditions my ex-husbands would have slept on the couch.

A rear-end collision in February had wrecked his car and his back. By April he was still having problems with muscle spasms. A week after the play, I went along to do the deliveries while he drove.

He laughed most of the night as his 'directions' for deliveries to apartments had me running all over the grounds. He pointed out the houses where he 'borrowed' the roses that appeared on my breakfast table every morning. "I get the white ones from this house and the house down the street has some great salmon colored ones."

At one house he prompted me to go to the bushes nearest the front of the house because "the pink ones there are the nicest." The outdoor floodlights came on as I approached. I ran back, jumped in the car and, laughing and scolding, said "Laudermilt, you're going to get me arrested." He chuckled and for the next few miles kept glancing at me with that mischievous grin.

But our life together was not to be. A few days later a bus made an illegal turn in front of him. For some reason, he speeded up his Harley, perhaps, as other riders surmised, to try and outrun the bus. He'd gone over the curb to the sidewalk to avoid the collision but when he hit a tree trimmed to look like a bush he and the bike flew. He was not wearing a helmet although the coroner told me that even with a helmet he probably would not have lived.

While death is not funny, the day of his wake was one to remember.

Repo had gotten Mike's bike from where it had been towed and brought it back to my house. The guys were going to determine the damage so I could get it repaired and ready for sale. Mike came from Indiana. I was the only friend in this far off place who knew enough about motorcycling to be able to sell the bike and send the proceeds back to his mother.

Repo tried to kick start the bike (no electric starter) and after the third kick, the starter pedal swung around and cracked Repo in the shin. Dave's dream girl who was now dating Repo took him to emergency. Before he left, someone said, "Mike is up there, laughing his ass off at you."

He replied, "I guess Mike just doesn't want anyone riding his Harley yet."

Later that afternoon he returned in a cast. His fibula had been shattered. Paul commented that many mornings he had heard Mike cursing when the kick start pedal whacked him in the leg but had never seen it quite so serious. A few days later Repo hobbled into the garage with a battery-charger and struck his forehead on a metal ladder hanging from the garage ceiling. After he finished swearing, he declared, "This garage is cursed."

One of my renters replied, "It's not the garage, it's the bike." So we started calling the bike Christine after the Steven King book.

Scott, a renter, was very good with pen and ink drawings. I still have two he made for me, one of a barn owl and one of Mike. I wonder if Scott ever reached his dream of being a graphic artist because he certainly had the talent.

After Mike's death someone asked me why I would continue to ride motorcycles. I asked, "If he were killed in a car accident would I stop driving?" Times like that I understood the great divide between riders and non-riders. Yet even today I will see something or go somewhere and think Mike would really have loved this. He definitely left his mark.

THE SMC, MOM AND DAVE
San Diego, 1991-1992

During this time one of the motorcycle riders, Kelly, had an altercation with Steve. Kelly had a dry sense of humor that was evidenced when I mentioned his name to the guys in a newsletter as someone they might want to contact for a passenger. When he called he used a falsetto voice, saying that while he thought the men on their motorcycles were very macho he didn't think they'd like a passenger with a beard.

In my message announcement, I asked people to speak slowly so I could write down the information. On his message, with every word distinctly enunciated he said, "I am speaking slowly because I know you cannot hear fast." On a ride, he accidently cut someone off in traffic and the other person wouldn't stop yelling. Kelly replied, "I apologized. Why are you yelling? Didn't you have some place to go? Weren't you in your car for a reason?"

On many occasions, Steve complained about the bikes parked in front of his house on the mornings we had a ride. Based on the incident when Steve had made his brother park his junk car in front of the house across the street, I didn't think his territorial rights had much merit.

The bikes were generally there 45 minutes and occasionally someone would have the tip of a wheel jutting into Steve's 14-foot-wide driveway. On this particular day, Kelly's bike was the dirty culprit with the tire about two inches over the limit. Preparing for the ride, we came out of the house donning jackets, gloves, vests, chaps, and helmets. Steve came storming out of his house, addressing Kelly with a belligerent tone.

"You're blocking my driveway."

Kelly looked at his bike tire and the driveway, bent down to measure with his thumb and forefinger, stood, his thumb and forefinger still positioned, then quietly said, "Well, I'm getting ready to leave so it won't be 'blocked' for long."

"I want you to leave now or I'm calling the police."

"I can't leave until I get ready and that includes putting on my helmet. I can't put on my helmet until you stop talking to me because then I can't hear you."

"I'm sick of you bikers blocking my driveway and parking in front of my house. I want you to leave now."

"We are trying to leave but again, we can't because if we put on our helmets, we can't hear you. That would be rude. If you'd stop telling us to leave, we could."

The more Steve sputtered, the quieter and politer Kelly became. Unfortunately for Steve, no one else was quiet or polite. Since most of the group had heard my tales of Steve's reality issues we were laughing so hard that some were sitting on the sidewalk. At one point, Steve pointed to his garage.

"I can't get out of my garage with your bike blocking my driveway.

Kelly replied, "Oh, I'm sorry, I didn't notice you were backing your car up. In fact," looking around Steve's shoulder, "you aren't backing your car up. And even if you were backing your car up, you'd have to go over the curb for my bike to block your car."

Steve finally realized he'd lost the round and went inside to call the police. A few people, when they were able to control themselves, commiserated with me about having such a terrible neighbor.

"Nah," I pointed out, "he's the reason I don't watch television. He's all the entertainment I need."

In May my mother died. With Mike then her then a good friend from the Housing Commission dying in September it was kind of a trifecta for 1991. But when my Mom died it was interesting to see how it affected Josh.

He had been given two options, college or work that included paying rent. He took the work option but the rent part left a lot to be desired. I told him to move out. Grandma couldn't accept her grandson not having a place to live so he moved in with her. John had lived with her while he attended college and he was the compliant type. I knew she would find it hard to take Josh's flippant attitude and ability to ignore her nagging. But even after I had detailed what she was going to be up against she made her choice.

Josh still came to my house to regal my friends with his exploits. (One was when he was stopped for speeding while driving Grandma's new car. When the officer realized my Mom's Geo couldn't go the speed that Josh had been clocked at, the officer walked away muttering he needed to get his motorcycle speedometer calibrated). So I was very surprised when I answered the phone one night and heard this tiny, tearful, soft voice. "Mom, Grandma's dead and I don't know what to do."

When I got to her house he was sitting on the front porch, his eyes brimming with tears. My cocky, brave man-child had been hit between the eyes. She was lying on the couch and had been dead for some time. At 80, watching television then sleeping on the couch until morning had become a regular habit. Josh had returned from his morning paper route, saw her on the couch and assumed she was asleep. He went to sleep himself, figuring she would, like always, wake him in time to take her to her doctor appointment in the afternoon. When he had gotten up it was long past time for her appointment. That was when he determined she was not going to be waking him up anymore. He was definitely a little more subdued for the next few weeks.

Sometime in the spring, Dave and I used two-for-one paragliding tickets we had purchased at the Singles show. I figured out the process pretty quick but Dave just couldn't get airborne. After a number of frustrating crashes I finally got him on the path and we were ready to soar from the 300-foot hill behind the training area.

We were driven up in trucks. The instructor gave us our final rules. Run down that direction, at that point begin your lift, at that point push off, etc. Most important if you felt you were not going to make it, abort the run, get back up the hill and try again. The area between the start and liftoff had been cleared of vegetation to ensure the trainees would have little to impede their path.

Keep in mind this is Southern California with rocky hills of prickly dry grass and thorn-type bushes. The more confident (or dumb) individuals started off with each soaring into the air forming colorful ribbons gently floating down to the landing area. I held back because I wanted to go after Dave to ensure he made it off the hill.

Finally there were five of us left. The guy in front of Dave started running down the hill and Dave and I saw he wasn't going to make it. The instructor and another student saw he wasn't going to make it. But the guy evidently didn't see he wasn't going to make it because he kept running. The instructor, Dave, the other student and I started yelling, "Abort! Abort!"

The student finally realized this flight was not going to be and started to veer off the course to abort. Only by now he had gone past the cleared area and was in the dry grass and thorn-bushes. He was out of sight but the sounds carried very well in that area.

Crash! Bang!

"Oww!"

Thump, thump, thump!

"Ohhh!"

Bang, bang!

"Ouch!"

"Damn it!"

Thump!

This went on for a minute or so and at each sound, whether body contact or voice, Dave, I and the other student (and the instructor if the truth be told) laughed. And we didn't just laugh bending over with our hands on our knees we laughed so hard we fell down. We rolled on the ground in laughter. I fully understood this guy was getting the shit knocked out of him and was going to look like a pin cushion but it was a total Wiley Coyote cartoon in real time.

By the time the flyer got back to the take-off spot we had ourselves under control. Mostly. He gestured for the rest of us to take off as he needed to get calmed down (and a little first aid). I decided to go because I was almost choking trying not to laugh and I knew Dave would not be paying 100% attention to lift-off if he knew I was back there still laughing. So I soared into the air and learned what it is like to be a bird. I only did it maybe two times (the cost was astronomical for the time in the air) but it was definitely something I am very glad I did. To know what a bird feels like. (Of course Dave's excited scream when he became airborne probably was a little unbirdlike.)

The last memorable ride was the Kings Canyon 1991 Labor Day weekend overnighter.

The plan was to arrive at Kings Canyon on Saturday night, camp out, tour the park, tour Sequoia National Park on Sunday, camp that night on the coast then return to San Diego on Monday via Highway 1 that borders the Pacific. A friend of Dave's would drive a truck with the tents, two coolers, four sacks of food, cooking utensils and numerous backpacks filled with clothes, wine, and beer. Since the truck couldn't maneuver as well as the bikes, the driver would have a different route and meet up with us at certain points along the way. That was the plan. Then Dave took over preparing the route.

Now it's 344 miles from the city of San Diego to the park, about a six to seven hour trip by bike. (Riders have to take a few more 'butt breaks' than drivers.) If you push it and plan carefully it can be easily done. But not if you rely on a route prepared by someone who is not too hot on calculating the mileage.

Sometime in the early afternoon as we blazed along, the lead bike (Dave) came to a screeching halt. The road ended. Not it was blocked because of construction or it turned into dirt. It just ended. As Dave studied a map we looked around and spied blackberry bushes. Lots of blackberry bushes. By this time we were hungry (I think we had also missed lunch) so the blackberries filled a need and we crawled in the bushes for about a half hour getting our fill.

Dave Larsen, a Navy man I'll call Larsen, asked Dave if he'd checked the mileage when he set up the route. Dave turned to him and measured a distance with his finger and thumb. "It was only that much on the map." Larsen shook his head as he walked away.

We regrouped at a restaurant and continued on our trek. The day wore on and Larsen was getting really low on gas. Since we hadn't passed a gas station to return to we decided to forge ahead and hope for the best. If worse came to worse we could siphon gas from the truck.

Finally we reached a gas station but the sun was setting and the station was closed. The guys tried to figure out how to get the pump working but no luck. At that point one of the guys pointed to the floodlight next to the station garage and said, "Wow look at all those birds flying around. Are they sparrows or something?"

I looked up then commented, "Those aren't birds, they're bats."

It took three of the women passengers to get the guys out from under the truck so the driver could check out the road ahead. Luckily there was a Koa campground about five miles away and Larsen could make it.

Larsen's girlfriend Wendy, who he'd met through the club, was with him. He'd rented a tent from the on base Navy store and had not put it up before the trip. So we sat back and watched his and Wendy's efforts after he made it clear they did not need any help. Thirty minutes and lots of blue air went by. He and Wendy got it partially standing, at least enough so they could use it. The rest of us had turned blue holding our breaths to stop ourselves from falling on the ground laughing.

The next morning I saw him walking in the field on the other side of the road.

"Hey Larsen, taking a morning stroll?"

"Yeah, didn't get much sleep. A dog was barking."

"How was the tent?"

"OK. We could get comfortable."

"Why do you keep looking down? Is the field that uneven?"

He glanced up, his face red. "No. Just walking around, getting some exercise."

"Looks to me like you're trying to find something. You're walking a little slow to get any exercise."

"Just checking things out."

"Gee, like what?"

"OK, OK, I'm trying to find the stakes I threw last night. Don't you dare put that in the trip report."

Hiding my grin, I mumbled, "Course not, mum's the word." We did find most of them.

The station with the bats was closed permanently but there was one up the road. I don't think Larsen had enough gas to get to the station because I had a notation in my newsletter that we learned how *not* to siphon gas from a truck to a motorcycle.

The truck guy had been gone when we first woke but came back by the time we had finally gotten everyone up, fed and ready to ride. He was real excited about some treasures he'd obtained from a rummage sale up the street. We discussed the route. He decided to go ahead on the straightest line to the Kings Canyon campgrounds and stake out campsites for us. At the time, sites were first come, first served. But I had been told by others in the club, who notably were not on the ride, that there would be plenty of sites available Saturday afternoon. Of course that was based on the assumption we would *be* there on Saturday afternoon. No one had bothered to ask about Sunday.

By the time we got to Kings Canyon it was dusk. The weather was really hot and we had stopped at two river pool areas to swim. But we weren't worried because Dave's friend had gotten us campsites and had left a note at the entrance noticeboard telling us where he was. At least that was what he was supposed to do. But he didn't.

We rode through the campground at least three times trying to find noticeboards where he might have left the note or campsites that had our names on them or the truck but to no avail. This was kind of critical since the truck not only had all the camping gear it had all the food. Finally I punched Dave's shoulder and said, "I'm hungry, I'm tired and I want a cigarette. Stop in at this camp store so I can buy some smokes."

He pulled into the parking lot with the rest of the tired, mad and hungry group behind us. I went in and got my cigarettes, came out and just then saw the truck slowly going down the road toward the exit. Running and screaming I alerted the others and they started running and screaming and we at least had the truck and our gear.

The friend asked, "Where were you, I've been looking all over for you?"

"We've been looking all over for you. Why didn't you leave a message?"

"There weren't any sites."

"Well, couldn't you have left a message about where you were so we could at least find you?"

"Wow, I never thought about that."

A ranger said we could camp on one of the fire roads but could not have an open fire. That put a damper on the camping idea with no campfire but we did have two camp stoves and could cook the chicken on high, eat the vegetables slightly raw and the salads would be fine. As we left the parking lot heading for the fire road Dave remarked, "This is the first time I'm glad you smoke."

We set up fast with the guys shuttling the women back and forth to the bathrooms for water and personal hygiene. Larsen got the Coleman going and we turned to the coolers. Unfortunately, someone had seen the city slicker coming and sold truck guy a leaky gas can. That he'd filled up and set on top of the coolers.

I was proud of the guys though. They didn't kill him. However, we didn't stop hearing comments about people who put gas cans on food storage containers until well into the next month.

We were able to salvage enough to feed everyone and breakfast would be OK as long as we could get most of the gas off the eggs. The camp stoves were set up, the leaking gas can removed from the truck and we started dinner preparations. As people were wandering around setting up their tents I glanced down and noticed the gas can was a) sitting next to the truck and still leaking, b) the leaking gas led from the can to one of the camp stoves and c) the gas near the camp stove had a wavering flame. You might have realized by now why Dave's friend does not have a name.

Finally with the fire out and everyone fed and in bed the quiet of the night enveloped us. Suddenly we heard thrashing in the bushes. The sound grew louder. Then we heard a bear. Or what we thought was a bear. Woofing, snuffling, running up the hill towards us. Then gasping, wheezing, halting to get air before it dropped. Larsen yelled, "My God Dave are you that out of shape."

Dave came into the camping area gasping and huffing, "I was trying to scare you and almost had a heart attack."

Later that night truck guy tried the bear routine. Then I heard a 'Whack' like someone getting hit with a riding boot and truck guy quietly crawling into his tent. Effective bear repellent.

The next morning we toured Kings Canyon and Sequoia. When a group of us decided to take a hike some of the less energetic riders decided to head back to San Diego or to the coast. After our hike, where Dave had been able to use his new water purifying kit, we headed for the coast. We went through fields of corn as high as an elephant's eye. In fact it was so high Dave decided to let it all out and jacked the bike up to his normal supersonic speed. As he passed a car I noticed a stop sign dead ahead.

"Dave," I screamed pounding his arm, "there's a stop sign ahead."

Slamming on his brakes he swerved from one side of the road to the other. At the stop sign I glanced to my right and saw the car we had been attempting to pass. The driver, terror in his eyes, was sitting in the passenger seat holding the steering wheel in his trembling hand.

Dave's reaction to all this? "That's a silly place to put a stop sign."

The closer we got to the coast the more fragmented became the group. In those days you didn't use cell phones to keep in contact you had to call an answering service and leave messages. We stopped in every town to make these calls but never quite connected. After we got home we found out the group we had been trying to find was in the same town in a restaurant two streets over but the answering service gave us the wrong message.

We tried to find one of the riders at Pismo Beach and I was amazed that Dave could handle the bike over all that wet sand. We watched the ATV drivers jump the dunes and saw hundreds of camp fires strung along the beach. People set off fireworks and it was quite a display with the exploding colors reflected in the ocean's surface. Another sight I would never have experienced if it weren't for Dave.

Dave, Brenda and I shared a real rattrap motel room that night. She was gone when I woke up. Dave and I took the long way back so we could ride by the ocean on Highway 1 as far as possible. The way back was beautiful scenery but by then we'd gone over 1,100 miles and I wasn't wearing underwear suited to that kind of mileage. As a result I stood up for the last 300 miles home.

Within three days everyone who'd been on the trip had called me to complain. Then I'd tell them something funny that happened to us when we all got separated, they'd remember something funny that happened to them and in the end Dave was forgiven. As one guy said, "Yeah, I guess the great roads and laughs made up for the inconveniences. It was a fun trip."

A campout was planned for the Anza-Borrego Desert for October 26 and 27 with the admonition from Kelly that, "We should not experience the typical, normal mishaps that occur with the Singles Motorcycle Club." No one signed up.

Dave was a general contractor and was working on my house. The downstairs bathtub faucets were leaking at the valve fittings and because the tub/shower was formed fiberglass the outside wall had to be torn out to replace them. He called me at work and the conversation went like this:

"I have two things to talk to you about but I'm saving the best for last."

"O.K. Shoot."

"Well if I use opaque glass on the bathroom windows we're replacing, we have to wait four weeks to get them."

"I want opaque so go ahead and order them. Now, what's the best?"

"Well we almost had a minor-near-catastrophe."

"A minor-near-catastrophe. What was it?"

"I almost burned your house down."

"What," I yelped as I started laughing. "What happened?"

"I was using a torch to sweat the fittings off the pipe and caught the fiberglass shower on fire. The water was turned off so we decided to use glasses of water from the pool to put the fire out. It looked like it was out so we went back to work. That was the wrong decision because now it had spread to the space over the bedroom. So I ran around front and turned on the water so we could use the hose. I wanted to tell you so you wouldn't get all upset when you came home and found the burn marks on your shower."

"Great. Now when I recommend you to people for construction, I have to say he's really good as long as you keep him away from fire. What would it have been if you had burned down the house?"

"Oh that would have been a major-accomplished-catastrophe." He hesitated, "This has never happened to me before."

"Why is it things like this always happen when you're around me?"

"You're just special I guess."

When I hung up, still laughing, Sue asked what had happened. After I explained, she noted she would have been furious.

"Well, getting mad wouldn't have changed anything so what would be the point? He'll fix the damage and no one will ever know."

When I got home dirt was all over the kitchen, hallway and bathroom tiled floor. "God, you guys make a mess."

Dave responded, "You should have seen the mess before we cleaned it up."

"What mess?"

"Well we'd taken off the shower faucets and shower head so when we turned the water back on it shot all over. I think there are water stains on the ceiling in the bedroom next to the bath and in the living room." (The living room was directly opposite the bathroom.)

"Where's the bathroom rug?"

"It's on the fence, draining. Notice I didn't say drying."

A few months later a woman at the Commission got keratotomy (this was wayyyy before laser vision correction) and I got the bug. Too many crashes while skiing because my goggles fogged up my glasses. Too many headaches from wearing glasses with a motorcycle helmet. The fear of losing the glasses if I seriously took up white-water rafting. Contacts had never worked and the last pair had caused scaring in my bad eye. It was time for new eyeballs.

Despite numerous people telling me I was crazy and would be blinded, my first stop was my health plan. They could only promise 140/20 in my bad eye. I would still have to wear glasses. Then I went to the top ophthalmologist in San Diego. He could guarantee 20/20 in both eyes. Sold!

The left eye, the one with minimal problems, was done first and healed in a day. The right eye, the mountain range cornea, took ten days to heal and was pretty painful for the first five days. Worse, the usual procedure was to fix one eye for far vision and one for reading. The reading one was the right one and that was the eye I used on rides to read signs for turns. When of course I wasn't yapping with the rider and totally missing the sign. Once it was healed it had to be re-cut and took another five days to heal. With both eyes set for far vision I had resigned myself to needing reading glasses but miracle that it was, I could read the tiny print on a road map.

My eyes didn't start going bad again until around 2006 when age did its damage. But I could see without glasses for all those years. Never listen to the naysayers.

In July 1991 Dave had taken me to a Guns N Roses concert in Costa Mesa. As he noted I was probably the oldest person there. In December I took him to *The Nutcracker*. We arrived in our leathers with helmets in hand, Dave's hair in its Indian headband. The people around us leaned as far away as their seats would accommodate.

At the end of the ballet Dave said to me, "Thank you for inviting me to this ballet, it was really beautiful."

I replied, "And thank you for taking me to the Guns N Roses concert, it was great headbanger music."

The woman to my left looked at both of us and burst out laughing. Her comment, "I wish I could live a little of your kind of life."

THE FIRE DEPARTMENT (AND DAVE)

San Diego, 1991-1992

The Housing Commission not only had memories of Mike it had no prospect for promotional opportunities. I had not started at the bottom as had others nor was I deferential enough. While others often left the Finance Director's office in tears, I would not be intimidated (and told him that). When managers said something couldn't be done because they didn't want to bother I showed them how it could. Now they had to do it or justify why not. Nor did they appreciate my finding questionable expenditures. Just as in the corporate world, government management did not like someone who could find cracks in the armor.

The National City Fire Department interviewed me for the position of Management Assistant. However the real job was Systems Administrator and that included introducing the firefighters to the new world of electronic incident reporting. The State Marshal had mandated electronic records within the next few years and the National City Fire Chief intended to be one of the first. In the interview I noted that doing the job might be a little hard since I had no idea what a Systems Administrator did. They demurred. My experience with personal computers and training made me a good choice.

This confidence was based on my buying a Franklin Ace (the first Apple II clone) in 1982, teaching myself word processing and spreadsheets, implementing a PC to mainframe system at DatagraphiX and developing and presenting software classes often with programs I had to learn to teach. I figured if they had the faith, I had the time.

By this time Gary's 'warm fuzzy' station wagon had been repaired. I had used the bus and trolley to get to work at the Commission for about three months until a homeless man had walked in front of the bus stop flinging blood from his hand into my face. This was after a bus ride where the driver was reading a brochure on pelvic exams while entering the freeway and another driver, when asked for the stop closest to Dave's street, had just stopped in the middle of the street to let me off. This to the chorus of other riders saying, "Wow, we just got a new stop." Feeling my mental calm trumped my bank account, I had found the means to get the car fixed.

Well, not a hundred per cent fixed. It ran but not well. The muffler had fallen off and it was belching black clouds of burning oil to the tune of a quart every other day. I had used letters on the back to spell out the Singles Motorcycle Club with my phone number. The paint was peeling, I think maybe a light or two was out and a window or two was definitely cracked. The day I started for the Fire Department I rolled into the parking lot trailing smoke after setting off every car alarm within five blocks prompting the firefighters to come out prepared for a fire. At my farewell luncheon a year later the Deputy Chief confessed that he had looked at the Chief that morning and both had said, "Did we make a mistake?"

They soon learned they had not. I figured out what a Systems Administrator did and re-installed the network to fix what had been botched by the Sears Business Network consultants. This did not sit well with one of the firefighters who had been sent to school for Certified Network Engineer certification. According to him, the problem with the network was directly attributable to the firefighters refusal to learn the new system. His training 'method' had caused deep resentment. I had to make the system work while convincing everyone to love their computers. Plus figure out why the incident software didn't work. I found the bug and the software vendor fixed it. The problem was not the firefighters' resistance and the engineer was not pleased. He was even less pleased when the oldest firefighter, who had made it clear he was not going to learn any new stuff that didn't directly relate to firefighting, became a one-man campaign for learning the new system.

Just keeping viruses off the server was a job in itself. Following is an email thread to everyone relating to this issue.

> *Subject: BUGS*
>
> *A week ago we had the MichaelAngelo virus scare. According to what I am reading, we should soon have a "Virus of the Week" club (someone wrote a book on how to create viruses).*
>
> *Some of you have computers at home and want to bring your work into work. However, I really don't want to spend three hours a week checking the PC's and network for viruses. So, please take the following precautions before bringing disks into work.*
>
> *(Here was a paragraph on how viruses get into systems and where they were most likely to occur.)*
>
> *1. Local bulletin boards (where you use modems to leave and receive messages and copies of programs, files, etc.*
> *2. School computers (secondary to college). Creating viruses has taken the place of dorm raids and paper toileting houses.*
> *3. Copies of commercial programs, i.e. copies of copies of Quattro Pro, etc.*
>
> *If you are involved in any of the above, the probability you will infect our system if you bring work from home is very high. The probability that I will personally kill you if that happens is also very high. So, please, get Norton Virus checker and test your home system before making copies to be brought to work. Your extra few minutes of checking will be greatly appreciated (and you will live a lot longer).*

Dennis Sheean, the Deputy Chief and my supervisor, responded

What is 'paper toileting' a house?

I replied:

> *'You've never paper toileted a house? Where have you lived all your life – in a monastery? Paper toileting is to houses what spray painting is to highway overpasses. A true expression of art – and it really gets the paper toiletee teed off. If you ever get bored, I have some funny stories about paper toileting houses.'*

Dennis, who knew I was from Michigan, replied back:

> *Flo*
>
> *I think you're referring to TOILET PAPERING, or T.P. ing houses. What is PAPER TOILET? Is this some weird Midwestern weirdness, or are you dyslexic?'*

I replied: '

> *You were the only one to catch that. You're the only one who said anything. Are the others being polite? Or do they think we Michiganders have some new, esoteric, kinky thing to do and they're a little nervous about finding out what it is?'*

In 1992 the helmet law went into effect and Dave showed his displeasure by wearing a helmet outfitted with six-inch horns. On one ride one of the horns broke loose and was hanging downward. The guys decided this type helmet would more likely be worn by a gay rider so Dave fixed it immediately instead of waiting a year.

Sometime that year he had gotten a Harley. I can't remember how (although I think I may have loaned him the down payment) but he was in Hog Heaven. Now he would have no problem getting girlfriends. In a way, he was right. However he soon realized that women who went with him only because he had a Harley might be lacking in some other admirable characteristics. When we discussed it I said, "Let me see if I understand this? These women are attracted to you because you have a Harley. They wouldn't look at you before you got the Harley. And you're asking me what's wrong with them?"

It wasn't until I got to the Bay area that I met the really hard-core Harley types. Such as the woman who promised her male friend on his deathbed that she would never be a passenger on anything but a Harley. How sentimental.

On the other hand, the girl of his dreams would now condescend to ride with him no matter how fast he went. (Although he did mention her often nagging him to slow down.) One ride was to the 10th Annual Laughlin Run and this time the girl of his dreams was on the back seat with her waist length, curly, purple-dyed hair floating around her beautiful body. Coupled with his horns their picture later appeared in *Easy Rider Magazine*. Dave bought at least thirty copies to hand out to friends. (I still have mine.)

In April and May he took me to the San Diego County waterfalls. Despite Balboa Park and our many green golf courses, lawns and community parks, San Diego is pretty much high desert. When he mentioned waterfalls I envisioned little rivulets maybe ten feet tall at the most. But, true to Dave's ingenuity, he took me to the 90-foot Cedar Creek waterfall where we could jump off rocks into a 50-to-60 foot wide pool. Getting there was another matter.

The road to the falls was not well-maintained. Let me rephrase that. It was not maintained at all. Not only were there potholes, there were long ruts at least six inches or more deep and two to four inches wide. Dave steered the bike along the raised sections between the ruts. I panicked and jumped off. Laughing, he continued down the road never making a slip as I jogged alongside.

During our hike he sat on the edge at the top of the falls and looked down the 90-foot drop while I shook in my tennis shoes waiting for him to plunge to the pool below. Characteristically he just laughed at my fear, jumped up and led me down the path to the pool at the bottom. On the way back I stayed on the bike with my eyes closed until we were out of the ruts.

The second hike two weeks before Memorial Day weekend was to the Three Sisters waterfalls that are part of the Boulder Creek drainage. These seasonal falls are a four-mile round-trip composed of scrambling up and down five-to-eight foot cliffs and lots of boulder hopping. On this hike he brought Sue, a lady he had just started dating. We went to each 30 to 50 foot fall and took dips in the pools at the bottom of each. Wanting to cut out some hiking I tried to go up a sharp slope and got caught in an impassable overhang. Looking down that long rocky slope I thought of my mortality for the first time. Luckily Dave and Sue were around to guide me out of my self-made trap.

One thing about this hike was the poison oak. I'm very allergic to poison oak. When it takes over the welts drain an oily, yellow fluid for days. It has been so bad I've had to wrap sanitary pads around my arms and legs to soak up the mess. Sue and Dave, being the intelligent souls that they were, had worn long-sleeved shirts and jeans. I, always wanting a tan, had worn shorts and a halter top. When I looked at the pictures I had taken I noticed all the bright green poison oak that I had stood next to or grabbed on steep slopes. Suffice it to say, within a day I was one weeping, itching, raw sore. The weekend after next, Memorial Day weekend, was my planned whirlwind tour to the Southwest National Parks. All of them. By now Gary's 'warm fuzzy' had been junked and I drove a fairly new four-door Mazda hatchback so I would be touring in comfort.

(I bought the turbo-charged Mazda at 77,000 miles against the advice of many who warned me that I would have to replace the turbo very soon. My instincts said no and it was not until the car had 187,000 miles that the turbo went out. Not due to wear but due to using synthetic oil at the suggestion of an auto buff who shall remain nameless.)

The weekend after the hike I went to somewhere near Bakersfield to learn how to kayak. It was a small creek, not very wavy but a fun experience. Unfortunately my body was weeping all over anything I touched so the rest of the group kept a wide berth. I used a lot of laundry soap to stop the itching. Tends to leave light scarring but at least you can get some sleep.

The Monday after kayaking I had an appointment with the doctor for a lump on my leg (which turned out to be an overly developed tendon) and the appointment turned into a poison oak lesson for the doctor. He'd never seen such a virulent reaction. He gave me some medicine called Atarax to stop the itching and also an antibiotic as some of the poison oak scratches had become infected.

I was not at work Monday and Tuesday because I wasn't getting any sleep and the medicine made me so loopy I couldn't think straight. I worked Wednesday through Friday and by Thursday night the poison oak was pretty much dried up and had stopped itching. However, Friday afternoon as I sat at my keyboard I noticed little bumps on my arms. One of the firefighters had said, "You know, you can get relapses on that stuff. It can come back worse than ever."

I had laughed but as I started itching again, I began to wonder.

Having run out of the Atarax I called the pharmacist on Friday but she had been unable to get a hold of my doctor to get a renewal on the prescription. Friday night the breakout worsened and I realized I had the hives. Saturday morning around 3 a.m. I woke and watched the blisters appear on my hands starting out as little bumps than spreading and swelling. As soon as the pharmacy opened I rushed to the store, showed her my arms and just said, "Help." She gave me enough Atarax to last to Monday.

On Monday I called the doctor about renewing the prescription and he wanted to see me. By this time the only parts of my body that weren't a hive was most of my face, my back from the shoulder blades to the waist and my chest. The rest was hives. And I mean *the rest* if you get my drift. Did you ever try to unobtrusively scratch your private parts in public? It's very hard and *very* embarrassing. Anyway, the doctor determined I had had an allergic reaction to the Atarax. The hives were a lot worse than the poison oak. I was wailing about looking so ugly with all the hives and the poison oak just starting to heal up. The doctor said, "Actually, you don't look that bad. You have on long pants and a long-sleeved shirt. From a distance, you can't tell anything is wrong. Now if you just get some gloves, no one will notice." Thanks Doc.

A WHIRLWIND TOUR AND RAFTING

Arizona, Utah and the Kern, 1992

On Thursday, May 21, I left after work for my whirlwind tour. The hives were still bothering me and I couldn't do the old 'break the skin and drain' routine like I had with the poison oak. I couldn't take any medicine so I was not anticipating a lot of sleep. I was right but not just from the hives.

I drove to Yuma at 90 miles an hour and hit a patch of sand that started me fishtailing. That was an adrenalin rush. I had been getting sleepy but that skid was Vivarin in one second. About 500 feet from the Arizona border I got a speeding ticket, 75 in a 65 zone. Luckily there was an inspection station that I had slowed down for or the ticket would have been for 90 in a 65 zone. It reminded me of when my mother had moved to California from Michigan after my dad died. She had been hitting 95 in her white TransAm when stopped by the Arizona Highway Patrol. The officer sauntered up to her window expecting to see some young hot-shot. Looking at this little old lady with her gray hair and sparkly framed glasses he did a double-take. She batted her eyes in semi-dementia and said, "Why Officer was I going too fast?" He was so disbelieving he just gave her a warning and sent her on her way.

By eight o'clock at night I decided to try to make it to Quartzite where I intended to car-camp. At Quartzite I learned there were no camp sites. Acres of brush-covered land set aside for RV's but nothing with bathrooms or, heaven forbid, showers. The RV season ended May 1 so I had the whole area to myself. I pulled in near a seven-foot high berm and settled down to sleep in the car. My seats recline but it wasn't real comfortable. Between the cramped seating, accidently getting my feet tangled in the brake and accelerator pedals and jumping at every sound (while asking about camping facilities in the Quartzite store I had noticed some semi-unsavory characters), I didn't get a lot of sleep. Watching the moon was pretty neat though.

About five-thirty in the morning, I used my acres of land for a privy and stripped down to take an 'out-of-a-water-jug' shower. Halfway through my toilette I heard the long blow of a truck horn. I looked around but couldn't figure where the sound had come from. I continued my nude rinse off and there was another horn. Looking higher up the berm I realized I was closer to the highway than I had thought. A trucker waved, I waved back, finished my shower, got dressed and was on my way.

From there I traveled through Prescott, Sedona and Flagstaff, gathering numerous flipped birds and curses when I partially stopped on the highway to take pictures. (Arizona is pretty sparing with turnouts near vistas.) Cresting a 6,500-foot peak through a cleft of hills to see the plain in the distance ringed by red mountains, what else could I do?

In Prescott I visited an art gallery with paintings by an artist named Bob Quick. One painting was of three wolves whose eyes followed me around the gallery. I bought that plus another with a wolf and Indian. I was hoping I had discovered the next Bev Doolittle but no such luck. I have treasured those paintings though. People who come to my home have said they too can feel those eyes.

Sedona, Oak Creek Canyon, Jerome and onto Flagstaff are a photographer's paradise of red and black mountains, towns built into the cliffs, plains with huge mesas and monoliths of every hue. As a result by the time I arrived at the Grand Canyon all the tent sites were filled. Backtracking to a campground called Ten-X I drove through it three times then spotted a Harley with a very overweight guy sitting at the picnic table. Positioning the car so he could see the Singles Motorcycle Club bumper sticker I asked if he had room for another tent. As one biker to another there was always room. He rode a Harley but said this was his last ride as he had a heart condition and was not expected to last the year. One thing he said that I will always remember, "You wouldn't expect this of a Hell's Angel but when I saw the Grand Canyon I fell to my knees and cried." I wonder what happened to him.

While I didn't cry I was in supreme awe. Time did not permit going to the bottom of the canyon so I hiked eight-miles of the West Rim Trail to Hermit's Rest. I remember a tower but not its name. Every plateau that jutted into the canyon had a different look from the one before. A great day of discovery.

From the Grand Canyon I went to Canyon De Chelly via the Navajo Indian Reservation. Keams Canyon, a town of about fifty to seventy houses, was built right into a narrow canyon and the children playing in the shadows of those overwhelming cliffs seemed to come from a different age.

Canyon de Chelly was not under the Navajo Park Service at the time and I could hike down to the canyon floor to get close to the many Anasazi ruins built under the overhangs of gigantic cliffs. I was in awe not only with how high the ruins were above the canyon floor and the immense height of the cliffs above the ruins but that structures that big had been created by a group considered primitive by white Americans. Walking along the bottom of the cliffs gazing up began my romance with North and South American archaeology. Subsequently I have visited at least fifteen complexes throughout Arizona, New Mexico and Colorado. From that I started reading about Central and South American civilizations and have traveled to or targeted my travel to those areas.

Navajo hogans were scattered every half mile or so near the small river flowing through the middle of the canyon floor. They still used the bottom lands for farming. I heard the distant tinkle of a bell. Looking up the cliff wall over a set of ruins I saw a herd of goats with a Navajo shepherd dressed as he must have looked two hundred years ago. It was magical. The crowning touch was Spider Rock a multi-hued pinnacle that rises from the canyon floor. Gazing at that you could feel the spirits of the Anasazi and Navajos calling to you. One of my few mystical moments.

From there I traveled to Monument Valley via Mexican Hat stopping every mile to take pictures of the monoliths, plateaus and sheer cliffs of every color. Close to Monument Valley was a series of cliffs that looked like ocean waves, rock formations the likes of which I had never seen. Just past Kayenta a plateau was close to the road and the sun lit up the mist in the long narrow canyon that splits the plateau in two. I was so tired by then I missed the picture opportunity.

My next target was Lake Powell then Kanab, Red Rock Canyon and Bryce Canyon. Hiking into the canyon at Bryce I think I was on the Fairyland Loop. You can exit at a point where a long staircase has been cut out of the rock for a climb of close to 900 feet. I had run out of film before I ran out of things to photograph so I went up the stairs passing two women about my age. Soon I started back down with more film. One of the women looked at me in astonishment.

"Didn't you just go up?"

"Yes and now I'm going back down to take more pictures."

"But, but, how will you get back up?"

I looked at her, puzzled. "Umm, the same way I got up before?"

"But, but, we haven't even gotten all the way up yet."

I just smiled and continued down. At that point I decided that while I was 48 I'd never be THAT type of 48.

Zion was my next stop and I approached it via the road that went past Cedar Breaks National Monument, another natural amphitheater that had been formed by wind erosion the same way as Bryce Canyon. The route over the mountains to Cedar City displayed aspen and birch in bloom with the bright light green and white bark contrasting against the dark green and brown of the pine and fir trees. Zion was beautiful but after the Grand Canyon, de Chelly and Bryce, it just didn't have the same awesomeness.

A few weeks later Josh, his girlfriend and I went white water rafting. Because there will be a lot more rafting stories here is a short primer on white-water rafting.

White-water rafting is riding in a pontoon-like paddle boat with four to six others and either paddling like hell to get through the waves or having the guide oar like hell to get through the waves. Many white water enthusiasts use one-person kayaks, hard-shell or inflatable. While I have used an inflatable I cling to my paddle boats on the big rivers.

A river usually has a variety of runs from super easy, called Class I, to super hard, called Class V to VI. Super hard means not only do you paddle until your arms fall off but the reason you paddle is to avoid running the boat into rocks or getting trapped in a sieve (underwater openings between rocks that are impossible to escape) or going upside down over the waterfalls or into a backward, circling wave action, called a hydraulic where you might get tossed into the water, be sucked down and not be able to get out. The more dangerous the run the higher the class. Most people start with Class III with the adventurous graduating quickly to Class IV+ and the real adventurous (and physically fit) going on to Class V. Very few people run Class VI because of the potential for serious bodily harm and/or death.

With that in mind, we had signed up for the Thunder Run, a short Class V on the Kern River near Lake Isabella. But the water was low so they took us on the Lickety Split, a much tamer Class III. Since this was our first time the Class III was fun but Josh and I instantly knew that on the next trip we were going up a class. We saw three people fall out of paddle boats or inflatable kayaks and they were whipped from the effort of trying to get back to the boats. Two refused to get back in the inflatable kayaks and one, who we had rescued, wouldn't get out of our boat.

The people in our boat were amiable but the guide, an eighteen-year-old called J.J. who had been on the river since he was three, was not certain if his off-color jokes were acceptable to me or an older couple. For one joke J.J. had a twinkle in his eye while constantly glancing at me and the couple.

At the punch line to one dirty joke we hit a rock because J.J. wasn't watching the river and he fell out of the boat. As people threw him the life preservers he kept shouting, "No, no, I don't want anyone to know I fell out of the boat."

Later on the boat ran upside a one-story boulder.

He yelled, "We have to get off this rock. Everyone run forward." Everyone, but me, ran forward. The boat bent in two.

"No, no," he yelled, "that isn't working. Everyone run to the back."

Everyone, but me, ran to the back. See, I had been in the kayaking class and I knew that what he was telling them to do wasn't what had to be done to get us off the rock. Finally, after having them run back and forth a few times, he got us off the rock. As we were progressing down the river, I said, "You know, for someone who's been on this river for fifteen years, it's amazing you didn't know that rock was there." He grinned.

Sometime in June I had a mammogram where I squirted bloody fluid during the procedure and the radiologist detected clouding in the milk tubes in the left breast. To be on the safe side, my doctor wanted to take them out. I then embarked on one of the weirdest operations in my life. (Well, weird until I broke my knee cap in 2001 but more about that in my second book.)

I was first sent to the pre-surgery waiting room. Usually from this point you are brought to the operating room in a wheel chair or on a gurney. But due to major construction I was led to the operating room while dodging scaffolding, thick electrical cords and temporary lighting. In the room I was asked to get on the table and the anesthesiologist started prepping me for a local, as in just numbing the breast. When I politely asked what the hell he was thinking the surgeon noticed my consternation and told him I was to be under general anesthesia.

I don't know if it was due to having thin veins in the back of my hand or the anesthesiologist was in training but he poked me at least five times. Finally he got what he thought was a vein and started the IV. The skin on the back of my hand started to swell then little geysers started shooting up from the holes he had previously made.

Seeing the fountains springing from my hand, the surgeon exclaimed, "For Christ's sake," grabbed the needle from the anesthesiologist, got it in a vein and re-started the IV.

"You can handle it from here can't you?" the surgeon asked, to which the anesthesiologist meekly nodded his head. By this time the dope was doing its job so I had no time to think about my impending death.

I went back to work two days later with one breast three times the size of the other. I was not big-breasted to begin with so the contrast was pretty obvious. I could tell the guys were making an extreme effort not to notice.

By July I had things so under control the secretary could do the network administration. When word came down that budget cuts would most likely eliminate my job, I made a decision. San Diego had gotten too big and its open spaces too small. The view from my bedroom of mesas and mountains was now filled by condos and shopping malls. It was time to leave. One night I had a dream. I saw a small hill with office buildings. The buildings dissolved, the hill grew trees, took on a layer of snow, and a lake appeared. I woke up crying, "I want to go home."

Well, home was Michigan, with 18-degree-below-zero temperatures, six-foot snowdrifts, and no ocean. I didn't want to go home that bad!

Looking for the next best thing, Southwest Oregon popped up. Not a lot of people, a rural environment that, in my mind, would produce a more laid-back attitude, a mild climate (annual rainfall was close to San Diego's), close to the ocean according to the map and plenty of outdoor activities. What I thought and what I learned diverged widely at many points. But Oregon beckoned. Oregon, real estate and my newsletter *Oregon Ho!*

Before I left for Oregon the doctor who had done the milk tube surgery said I was all clear. The tubes had pre-cancerous cell structures but with them out I shouldn't have to worry. Not that I had been worried, he had to contact me. At least I didn't have to worry in the future.

OREGON HO! – GETTING THERE
Oregon 1992

My last day at work was Friday, August 7. I had a farewell party with the SMC planned for Saturday. On Sunday, Josh, and I would leave by six or seven in the evening and drive until we were north of Los Angeles thereby missing the LA weekend travelers and the Monday morning 'LA crawl.' I would drive the van and Josh my Mazda. The van would carry my household furnishings that I intended to store until I had work and a place to live.

I'd bought the van for $1,500 because renting a moving van would have cost $1,700. I figured I could sell the van in Oregon thereby making the move for nothing. Based on Josh's moving violations record if he got stopped my car would be sans a driver. It was Josh or flying back to get my car so I forged ahead.

I had the van tuned-up and the brakes checked then returned to my house, parking the van in front of my car that was sitting at the curb. Well, almost in front of my car that was a little closer than I had calculated. As the van seemed to lose power I heard and felt the sickening crunch of the Mazda's left front fender against the van's rear panel. I realized I probably was going to need a little more practice driving a vehicle that big.

As we started moving boxes and furniture into the garage, I also realized that what I had to move and my van were unequal by a 2 to 1 margin. My choices were to leave a lot behind, make UPS rich, buy a trailer or a combination thereof. Someone at the party facetiously suggested I make two trips.

On Sunday, after determining that returning Josh to San Diego would be $200 airfare, buying a trailer $400 (no one-way trailer rentals) and I still would have a passel of boxes to send UPS, the two-trip scheme took on new meaning. Gas, round trip, would be about $160 and I would only have to drive an extra two days.

Well, it looked good on paper.

We packed the van under the direction of John and his girlfriend, both of whom were methodical doctoral students at Indiana University. While the van's contents were well arranged the effort took a lot longer than I had planned. We then waited for Josh. And waited. Finally he showed up with his friends that meant more waiting while they made phone calls and he packed two boxes of CDs to take on the trip. He did not pack contact lens solution, storage vials or a toothbrush but he did get all his favorite CDs. Then they had to go get something and we finally left – at nine-thirty at night not six.

The first adventure was trying to use an exit ramp with no rear vision. The boxes were stacked so high I couldn't see out the back and I'd forgotten to clean the side mirrors before we left. After cleaning the mirrors (by golly, that there was a road back there), we got ready for the Grapevine (I-5 through the Tehachapi Mountains north of Los Angeles).

Empty the van could get about 45 mph on a hill. Full the wheezing and chugging was like prodding an elephant to run a marathon. Going down the Grapevine also made me realize that when loaded the van's brakes weren't too hot either. When we stopped for gas or to take a break, I also noticed the van stalling as I rolled to a stop. At the time, I thought I could handle it.

On the way to Oregon I wanted to stop at the jellyfish exhibit at the Monterey Aquarium. We decided to drive as far as possible so we would be close to Monterey when we collapsed. The closest camping area between Bakersfield and Monterey was San Luis Reservoir at I-5 and State 152. We rolled in about five Monday morning, threw our sleeping bags on the ground and crashed.

Let me say one thing about this campground. DON'T EVER USE IT!!! We woke up about eight in the morning and after using the showers we started to repack the sleeping bags when we noticed this 'odor.' Like being in the middle of a landfill. We thought it was the garbage bin. Three hours later we realized it was the dirt. The campground must have been built on an old landfill. It took two days for the stink to get out of the sleeping bags and car. Not pleasant. (The jellyfish exhibit was awesome enough to make the lingering stench worthwhile.)

From Monterey to the Golden Gate the van stalled at every light. At Sausilito we decided to take the coast route, Highway 1, to Stinson Beach and on to Bodega Bay where we would camp on the beach. Unfortunately I wasn't aware that the road to Stinson Beach was a series of switchbacks that only a motorcyclist could love – a good motorcyclist. Besides the terrors of driving an over-packed van with bad brakes on twisty mountain roads the constant stalling at low speeds really added a fillip of fun – particularly when it stalled on an upgrade and start rolling backwards. The views were spectacular but not worth the jangled nerves. At Bodega Bay Josh suggested a different route for the rest of the trip since we had taken four hours to go fifty miles. Prying my hands from the steering wheel I agreed with him whole-heartedly.

After a chilly night camped on the beach at Bodega Bay, Josh, who'd opted to sleep in the open, found more water on the inside of his sleeping bag than out. He was not too alert. I checked the oil and, lo and behold, there wasn't any. Luckily I had some but the oil depletion grew greater as we neared Oregon.

We cut cross-country to get to Highway 101. In Santa Rosa the van stalled at an intersection and wouldn't restart. I had jumper cables but with my usual practicality had safely placed them in the van's storage bins that were now buried under boxes and furniture. While Josh went to find a Kragen I directed irate drivers around my van. I was amazed at the polite people who sat behind my van until I told them they would be there a long time. I mean if you saw someone standing behind a van pointing to other lanes, wouldn't you think there was something wrong?

Josh came back to get the map so I figured, "One more try for old time's sake." And the darn thing started. I immediately drove to the nearest service station and had the battery charged. Again, we were on our way – with the addition of six quarts of oil. By the time we got to Eureka, we had used three more quarts, the van's rear quarter panel was a blackened mess from the burning oil and the van had stalled one too many times – it had rolled backwards as Josh, in my car, rolled forwards. Luckily only the license plate was dented but not as much as my nerves.

At Crescent City we took State 199 through the Jedediah Smith National Forest and even though the road was twisty-turny I was very happy to see the *Welcome to Oregon* sign nestled in the trees. Plus the deer-crossing signs where the deer had little red bulbs on their noses.

Past Cave Junction I almost hit a deer but the brakes worked fine. We found a campsite and the next day, Wednesday, I looked for a rental. By late afternoon I gave up so we went to a storage place where the lady apologized that the rate was so high. At $55 for a 10 x 20 space ($150 in San Diego) I had no problem.

Because Josh wanted to get back to San Diego we decided to drive non-stop. P.S. It's fourteen hours and nine quarts of oil straight through.

From Thursday to Sunday I recuperated at my house and on Sunday packed the van a second time. This time I didn't have my doctoral students. I had to leave my box springs, headboard, three boxes, my mother's paintings and a horse print from college high up on the living room wall. I never saw any of them again.

I intended to leave at six in the evening and made it by ten-thirty. With two half-hour snooze stops I drove straight through until I was two hours out of Grants Pass. Not wanting to drive the mountains half-asleep at night plus being continually bopped by poorly stored boxes I stopped at a Klamath River rest stop and slept for ten hours. I got to Grants Pass around nine-thirty Tuesday morning, stored my furniture, took a shower and started looking for a rental and work.

Amazingly, unloaded, the van stopped burning oil. Now it just burned power steering fluid. And coolant. And alternators. And fan belts.

Grants Pass was a little strange with the southern entrance running past a scrap yard and the northern graced by one of the ugliest statues of a caveman I've ever seen. This was, and still is, the Grants Pass mascot based on some citizens dressing up like cavemen for a long-ago parade and thinking it would be really cool if the city adopted this motif for its future parades and advertising. Like my Mom said when she saw *Who Framed Roger Rabbit*, "The guy who thought that up must have been on drugs."

One building in the city was six stories, the rest not over four. By San Diego standards, with 17,500 people Grants Pass was a village. The city was in Josephine County with adjacent Jackson County holding the two other major cities, Medford and Ashland (of Oregon Shakespeare Festival fame). At the time the two counties had a combined population of about 210,000 residents in a land area of 4,400 square miles. (Twenty years later population is close to 288,000 so it's still a rural environment.)

The street system was 'different.' North/South streets were numbered and the main streets, Sixth and Seventh were one-way with Seventh being the Caveman entrance off I-5. The cross streets went from names to letters, i.e. Evelyn then A, B, etc. Then there were the direction designators.

Numbered streets were designated as 'N.W.' or 'S.W.' or 'S.E.' and the point of change was 'G' street (not 'A' as one might assume). But this directional identification did not always hold.

Fifth was 'N.W.' and 'S.W.' Where Fifth was 'N.W.,' so too was Sixth.

However where Fifth changed to 'S.W.,' one block over Sixth was 'S.E.' The Yellow Pages said 'S.W. Sixth' but the identified companies were located at 'S.E. Sixth.' The only explanation I could figure was they had run out of S.W. stencils.

If you were looking for 300 S.E. 'F' Street, you didn't look on Third and F because the change point was Sixth. Therefore, 300 S.E. 'F' was at Ninth. Confused? And you weren't even there trying to find things!

While looking for a rental I lived in my van, parking it at the Valley of the Rogue rest area south of town. A few other 'campers' had been there for two to three weeks and assured me it was perfectly safe. The bathrooms were open all night, the nearby campground had showers for two dollars a day or I could join a health club and take my showers there. Doing the math I determined it would be cheaper to join the gym then pay the combined campground fees and shower charges plus I could work out. Living in a motel was financially out of the question. To underscore the complete change in attitude between Oregon and San Diego I was congratulated by many at my ability to find a cheap solution to my temporary lack of housing.

The Grants Pass Chamber of Commerce meeting that I attended to find job leads was a far cry from similar meetings in San Diego where fellow computer pros were downright nasty at the thought of competition. However I did note that several women hurriedly latched on to boyfriend's arms, waists or necks when I approached the male member of the couple. I soon learned that the ratio of women to men was so lopsided that single men of any age were the prime rib of the area menu. This ratio was made worse by the fact that the majority of men were significantly undereducated most having quit school in the eighth grade. In logging you needed a strong back not a strong mind. An educated man could have his pick.

My temporary home wasn't equipped as a livable van – it was basically a shell. My mattress was in the front part of the cargo area and my cooler and eating utensils in the rear. My spare tire was mounted on the van's backdoor with a rope because the tire mount was missing. In San Diego I had been told I needed to order the part at considerable expense.

When the tire went flat I took it to a Grants Pass mechanic. After fixing it he threw it in the rear of the van. The conversation went something like this:

"You put the tire in my kitchen."

"Your what?"

"My kitchen. See, the cooler and plates and stuff. That's my kitchen. Up front is my bedroom where the air mattress is."

At that point he took the tire out and fixed the spare tire mount. Without charge.

Other incidents indicated the difference in attitude. When my alternator and fan belt went out I rolled into the nearest gas station and the owner stopped his planned work, fixed the problem and charged me $30 for labor, half what I would have paid in San Diego. The local Mazda dealer had my Mazda for two weeks waiting the adjuster's OK on the crumpled fender. No storage charge. Building walls were graffiti free. The streets and sidewalks were clean. No homeless people in your face for money. No one pulled to within a foot of your bumper and flashed lights or flipped you the bird to move over. You could park directly in front of or within a block of any store or drop off mail while leaving your car running. You didn't have to lock your car doors.

The gas station attendants were friendly. Since you couldn't pump your own gas in Oregon, you got to know them. They checked your fluids (the car's not yours) and gas cost less than in San Diego.

Compared to Southern California crime was almost non-existent. High school students carrying cigarettes were suspended. Newspaper reports of arrests and convictions included the names of juveniles. Perhaps the stigma of disclosure and community disapproval bore on the low rate. I soon found this innocence was a façade for some real problems.

Jobs, as in a company with benefits, were not in large supply. Minimum wage was the norm. The person starting a business could make it. The person who had to have a 'job' was in for a tough time. My interview for systems administrator bore this out. The job was expected to be a minimum of 55 hours a week for $20,000 a year with few benefits. Doing a quick calculation, I determined the hourly rate would be about what I could make at Burger King. When I pointed that out to the owner he retorted that 100 people had applied for the job and were more than willing to take it at that pay level. I wasn't one of them. (The owner telling me I would be under tight supervision until he felt he could trust me didn't win any applause either.)

I found work as an assistant to a real estate broker who worked with both houses and raw land. As in California I obtained a broker's license. The four-page newsletter that I started, *Oregon Ho!*, was sent to people who had inquired about moving to the area. Designed to help the broker I worked for, and eventually me, find clients for real estate transactions it covered everything –things to do, places to see, schools, politics, housing, jobs, business opportunities and the many quirky things I observed or read about. As a result of the newsletter a lot of subscribers did *not* move to the area but they continued to take it because they said it was so funny.

The health club I joined, the Riverside Athletic Club, did not have the variety of equipment as my San Diego 24-Hour Fitness but there was no waiting for the machines they did have, a significant compensation. What I found interesting was in a community where close to 60% of the residents were retirees, the workouts were pretty tough and the step classes were killers. Step/high impact classes lasted one and a half hours with many including weights for upper body.

The smaller population led to fewer cars on the roads, a bicycler's dream. After I finally moved into my house a fifteen mile ride in late afternoon became the norm. The only things I saw on the road were cows, horses and maybe deer.

During this time I went out with Stan. Once.

One of Stan's properties was managed by the real estate firm where I worked. An old hippie he had lived in the area for over ten years and frequently lamented to the property manager that he just couldn't meet any nice, intelligent women who were in shape. Since I met all the criteria, she fixed us up.

I met him at a bar in Jacksonville and was a little startled by his emaciated appearance. Long, thin, stringy gray hair was held back with a rubber band and his arm was in a sling. I can't remember the reason for the broken arm but it had been taking a long time to heal and he was not pleased.

We sat down to order dinner and the discussion turned to our personal past lives. Stan had been a '60s rebel and expounded on what it had been like to live on the fringe. Then he began to relate what had started the hippie movement.

"It's Masons you know. They control the government and our financial institutions. They're world-wide. That's why they have rings and secret handshakes so they can recognize each other. They've been responsible for the overthrow of legitimate regimes."

Noting my somewhat dubious expression he pressed on, "A lot of people knew about this and they tried to stop it. But the Masons, they controlled the FBI and the CIA. The FBI went after the people who knew but they didn't get them. You know why?"

I was afraid of the answer because I've always found it hard to refrain from laughing when talking to lunatics but I murmured, "No, why?"

"They dropped out," he exclaimed. "They disappeared. So they couldn't be arrested because no one could find them." He sat back a triumphant smile on his face.

"So," I asked, because I've also found it hard not to bait lunatics to see how far they'll go, "if they dropped out how was that supposed to stop the Masons from taking over the world?"

"Well," he sputtered, "it wasn't. It just prevented the FBI from arresting them."

"So what good was that?" I asked.

"Well," he responded, his voice going up in irritation and volume, "they were free."

"To do what? From what I remember, since I wasn't a part of the culture, the only things they did were take dope, have sex and live in tents. That doesn't sound too commendable in my book if their original objective was to reveal the Masons for the terrible people they were."

"You don't understand," he roared, "you weren't a part of the time. You couldn't see what they were trying to do."

"Yeah I could. I just said what they were trying to do. Remember, the drugs, sex and tents? I'm asking you how that helped them accomplish their goal of exposing the Masons?"

"I can't talk to you. You don't have the intellectual capacity to understand."

The conversation continued this way as we discussed a number of other issues such as the people who lived in southwest Oregon, local, state, and national politics and politicians, automobile repair shops, etc. For each topic Stan had some negative comments and at least one conspiracy theory as to why that issue was unsolvable. And, of course, the standard response to my objections was that I wasn't intelligent enough to understand.

Finally I asked him, "Is there anything you like, anything you can say something positive about?"

Taken aback he stared at me balefully, thought for a second then responded, "Well, yes, I like my daughter."

"But just a little while ago you were telling me how lazy she was, how she didn't want to find a job and hung out with bums."

His next remark was the killer.

"I don't think this conversation is going too well."

"You know," I responded, "that's the first thing you've said all night that I can agree with."

When he left me off at my 'house,' he said, "I've never left anyone off at her van before."

I replied, "Well there's a first time for everything. Good luck in finding someone 'cuz I'm certainly not her."

Finding a rental was frustrating. Calling on ads was the worse. Most landlords had answer machines asking me to leave a number. Which was difficult when you didn't have a phone. In the days before the proliferation of cell phones if you didn't have a permanent address you probably wouldn't have a phone. Worse, the area had multiple local and long distance carriers making what would be a local call in one spot long distance in a spot a few miles away. The pay phones were highway robbery. A call within the county at one pay phone was $1.00 for three minutes but $1.45 at a phone half-a-mile away under a different carrier.

To counteract the problem I bought a message service and paid business owners or local merchants to use their phone although many wouldn't accept money for calls within the two-county area. Out-of-state long distance was a problem even with collect calls. I needed to make the calls collect to ensure I didn't waste money on answering machines. Remember, no one could call me back because I had no phone. When I tried to call Josh in San Diego the operator said she could only make collect calls within Oregon. I had to connect to my long distance carrier to make out-of-state collect calls. But I couldn't connect to the long distance carrier without a special code and by giving the special code the call ended up being charged to the business – no operator came on to ask if it was collect. John, going to school in Indiana, thought I had disappeared because I didn't return his messages – I couldn't find a phone to call from.

SCOPING THINGS OUT
Grants Pass, 1992

On the Sunday of Labor Day weekend my van broke down in the parking lot between the Riverside Inn and my fitness club. I had a choice of having the van towed (but to where) or leaving it there, finding a room for the weekend and letting the police department tow it. However the managers of the Inn and the fitness club along with the police nicely resolved the issue. The van, with me inside it, could stay there until Tuesday morning when they would arrange a tow to the nearest mechanic. (Luckily the best in the county. I took my cars to him thereafter.) While the van was beached, all three parties would check the area each night to ensure I was safe. Can you imagine that happening where you live?

Entertainment was different. At the Josephine County Fair I watched the 4x4 Pulls where various classes of modified and unmodified trucks pulled a dead weight until they went farther than others in their class or their clutch burnt out, whichever came first. I had not seen these in San Diego although a relocated San Diegan told me they do occur. One guy said, "We think up some pretty strange things to entertain ourselves. There isn't much to do around here. Wait until you see the barstool races."

The annual 'Gold Beach Antique and Crafts Fair' consisted of about fifteen tables which leaned heavily towards yard-sale goods and domestic crafts. An art/sculpture show had ten artists. The quality was not an issue but the number of artisans took on significance when you considered the driving time to get to some of these shows. My first attempt to drive to Gold Beach over the mountains separating the Grants Pass valley from the ocean resulted in burnt-out brakes on my van. The second try in a Jaguar (not mine but indicated what was available if you went on a date) was successful although at least 60 miles was a paved one-and-a-half lane 'hair-raiser' due to the many blind curves. My date's knuckles were white for about three hours.

I asked around about places (bars) where you could dance but was told that the closest non-shabby place was Medford, 28 miles south. I went dancing at one Grants Pass 'sleazy' club after someone told me that when she was there it got so rowdy some guy had to be maced. "Hmm," I said, "sounds like my kind of place." However the most exciting thing was a pile of people on the floor. Someone said it was a fight but I think they just danced different in that part of Oregon.

The Jedediah Smith Rendezvous was a weeklong gathering of mountain-men and women who lived in log cabins or teepees deep in the forests covering the mountainsides. They had shooting competitions and sold mountain-man related merchandise such as guns, hides, beaded clothing and badger, raccoon or skunk fur hats. More intriguing were the many artisans who sold their wares by mail-order to places around the globe. Maybe the remoteness of the area allowed them full rein to their creativity.

The Labor Day Buffalo BarBeQue at Sportsman's Park, about three miles north of Grants Pass, was another peek into a different world. I met two women and their father, an ex-logger. His daughter told me they had four freezers to accommodate her dad's hunting. One for bear, elk and moose, one for geese, ducks and other fowl, one for fish and a portable one for the RV. They invited me to stop in any time but my city ways made me uncomfortable with this sudden offer of friendship. That Dad weighed 400 pounds and was eying me might have influenced my decision. Too bad, the culinary choices would have been fascinating.

The National Fish and Wildlife Forensic Laboratory located in Ashland, investigated the death of wild animals for international, national and state agencies to determine the cause of death and prepare evidence, if necessary, for prosecution. The forensic capability rivaled many police labs. An example was the deaths of eleven golden eagles. Through serology and inorganic/organic mass spectrometry they determined the eagle's last meals had been from the cat family and they had died from pentobarbital used by local veterinarians to kill cats. Lab personnel determined that the vets had been leaving the cat carcasses in the public dump, the eagles had feasted and died of secondary poisoning. Without the lab many more golden eagles would have died.

Wildlife Images Rehabilitation Center was one of the largest in the United States, working with three to four hundred wild animals a year rehabilitating them to return to the wilderness. They also provided an endangered species program for the public schools and gave presentations throughout the United States. Near Grants Pass, Wildlife Images was three miles from a bar called the Hideaway Lounge where I had gone for about ten minutes to check out the local scene. "Oh yeah," said a former patron, "we call that the 'Hug-N-Slug.' About one o'clock in the morning, they're either in the parking lot smooching it up or punching each other out." Wildlife of a different type.

I hiked in the Kalmiopsis Wilderness area to Babyfoot Lake. The first sign on the trail read 'Babyfoot Lake 3/4 mile, Canyon Creek, 4 mile.' I figured I'd go to Babyfoot then on to Canyon Creek an area supposedly heavy with waterfalls. That was the plan.

Next sign had an arrow pointing to the left with the notation, 'Emily Cabin.' Right arrow had 'Babyfoot Lake.' At Babyfoot Lake there were no more signs. I saw an older couple. He was fishing. They asked if I had left a checkout message in the parking lot box telling who I was and where I was headed.

"Why?" I asked.

"So the rangers know you're out there if you get lost."

"I come from San Diego," I said, "you can't get lost. Someone will be along the trail eventually."

"Not here," they warned.

They offered me coffee and crackers but I wanted to go on to Canyon Creek.

"Well," said the man, "there's an arrow on a tree back about 100 yards. Maybe that's the trail to Canyon Creek."

I followed the arrow feeling a little like Alice in Wonderland and after a twenty mile, 90 degree uphill climb (well, it seemed that way) I saw a sign that read 'Babyfoot Lake Parking' to the left and 'Hilltop Mine and Davis Mining Road' to the right. I figured maybe the Canyon Creek sign would show up. No such luck. After two hours and no mine, road, humans or signs I gave up and headed back. Saw the 'Babyfoot Lake, Emily Cabin' sign again with the Emily Cabin pointing back up the trail I had just come down. Never passed a cabin. Strange.

Three weeks later at the Sierra Club I saw maps of the area. Found out I was at the Hilltop Mine although I did not recognize it as a mine, was within a mile of the Davis Mine Road and a mile and a half from Canyon Creek. There were no waterfalls. I was told, "They don't do real well with trail signs around here."

A few days later I went to the Jacksonville Yard Sale that engaged the town's entire commercial and residential area. No problem parking. No crowds. Everyone was friendly. I bought a 27" console color television for $5 that the seller said just went blank and they didn't know why. With its ornate molding I figured I could remove the picture tube and have a nice bookcase. After moving it from my car to my van then back to my car to storage then back to my car and into the house I had bought I hooked it up for the heck of it. Worked fine.

The evening of the yard sale I went with a friend to a pot-luck sponsored by the Slopes and Trails Singles Club. The place was so rural I thought we'd need a four-wheel drive. The owner lived on a farm with sheep, donkeys, chickens and other livestock. I later learned about half of the club's members lived on farms. Finding her house was a treasure hunt. She'd said she would tie balloons at the cross road because the roads were not always marked. (True.) Even when they were marked the house numbers bore no resemblance to any logical progression. We had gone up and down one road three times before we saw an address that gave us a clue as to which road led to her house. When I mentioned getting lost at the party she asked about the balloons. Someone interjected, "When I got here I saw two little girls walking up the road carrying balloons."

I now had first-hand knowledge of how the timber industry manipulated people and the media, something I never would have seen in San Diego. I attended the Takilma Fair at a village populated with residents wearing tie-dye shirts. The women were in long skirts or jeans and had long hair parted in the middle. Recycling bins and a communal schoolhouse rounded out the ambience. I returned to Grants Pass via Grayback Road, a two-lane artery that is paved for a few miles then washboard dirt. Along the paved portion the forest was beautiful and abundant. On the dirt part, where most 'Las Touristas' would not venture, it was all clear-cuts. Well over 50% of the replanted steep-slope trees were dead. Erosion was evident. I returned to the paved portion and a short hike revealed the trees were hiding the rest of the clear-cut. Not only were we not being told the truth about forest recovery but the locations of cuts were being staged to fool us otherwise.

The Grants Pass Chamber of Commerce 'Project Awareness Program' was designed to train people for leadership roles by making them aware of their community. I went up in a two-seater airplane to survey the county from above. What a gas!

Art Schmidt, the pilot in his early 70's, had moved there from Palo Alto in 1981. He had built the plane from a kit costing $50,000. He was very proud of the plane but more importantly he was very proud that he had lived his dream. He said, "I wanted to do this before I was too old to enjoy it." Enjoying it he was.

The area was vast with few houses, swimming pools, shopping centers or tall buildings. But besides the vastness, you could see the thousands of acres of earth barren from clear-cuts and fire damage. A native of Grants Pass told me that while the Forest Service and timber executives had assured everyone the forest would grow back it had not done so in her lifetime and she was in her 40's.

I talked with Craig Brown who worked for Grayback, a fire-fighting, tree planting and tree protection contractor. When not breathing smoke he planted trees or put wire cages over little seedlings so the deer couldn't eat them. He described being in three fires in one week including being dropped into the middle of a fire on the top of a mountain in Ashland. Singed hair, no breathing devices, getting bombed by aircraft dumping flame retardant and having sticky yellow stuff that smelled like ammonia all over your body. The pay ranged from $8 to $12 an hour. Why did he do such dangerous work for such low pay? He grinned and replied in a voice still husky from breathing smoke for a week, "The adrenaline rush."

I soon learned Mr. Jaguar was an out-and-out racist. He had moved to the area because he felt it better suited his militia viewpoint particularly his hatred of blacks. He blended right in with the types attracted to that part of Oregon. Bo Gritz who in 1988 was on the Populist Party Presidential ticket as the running mate of former Ku Klux Klansman David Duke. The woman who shot a doctor at an abortion clinic. The state leader of the Aryan Nations, Dennis Hilligoss. The organization that consistently promoted legislation against gays. Luckily Ashland was the liberal heart of the area so I could go there when I needed to breathe normal political air.

Mr. Jaguar had found an old cabin on ten or so acres for $30,000. Wondering why it was so cheap since it was on a creek and not too far off State Highway 99, he asked my opinion of the proposed purchase contract. I determined that a) because the cabin might have historical significance he would not be able to tear it down and build new and b) the property had been used for a meth lab so would probably require at least $30,000 to clean it up for resale. That was why the property was being sold 'as is' with no rights to recourse. He pooh-poohed my analysis. I was pretty smart to understand all that legal stuff but he'd find a way around it. He'd tear down the shack, dam the creek to make a swimming pond and find a cheap way to get rid of the chemicals.

He settled into his little kingdom. Three years later I visited before I left Oregon. I had to duck to walk through the doors. He contended he loved it just the way it was since he had learned it was going to stay just the way it was no matter what con he tried. The meth cleanup would indeed cost about $30,000. When his dam caused the place to flood during the spring run-off thereby making his illegal dam obvious to people concerned with water rights he got a hefty fine. He was not a happy camper. (Although one man north of Medford had built a sumptuous home in the mountains visible from Interstate 5 with no permits at all because he didn't recognize any government unit including the United States.)

Even with the negatives my first six months had met my expectations. On my morning drive from the city of Rogue River to Grants Pass the mountains seemed to drift off in the distance under a cloak of mist. At night they glowed light-burnt-orange from the setting sun. The peaceful feeling was almost mystical. At 9,495 feet Mount McLoughlin, north of Medford, is the tallest mountain in the area, a volcanic cone whose top half is black and devoid of vegetation. Driving to Medford one day, I wondered why the sight of snow half-way down the mountain was so impressive. Then the reason became clear.

I could see it. No smog.

MY OREGON HOUSE
Rogue River, Oregon 1992-1993

By Labor Day weekend I had given up finding a rental. Using money from Josh's inheritance from my mother I bought a house in Rogue River, a town of 3,300 population seven miles south of Grants Pass. I closed escrow on September 22 but the tenants wouldn't be out until October 18. My adventures were about to move up a notch.

The house I bought was 1,346 square feet with two bedrooms and two baths on .42 acre. The style was comparable to California ranches built 25-years ago. The price was $75,000, the house a cosmetic fixer although I soon learned that my initial concept of cosmetic was comparable to thinking a liberal dose of makeup would make Bela Lugosi look like Cary Grant. When I first saw the house I also saw thickets of blackberry bushes. Clapping my hands I ran to the bushes, "Wow, blackberries and right at my doorstep."

The agent looked at me weirdly as I gathered berries in my hand. "They're considered weeds in Oregon." I later learned how bad they were when I tried to clear the land that came with the house.

The cosmetic included tearing out the dark paneling in living and dining room, patching the holes in the sheetrock and painting, replacing the carpet with new carpet and wood, tearing out the vinyl kitchen floor and countertops, replacing them with tile, some rewiring, painting the bathrooms and bedrooms, scraping and painting the exterior and replacing the garage/workshop roof. With a 15-foot breezeway, double garage and workshop, it was a lot of roof to replace. Luckily a guy I'd met and my next door neighbor and his son did a lot of the heavy work. I'm an independent woman but not stupid. (But I did tear off the existing roof, helped get the bales of tar paper and composition shingle up on the roof and laid some of the shingles so they were duly impressed.

Going through the neighborhood I soon learned there was no 'normal.' A 2,000 square-foot, executive-level home could be within 500 feet of a mobile home with three junk cars. Nor was it unusual to have the junk cars in the executive-level home's yard. Well I had expected laid-back.

I finally moved into my house in mid-October. I now had a shower that I didn't have to drive to. And a refrigerator. And a stove. And heat. You couldn't imagine how important those things are until you've done without them for a few months. (When the weather had gotten cold one of the realtors had let me stay in a rental until he could get it rented. A week with mice running across my chest drove me back to the van, cold or not.)

The house had a story. I left California without selling my home there because I had a dream. I bought the house in Rogue River from an Oakland, California man who purchased it in 1988 because he too had a dream. His mother had a heart attack and refused to move so he stayed in California (living his life for someone else). His mother recovered but his girlfriend didn't want to move (living his life for someone else). He sold the house because, at 52, he was dying of cancer. I was going to live his dream. There was something to think about in this.

I had to keep my house at 60° due to my heating bill. Everything in my house was electric, not typical of many homes there. Most houses had heat pumps, like electric heaters but 25% more energy-efficient and a number had switched to gas. Most pre-85 houses also had wood stoves or fireplaces with inserts. My October electric bill for 28 days, not much cold weather and a 70° heat setting was $98. A friend's bill for a 1700 square-foot house, lots of windows and four people was $60. I figured something was wrong with the furnace or thermostat so I had the filter and thermostat replaced. Normally

I did my own work but the wiring from the old thermostat looked nothing like the wiring in any of my books.

The November bill was $156. I called Pacific Power and asked for an energy survey to find out what was wrong. The conversation with customer service was surreal.

"You are only using 100 kwh more than last year."

"Last year three people lived here. Now there is only one."

"We don't work on equipment. You need to have someone check your furnace and other appliances."

"But they won't know what to check unless your company does an energy survey so I know what's wrong."

"Are you running out of hot water before the second or third person takes a shower?"

"Only one person lives here. I thought we'd gotten past that point. Is anyone home there?"

I got an appointment for an energy survey.

While waiting for the survey I despaired. My fireplace had an insert but burning wood didn't give off much heat. I can burn down a forest when I go camping but couldn't get a lousy fire in my fireplace to stay lit for more than five minutes. My neighbor, Rebecca, showed me how to get a fire started. My other neighbor, Paul, showed me how to clean the insert so I could get some heat into the room. I finally got some heat. Not much but I wouldn't get pneumonia.

Fireplaces there were definitely not used for contemplation. I bought a cord of wood. Josh was moving up to stay with me since he had no job and no place to stay in San Diego. I thought wait until the city boy sees the wood he's going to have to split to avoid freezing. Considering he couldn't put up a tent when we went camping, I wondered how long he'd last.

I got the survey but not in time to affect the December bill which was estimated at close to $200. At the time Oregon power rates were 66% of the national average. No double-pane windows so he suggested I keep the curtains closed. Now I knew why the houses I'd been in seemed so dark. He also commented that I had old style heat return ducts under the house, just the kind animals like to tear up so they can keep warm.

After he left I noticed the crawl space entrance was open so I crawled in. Yep the ducts had been torn down. Instead of reheating 60 degree air the furnace had been reheating 30 degree air. The ducts were about four feet in circumference. I had to lie on my back with fibers falling in my face getting the ducts up and taped together. Of course the duct tape didn't stick to anything but itself but finally the ducts were whole again. I blocked off the crawl space with a wire-frame and hoped the repair would help January's bill. (Which it did considerably.)

Two nights later, Rebecca came over. "I'm so sorry Flo. I had to tear out your crawl space frame." We'd been co-feeding a family of feral cats and the kittens had been in the crawl space when I put in the frame. I wondered where the little stinkers had gone to. Rebecca said she knew I wouldn't mind because if they had died under there it would have been really smelly and they would have been all rotted and slimy and what a mess to clean up and ... I thanked her and mentioned that I'd get in touch any time I needed to write a description for a horror story.

Pacific Power had a program that evened out payments at $96 a month for all months. At least I wouldn't starve to pay the electric bill. My friend with the $60 bill also mentioned his November bill was $250. Now I didn't feel so bad. And the insert *was* giving off more heat.

I had to pay a traffic ticket at the Rogue River Court House for going 39 in a 25 zone. This had happened because I didn't realize I had entered the town and the lower speed limit. Before my case was called a guy addressed a similar ticket telling the judge that where he got the ticket there were no traffic signs. Not being one to let someone get off what I knew I had to pay, I piped up. "Sorry kid but you got nailed right where I did which is about 100 yards from my house. I know there's a traffic sign there because people are being stopped almost every night. The police lights wake me up." If looks could kill.

I told the judge, "Where I come from, the country is the country and the city is the city and here the country is the city." His reply made me laugh even though I had to pay a fine (they did not have traffic school). "Well, you're a country girl now so you have to watch out."

Getting my cars registered and my Oregon driver's license was interesting. I ordered personal plates for my Mazda. They did not take your out-of-state plates suggesting I use them for target practice. The letter I received for the personalized plates said it all.

> *'A temporary registration permit is enclosed if we thought that you needed one.* (None was enclosed.) *If a permit is not enclosed and you need one, please let us know. If you do not receive your new plates before your current plates expire (or before your temporary registration expires, if you are using one), please let us know.'*

My take: we have tried to cover all bases and if we missed one, please let us know.

SINGLES AND GOING PLACES
Oregon 1992-1993

During my twenty years in San Diego, I skied maybe three or four times a year with many years being zero. Major factors were money, husbands or boyfriends who didn't ski or the three-hour drive. But in Oregon things were different.

The Mt. Ashland Ski Area, 38 miles south of Rogue River, had been owned by a Portland company. In 1991 they decided to close due to a number of bad seasons from the drought that had plagued Southwest Oregon for seven years. The people of Ashland and surrounding cities disagreed. With funding from the state, the cities and locals, they bought the resort. As a thank-you to the locals the first three days of the season plus Christmas Day were free. Naturally I took advantage of it. Day lift tickets were $23, half-day and night $15 and equipment rentals $14 half that of resorts in California. I could get there in less than an hour if I didn't have install chains on my tires.

As of New Year's Eve two months into the winter season I'd skied three times with plans for using a January package for $70 that included six hours of lessons plus three days of lift tickets. I was in heaven. Well, almost heaven because Ashland did have its quirks.

The first day I stood outside the lodge looking down a long mid-intermediate bowl-shaped slope that funneled into a narrow shoot. Turning to a fellow skier who looked like she'd been there before I asked, "Where are the lift lines?"

She pointed towards the narrow shoot. "On the other side of that shoot."

"You've got to be shitting me," I said, "I need to warm up before tackling that."

She shrugged her shoulders and said, "Welcome to Mt. Ashland."

Fifty percent of the slopes were (and still are) expert. Ashland's intermediate slopes would be classified low expert at Big Bear in Southern California. Some of the intermediate could only be reached via a low expert. If you didn't keep close track of where you were going one intermediate segued into an expert. This was not a beginner's ski area. I was told that if you could ski Mt. Ashland you could ski anywhere. I believed them.

At Ashland I met a group who liked to drink, have Monday Night football parties and ski. For Vinny (not his real name) the drink and ski combination were not the best. He hadn't skied in three years when I met him but started off with better form than mine. For the first few runs. Then he took a long trip off a short jump and had to suffer a little kid picking up his equipment. As the kid brought back each piece Vinny kept repeating, "That's OK kid, you don't need to be doing this. I don't want my friends to see it."

On another run he veered off the groomed trail and was buried to his waist. While trying to slog his way out the ski patrol stopped by and asked if he needed any help. Pointing at me he snarled, "Yes, break her camera." (Well, I wanted memories of everything I did in Oregon didn't I?)

He did have his revenge. I was a third down a slope and tried to cut above someone just standing lower on the slope. I missed.

Vinny said he was watching me and suddenly an octopus was heading down the slope. I was on the bottom, the guy on top, skis, poles and goggles flying. Vinny noted it looked like we were doing something intimate and did I know this was a family resort? After collecting and re-donning all our equipment my victim skied a little farther down. As I started off he looked up, terror in his eyes, and cried, "You're not coming this way are you?"

Unfortunately right before the Super Bowl in 1993 the drink and the skiing clashed and Vinny skied into a tree. As he was being carried into the party house (a barn that had been partially converted to a recreation area with pool tables, a bar, a big-screen television and cows mooing in the background) he repeated, "I learned my lesson, no more drinking and skiing."

A few months later he was stopped on a DUI and lost his license. I mentioned that the 'no more drinking' should have been for everything but he didn't appreciate my comment.

That group had other encounters with the far side. The owner of the Monday night place was divorced. His ex was with him sometimes and away others because, as she said, he took too many risks. She didn't want to be around when he killed himself. One risk was when they were in Hawaii. He had either been parasailing and crash landed then went surfing or the other way around but by the end of the day he had a bad headache. Evidently he went out that night to carouse and the next morning to swim or surf while the headache got worse. She finally strong-armed him to a doctor where he learned his neck was broken. She had pictures of him in the body cast.

While still in the cast he set out to turn the barn into the Monday night party house. During this renovation the barn had to be lifted and part of the foundation replaced with concrete blocks. Rather than get a forklift or other logical equipment he and a few friends had attempted to lift it themselves. I can't remember what he broke doing that but the body cast that had started at his waist was now extended to his hips. They had pictures of that too.

In California I had my motorcycle buddies for fun, especially during the holidays. I had wondered if I'd have the same type buddies in Oregon. After a Halloween party, Thanksgiving with the Slopes group (at my house with 25 people, two turkeys, eleven bottles of wine, six pies and a cake), the Mt. Ashland Snow Ball, six Monday night football pot-lucks, two Christmas parties, one of which was catered, a New Year's Eve party, a New Year's Day Brunch and a Charger playoff game potluck, I realized being without my motorcycle group wouldn't be that bad.

Being with Slopes offered a picture into the difference between San Diego and Oregon. At a Mexican buffet they loaded cups with every sauce available. Silently one sauce after another was slid to me. After I had gone through the lot, they sat amazed. How could I have eaten such hot and spicy sauces and not reacted? Sadly shaking my head I noted most of the sauces would be considered mild in San Diego. Some looked at me as if I had walked through a fire.

Another issue was education. I didn't realize the illiteracy rate was so high until I was chastised for putting membership drive ads in the windows of local grocery stores. Club members wanted the ads in the newspapers to ensure that respondents could read.

Oregonian's concept of distance was also a change. In San Diego, 'Take the 52 exit off 5, turn right at the second light, left at the third street and I'm the fourth house,' meant 'No problem.' Here, the second light could be five miles from the freeway. The third street could be an unmarked dirt road and the fourth house could be set back three miles off a shared road that didn't have all the addresses marked. I was beginning to feel a deep kinship with Lewis and Clark.

I was also surprised by Oregonian's neighborliness. One Monday Night Football potluck I left my front door open. As in wide open. It faced a main road into town, although the 'town' was only 3,300 people. When I returned someone had brought in my paper and removed a cat that was tearing up my cat food bag. The door was still open. They must have thought I had just stepped out. I had over $1,500 in stereo equipment, CDs, and tapes within six feet of the front door. Nothing had been touched. In some areas of San Diego my wallboards would have been gone.

The Grants Pass paper published daily police calls. I noted four bank robberies since I had moved there in August. About one to three break-in or petty thefts occurred each day. This was for the whole county. In September, a murder-suicide. Even after such a short time in the area I knew one of the men. It was a small town. They had an evening memorial service for the murder victim outside the town hall. In San Diego, seeing it daily in the newspaper, I had become immune to death. Here they were people you knew.

In 1991 the city of Medford had a 100% increase in the murder rate. The previous year one person was killed. In 1991, two. One body was not discovered for three weeks. It was floating in a pond and the pond's owners didn't recognize it as a body until it was close enough for them to get curious and look. Even though the person who was missing for the three weeks was a neighbor, things like that happened so rarely what should have been obvious wasn't.

One reason for the low crime rate (a statistic that unfortunately changed in the next two years) may have been attitudes toward kids. Without national sports teams as a distraction, local high school teams were heavily supported. I was told to arrive at games two hours early for a seat. In the newspapers school sports coverage was double to triple that of state and national. Some officials showed logical initiative such as the coach for the Prospect High School football team. The interior lineman/part-time running back for the team was also one of the three senior princesses for the Homecoming Court. Headline front-page news in both the Grants Pass and Medford papers was when the 80 students at Butte Falls High School went to nearby Prospect to apologize for a fight that resulted in a Prospect student getting an injured hand. Can you imagine that happening in Southern California?

While I hadn't seen porno movie houses or bookstores in Grants Pass or Rogue River and girlie magazines were behind the counter, Gold Hill, about 8 miles south of Rogue River, was 'different.' They had legalized gambling and a topless stripper bar frequented by Hell's Angels-types. They danced waltzes and fox-trots to the 'Polka-Dots' on Saturday night. The city had signs stating: 'Gold Hill. A quiet city. All loud and unnecessary noises are prohibited.' Natives told me some strange tales about the residents.

The area was awash in the arts. The Ashland Oregon Shakespeare Festival is considered nationwide as a major festival and brings in 400,000 patrons a year. As a result the surrounding cities all have little theater groups with some excellent actors. People living in Jackson and Josephine counties were offered half-price tickets to the Festival for the months before and after the summer rush. Even if you weren't into plays, the Elizabethan Theater with its three-story stage was an awesome piece of architecture. The Jacksonville Britt Festival drew national music and dance artists during the summer. With the exception of ballet and big name modern dance companies, culture was equivalent to the big city.

In October a friend and I went to the Applegate Barter Fair. This was one event you really needed a camera and I had forgotten mine. The fair covered about ten acres and they were all '60s hippies selling '60s hippy wares. My friend commented "It's like everyone was caught in a time-warp." Ages ranged from seven months to the seventies. Applegate and Takilma had hundreds of hippies living back in the hills.

Another thing was the artists. No matter the event the wares for sale often exceeded what I had found in San Diego. Many of the artisans had world-wide markets. One man and his wife made acrylic paper weights, containers and pictures with extensive dioramas in each object. They shipped as far as Russia. Another artisan made rocking horses that sold nationwide. When I look through my picture albums I often wish I had purchased many of these creations because I have not seen their like elsewhere.

But the biggest change was the lack of traffic. According to natives Medford had traffic jams during work hours. I found that their 'traffic jam' meant taking five minutes to get through an intersection. One day I saw a surveyor with his equipment on Interstate 5. Standing right in the middle of the lanes. No traffic barriers, cones, nothing. Can you imagine that where you live?

Grants Pass had a banner across the main street saying "It's the Climate." A guy who moved here in 1987 said, "The first time I saw that sign, it was raining and freezing. The next time I saw it, it was 110 in the shade. I thought, 'Someone here sure has a great sense of humor.'"

JOSH AND THE FIREMAN
Rogue River, 1993

February, 1993 I returned to San Diego to move Josh to Oregon. He was going to work (spasmodically) on renovating the house while I worked on earning enough money so we could afford to renovate the house. The overall objective was to make a profit on the inheritance rather than spend it on frivolous things like everyday living expenses.

I had been using my van for a garbage truck transporting debris from the house fix-up plus my household garbage to the dump a few miles out of town. Considering weekly pickup of one can was $22 a month and the dump was $9 a load the drive through forests and mountains was worth the effort. In addition to the aforementioned garbage I had also stowed a number of 33-gallon bags of the pears that seemed to never stop dropping from the pear tree in my front yard. Needless to say the van's interior did not smell its best. It was half loaded so I figured I would hit the dump on Tuesday (the 2nd), wash out the van and head for San Diego Wednesday morning. As usual that was the plan

Tuesday morning the van wouldn't start. I had to have it towed. Because the important parts connected to starting the van were *inside* the cab, the mechanic practically had to work on it without breathing. Taking a deep breath he'd get in, work for about five minutes, then stagger out gasping. As another van casualty, the heater didn't work and temperatures were hovering in the 40s. He propped it open with some rubber to allow it to work all the time never considering that I was going to San Diego. (Obviously I didn't consider it either.) I wanted to get through Los Angeles before work hour traffic took over so I couldn't get to the dump. After unloading the garbage in my garage, I realized I also didn't have time to wash out the interior.

By the time I got to San Diego the heater was going full-blast in 75 degree weather. Stopping to gas up I noticed people looking at my broken-down van and sniffing the air. I bet their secret thoughts revolved around hippies. At Dave's house where I was going to stay, the van was parked in the street and his place was behind the main house. Even at that distance his first reaction was, "What is that stink?" With my heater and the weather the rest of the visit was odiferous.

What was my reaction after being gone six months? My chest was congested, the drivers were obnoxious. I repeatedly had to force people to let me merge onto the freeway before I ran out of lane. I couldn't wait to get back to Oregon.

Josh did not adapt to Oregon. He missed the friends that he'd had since junior high, never had been good at making new ones. Activities just didn't match those available in San Diego. But he did enjoy the skiing.

In mid-February of 1993 we went to Mt. Bachelor with 70 other people from Slopes. With eleven chairs and fifty-four runs, Bachelor is close in size to Mammoth (California) in ski area. If you combine the Sunrise chair's 807-foot vertical rise with the Summit chair's 1,725-foot rise, you have one very long run. Unfortunately I did a Leon by going to the top. I'd ski, stop for a rest, look for the bottom of Summit, ski, rest, look. I thought I'd never get to the end of that run. At least I wasn't using the F-bomb. I was still raring to ski but by mid-day on Sunday, Josh had petered out so we returned home.

I've always been long on stamina. In hiking I may make it up the mountain last but I will make it up when others much younger have pooped out. This was very clear the March weekend when Josh and I went skiing again at Mt. Bachelor with Slopes.

One club member, Ken, had told me he wasn't interested because, at 49, I was too old for him and wouldn't be able to keep up. He was 53 and in excellent shape. Or at least he looked like he was. We went dancing where he told me he would run me into the ground. By one in the morning he was still with me but grimacing through any set lasting more than three minutes.

The next day he left the Club's lodgings early to ski. I rode up with another member, Peter, who had also said he could outlast me. I skied with him and we hit an area designated intermediate but was now expert due to recent snows. Even expert skiers were getting winded. Peter kept lagging further behind and when he stopped once again I looked up the slope and irritably asked, "What is wrong?"

He panted, "I need to rest. I can't take it. You're a lot younger than I am."

Looking at him, I asked, "How old are you?"

"Fifty," he replied.

"Well I'm 49," I retorted, "so get your butt down that hill."

I finally gave up, finished the hill, went back to the ski lodge and waited for him. After an hour he showed, took a half hour to recover and we went out again. Despite constant whining, I made him ski the rest of the day. That night, after learning that Ken had quit skiing early, we all went dancing where I alternated with both men. The next morning, as Josh and I prepared to go skiing, Ken sneaked out and went home. Peter said "Well, you've danced me to death, skied me to death and…"

"You can stop there Peter, we didn't do anything where I could screw you to death." He was limping as he put his equipment into his car and looked as if he would have a hard time driving back to Medford. I only skied half a day because Josh was tired.

And they say women are the weaker sex.

By April, 1993 I had re-started the Singles Motorcycle Club, Oregon branch. The rides were sparsely attended but it did help me meet bikers with whom I could be a passenger. More important, because southwest Oregon wasn't exactly a hotbed for news, I was on television, written up in two papers and the story filed with the Associated Press wire service. It was reprinted in Canada and one day I got a call. "Hey are you the Flo Samuels who ran that club in San Diego? Well, damn, I live in British Columbia and I was in the club. I thought that was you." Wow, international fame!

On my birthday, April 14, I was in a grocery store and walked out to see this tall, good-looking, thin Sean Connery standing next to his BMW. In my usual manner I walked up and said, "Hey, are you single?" After he regained his composure and answered yes, I gave him the SMC card, told him about the club then asked for his address so I could send him a schedule. When he later introduced me to his friends he'd swear I never told him about the club just that we met because I had walked up and asked if he was single.

He was 53, a retired San Francisco firefighter from Sebastopol, California, but visited the Rogue River Valley often because, in his opinion, it contained the only decent BMW repair shop in the Northern California-Southern Oregon area. Bikers can be very particular about who touches their bikes and the shop, between Phoenix and Talent, had many out-of-state customers.

The weekend of May 7 to May 9 we explored the back roads of Josephine County including 'I wonder where that goes?' dirt roads. I fell in love with BMWs because most can easily do both highway and packed dirt. That ability came in handy later on.

On Mother's Day we went to Galice the only restaurant/lodge on the Rogue River within twenty miles of civilization. We met a 93-year-old woman who'd lived all over the world and finally came back to where she started. She introduced herself because she saw our leathers and told us that when her husband was alive, they'd both owned Harleys. We had a long conversation on bikes, biking and where she'd traveled. At 93 she still walked the half mile from her house to the restaurant. I thought, 'If I hadn't been on a bike I never would have met this remarkable woman.'

Another of our explorations was in the car due to rain. We headed to Coos Bay and after deviations to waterfalls and interesting trails we ended at a deserted ocean beach. At least we thought it was deserted. Using the recline function on the passenger seat, Paul and I were indulging, me on top, when a large van appeared. The woman driver looked at me, I looked at her, she smiled, I waved, she waved. Then she immediately backed up heading for another section of the beach. Paul never noticed.

On Memorial Day weekend Paul took me to the BMW '49er Motorcycle Rally in Quincy, California. We started our journey on Thursday, May 26 and got as far as Mt. Shasta through some torrential rain when he decided to get a motel. Since he was a died-in-the-wool camper, I asked if he was getting the room because I was along. He sighed, "No, I'm getting too old for roughing it like this."

The next day we took off in the rain heading for Lassen National Park where we were to meet two of his friends. Since my rain gear was yellow and I had multi-layers of clothes to keep out the cold, I looked like a fat BIC banana. I was sure they'd have no problem finding us. On the way we stopped to see Burney Falls. They wanted five dollars per person to enter the park for a twenty-minute hike to see the falls. I was incensed. This wasn't Yosemite and charging per person for a bike when they charged per vehicle for cars was patently unfair. I then got a lesson in the versatility of BMWs.

Paul tut-tutted, "No, worry, I'll handle it," and went back to the highway. We rode about half-a-mile from the entrance where a berm and wide culvert divided the campground from the highway. Despite two people on board with camping gear and heavy clothes, we popped over the berm, down the culvert then through the dirt camping area into the park to the shocked looks of many campers. The falls were beautiful, with rivulets cascading from hundreds of openings in the cliffs. After taking pictures, we dirt-biked back out. Now I understood the increasing popularity of BMWs.

We met his friends at Lassen but couldn't go through the park as the snow pack was still ten-feet deep at the crest. Rangers said they were working ten-hour days, seven days a week and didn't expect to have the road cleared until mid-July. Taking another way, we rode along the Feather and Indian Rivers and the scenery was spectacular. Deep mountain gorges and multiple plateaus in the riverbed resulted in small waterfalls tumbling every which way. Even the rain couldn't dampen the beauty. Greenville was a page right out of Small Town, USA. We arrived in Quincy in late afternoon.

The rally was at the County Fair Grounds across from a lumber mill. We set up our tent in one of the barns and watched people pretty up their motorcycles, some even pitching their tents outside in the rain so they'd have room to put their bikes inside the barns. That night we listened to a foghorn go off every five minutes. Since the closest water was the Feather River and they didn't have large boats, I wondered if there was some slightly mixed up ship captain in the local population.

While Paul was somewhat reticent about sex where people might hear, I wasn't. That night we made a little noise. One of his riding buddies in a tent next to ours sat at breakfast the next morning and commented that he had had a problem sleeping because we were going at it like 'two stallions.'

I quietly replied, "Uh, no, Brian, not two stallions. A mare and stallion. Not two stallions. We don't want to give anyone the wrong impression."

Seven years prior, Paul had been on a bicycling trip in the area and had gone eight dirt miles up the mountain then down a long, twisty, dirt road to nowhere. He'd run out of water and food and thought he was a goner. At the bottom of the road, he'd happened on a small bar with a 66-year old woman who served beer and made hamburgers. She'd saved his life. Not literally of course but it seemed that way to him. He wanted to go back and see if she was still there since no one believed his 'bar in the middle of nowhere' story. The next day, the 28th, we retraced his trail.

Marie, 73 at the time, was there running the Seneca Resort. With a beer and liquor license, her menu consisted of three items: ham, tuna fish, and peanut butter and jelly sandwiches. The building was about twenty feet long by fifteen feet wide. She served liquor in 8-ounce tumblers and filled them up for $2.75. The inside was plastered with people's business cards and was so dark someone had to loan me his flash for pictures. Outside there was a barbecue, three picnic tables and two tiny one-room cabins for rent. That was it, in the middle of nowhere. Now Paul had pictures to prove the place really existed.

That night I asked some of the locals about the foghorn. One replied, "What fog horn?" Not wanting to appear daft, I insisted I'd heard a foghorn. Someone finally acknowledged the lumber mill had some kind of horn it blew at night for shift changes.

"Every five minutes?" I asked.

"I don't think so," was the reply. No one knew what it was for.

Paul's concept of passenger comfort was zero. He'd brought me a helmet to use but it didn't have a face shield. He'd gotten upset when it took me so long to get ready each day. I had four layers of clothing to don. He had a heated jacket, heated vest and heated gloves. After his third venting in one day

I demanded he either shut up or give me his heated gear so I could dress faster. That eliminated the problem. He shut up.

At the rally we had run into his old girlfriend. It was evident he hadn't made the break. He said he was going to return to his pursuit of her because she was a challenge. She talked down to him, didn't like sex and basically treated him badly. I was too nice, liked sex and was therefore not a challenge. Dave, in describing the type of woman he wanted, had told me the same thing. He didn't want a woman who was easy to get, he wanted the ones who rejected him because then the prize was so much greater when he finally won. Men wonder when I roll my eyes at their contention that they don't understand women.

One thing I did regret about that ride. At the campground I kept seeing this tall, rangy guy with a thick mustache, killer smile and beautiful dark eyes. I never got his name only that he was from somewhere near Mountain View in the Bay Area (San Francisco for non-Californians). Over the years, particularly after I moved to the Bay Area, I thought about how I should have found a way to meet him. Obviously he had a BMW so when I started the club up there, I kept a look out. Went on a couple of BMW-only rides. But he never showed. If only I'd asked his name at least I would have known what happened to him.

I did visit Paul in his hometown of Sebastopol a few months later. Oregon was beginning to sour politically and economically. I was thinking of alternative locales. We rode around the area and somewhere near the Russian River he took me to this artisan who made, among other things, copper bracelets. At the time I smoked and drank alcohol. Paul was determined to stop the smoking even if we weren't going together.

He bought me this thick, intricately woven copper bracelet. Within a few days of wearing it, I lost my taste for alcohol. Now this was important because I have a dual addiction. If I drink, I smoke. If I smoke, I drink. No drink, no smoke. Eliminating one addiction eliminated the other. At least it did for two and a half years until I moved back to San Diego. After a few years back, smoking and drinking, I tried the bracelet again to no avail. Weird.

MARK, A RENTER AND RAFTING
Rogue River, Oregon 1993

In the summer of 1993 I met Mark, someone who shared my blithe spirit in some ways but not all. When we didn't have the money to attend a Britt Festival performance he found an area where we could scale a fence to watch the proceedings. His other side appeared for the Jackson County Fair. We had to ride the bike to a high school about three miles away and catch a bus back to the fair because the rain had made the parking areas into a quagmire. While waiting for the bus a woman with her husband made a bet with me on how many times the men would complain about waiting for the bus. Mark won.

One problem however was his Suzuki Harley clone, a bike that had been mistaken by many Harley owners as the real thing. Due to the high rate of motorcycle theft in the area, particularly Harleys, on any ride we could never be more than fifty feet from the bike. That put a definite crimp into any hiking.

The day we climbed Mt. McLoughlin I drove to the trailhead. At a height of 9,495 feet the mountain presented a 4,000 foot vertical gain that was five and a half miles each way, much of it over ancient volcanic rock. In a local hiking book for Southern Oregon and Northern California McLoughlin was rated third-hardest after Mt. Shasta and Mt. Theilsen. The first four miles took two hours. The one and a half miles to the top took two hours, sometimes three. On volcanic rubble that slid you back as much as you went forward. Uphill. Real uphill.

Mark, his niece Marla, nine other people from Slopes and I made the hike. We started about 9:30 a.m., got done about 6 p.m. I and another Slopes lady, both almost 50, completed the hike while five people in their 30s and 40s quit in the middle.

The scenery was spectacular and watching clouds actually form was fascinating. The mosquitoes were unbelievable. I was bitten at least 20 times on the way down. Back in Rogue River we soaked in a Jacuzzi at one of the local motels because Mark really knew the right people.

The next day we went to Indian Mary Park on the Rogue River with Mark and his two-year-old Tasmanian Devil, Aaron. We both had major thigh pain and since you have to do some hauling with your arms due to the steep slopes our arms didn't feel much better. Naturally, Aaron wanted airplane rides in the water. Many airplane rides. We took turns until we both gave out.

Mark and I were the only bikers who went to Lost Creek Lake with Slopes. (Not that the group welcomed motorcyclists anyway.) Mark tried skiing but found it's hard to do underwater although he did get up a few times. After getting sun fried and waterlogged we went to Crater Lake, always worth a visit. A woman there made it her civic duty to turn Mark and me into the Ranger for climbing on the observation station to get pictures.

I noted that he was commitment phobic, a contention he promptly denied. His breaking up with women after multiple years because they dared ask if there was a future did tend to underscore my observation. One relationship had resulted in Aaron but Mark wanted to move to Hawaii and felt that monetary contributions and phone calls from Hawaii would be sufficient 'fathering' for his son.

After our last ride I wrote him a letter outlining the flaws in his logic particularly relative to his relationship with his child's mother. Interestingly enough a year later when I was about to leave Oregon he asked me to meet him at the annual fair. It was to introduce me to Aaron's mother and announce they were moving to Hawaii together. It felt good that my nagging had had an impact.

At the end of the month another SMC recruit, Vern, took me to Emigrant Lake for the daylong Blues Festival. Vern rode a Harley, was about 6'4" and muscular. Unfortunately he also had a 'woman as property' mentality so friendship was the only option. We were floating in an inflatable two-person raft so we could listen to the concert while keeping cool in the water. But the 'Lake Patrol' decided we were too dangerous without life jackets even though there were no postings that life jackets were required. The guy was on a jet ski and decided he had to write us a ticket. I said, "Nah, we'll just go back to shore."

The guy insisted he had to write us a ticket. Vern grabbed the jet ski, looked at the guy, bulged a few muscles and said, "Nah, I don't think you want to write us a ticket."

The guy agreed with Vern.

On a Rogue River Jet Boat Trip I learned that osprey migrate over 5,000 miles each year in seven to ten days. They mate for life and have three to four chicks a year. Since their presence restricted logging, I did hear some comments like, "They taste terrible, just like an owl." Going under the Robertson Bridge that was about 40 feet above the boat, the guide mentioned that the flood of 1964 covered the bridge. In 1997, two years after I returned to San Diego, the Rogue flooded Grants Pass to the tune of $10 million in damage.

As I've mentioned traffic was pretty sparse. This dearth of traffic helped my exercise program. I was bicycling at least 15 to 25 miles a day between Rogue River, Grants Pass and Merlin or south into some of the little towns north of Medford. I passed maybe ten to fifteen cars on any given day. I really miss that part of living in the area. I've never ridden my bike since I left Oregon.

Labor Day weekend I went on a boating trip to Lake Shasta with a group from Slopes. As I pulled into the camping area, Mark was pulling out on his bike. Before he put on his helmet he nodded my direction.

"She'll keep you entertained. She has a story for everything." (Hence the name of this book.)

The group leader, my age but looking a lot older, had a speedboat and a toy dog. I've never liked toy dogs so when I didn't drool he was put out. I rode in the boat for a few turns with various skiers and at each turn he urged me to try water skiing. Despite my repetitive comments that I knew how to ski and wasn't interested he kept it up assuring me that he would be very careful and not rev the boat beyond my capabilities. (This episode was just one of many I'd endured in Southwest Oregon that women were weak creatures needing a man's protection and guidance.)

To shut him up I finally accepted his offer. He tried to start slow, which I knew was a sure method for swallowing half the lake, so I waved for him to go for it. I could see the doubt on his face, his need to not cause any harm to this flower of womanhood. He revved the engine and I got up immediately. As we went around the lake I jumped the waves, something the other skiers had not done. I rode to the far side of the boat and pulled on the tow rope. If you know what you're doing this can pull the boat off course forcing the driver to correct repeatedly to maintain control.

After about twenty minutes I singled to go back to the start point. I dropped off. He pulled the boat around and slide past me idling. Throwing the skis in the back of the boat I climbed up the ladder.

"OK, see? I can ski. I don't want to ski, so leave me alone."

Although properly chastened he still had a number of other passengers to get up on skis. Unfortunately, now that it was obvious I knew what to do I became the instructor for five new skiers. The only way to instruct is to be in the water holding the skier and telling them what to do and when. I thought my skin was going to slough off by the time I got the last one up.

A renter, who I'll call Stanley, was probably one of the dumbest and wiliest people I had met in all my years of renting. Dumb included his wanting to be a physical therapist despite his inability to speak an entire sentence with any semblance of grammar, logic or appropriate word usage. When I pointed out that he needed to be careful of his speech, he responded, "Why should how I talk do nothing with the cripples? All I gonna do is rub their legs, they don't need no talk."

However why he was a renter was the wily part.

Incredibly good-looking he was tall with dark brown hair and eyes, an infectious grin and well-built. Where it came to manipulating people he was spot on.

Married with two children, six and four, he was renting a room because he had separated from his wife. I soon learned this happened about every 18 to 24 months. While he was separated he threshed a path through all available women in the area. When satiated or exhausted, I never figured out which, he would reconcile with the wife. This had been going on for ten years and the wife still hadn't caught on indicating they did have one thing in common. Being dumb.

Stanley found a girlfriend, Delores (made up to avoid embarrassing her), who was as shy a few cards as he was. One day when he had his kids for visitation (both were child-star material with the daughter a duplicate of Elizabeth Taylor at that age) Delores came into my kitchen out of sight of Stanley and his kids in the living room. She clenched her fists, stomped on the floor and trilled, "Ohhhh, ohhhh, ohhhh, I can't stand it. They are all so beautiful. I can't stand it." She huffed and puffed a few times, re-stamped her feet, unclenched her fists and went back to the living room. My mouth was still hanging open.

His relationship with Delores went on for a couple of months until Stanley was ready to go through the reconciliation routine with his wife but not before Delores lost her mobile home.

She had brought her male renter- roommate to one of my motorcycle parties. He had made some comments about being a reincarnated wolf who would take down anything or anyone who thwarted him. He hinted at a date. I flat out told him to forget it. The guy was creep-city personified.

A month or so later, Delores came over to say goodbye to Stanley and tell me her sad tale. Right after the party Wolfman had gotten drunk with her booze, trashed her trailer and not paid his rent. When she called the police they refused to evict him since she had signed a rental agreement with him and he therefore had a legal right to be in the trailer.

Her solution was to move.

Out of her trailer.

That she had purchased.

I later learned that by the time he finally moved out the trailer payments were so in arrears that she lost it. And her $5,000 down payment. Which was a lot of money when you only made $12 an hour.

When she initially told us I asked why she didn't get an eviction order against him. She blinked and said, "But that means I'd have to go to court. I don't understand all that legal stuff. I wouldn't know what to say or do."

"I can help you. I'm a real estate broker. I know what papers to file. I can coach you on what to say."

"But they might ask me questions. I wouldn't know what to say."

"If you don't do something, you'll lose your down payment and probably the trailer. And your credit will be ruined so you won't be able to buy anything else."

"But at least I won't have to go to court."

In the fall of 1993 I went to a two-hour air show with Greg, a SMC friend. He had a Ninja so we got quite a few looks because sport bikes weren't that common in Southwest Oregon nor were sport bike passengers who were approaching 50. While at the show I saw one of the funniest things I'd seen in a while.

The show had started. In front of us two couples, one older, one younger, were attempting to erect a portable gazebo. The older couple argued with each other about the numerous parts with the man holding pieces, turning them over, looking totally puzzled. The four of them got it together but it was crooked. Someone tried to help. The frame leaned even more. It was taken apart and put together again. After three tries they finally got the frame right then realized the canvas needed to be put on so they had to take it partially apart to get the canvas on. They finally got it together, got the chairs under it, sat down and within two minutes the air show ended. I was laughing so hard when we left Greg had problems keeping the bike on course.

In September I went white-water rafting with Slopes on the Klamath River with Class III and one Class IV rapids. A guy named Bill, Baseball (a former pitcher in the major leagues who shall remain nameless) and myself were in inflatable kayaks. Baseball's son, Ralph, was in a hard-shell kayak and six others were in a large paddle raft with George, the organizer/guide. Both George and Baseball had guided raft trips for years. Ralph had taken many kayaking and rafting classes and Bill had rafted before. I had been in big rapids in a large raft with a guide. Once. (That had been the Kern trip.) I was now 49 and this was my first time alone in a white-water rafting craft.

The Class IV rapid included a ten-foot waterfall that could result in real damage if you went over it plus multiple boulders, deep hydraulics and other obstacles. With my limited experience I felt like I was in the movie *The River Wild* in the throes of the Kootenai where the final scene was filmed. (When I got the pictures back the waterfall was about four feet. Amazing what fear can do to your perception.)

Skirting the waterfall and holes was a left-right deal against heavy current. When he saw my nervousness Baseball told me I could ride the big raft and no one would think poorly of me. But I wanted to prove to myself that I could do it. Which I did! However when they asked if anyone wanted to run it a second time I respectfully declined.

The trip also included Cornish game hens for dinner, really good lunches and a hike to a waterfall that included climbing a cliff that was more frightening than the rapids. On the way back, I opted for swimming out via the creek over going back over the cliff. The water was so cold I could barely breathe. If taken in Southern California this trip would have cost a minimum of $250 plus gas to the river. Here it was $50.

When I got home Josh with his two friends, Andrea and Rodney, had come up from San Diego to take care of traffic tickets. The starter on their car had gone out and I told Josh we could get it fixed at the gas station where the car died. "No, Mom," he said, "those guys are Goober One and Goober Two. When the car wouldn't start the guy opened the hood, asked us to turn the key a few times, then said, 'I think your problem is that your car won't start,' which was when Rodney said, 'Wow, I'll bet that's why the engine isn't running.'" The next morning they pushed it to the next gas station, almost running into my car of course, then proceeded to hassle the mechanic to the point that he was laughing so hard he kept dropping parts.

Baseball had ridden motorcycles but quit when he had an alcohol-induced accident that tore up his leg and severely limited his life in the Majors. His encouragement on the Klamath trip had gotten me interested in not only more challenging rafting but in him. I'd gone out with him for coffee a few times and since he was sexy, we soon ended up in bed. He was great company. Once, while watching Stanley trying to put up Christmas decorations he had told him, "You have to be smarter than the bulbs." But his personal life was bizarre.

He'd been married, had two children (one of which was Ralph), got divorced and his ex-wife had moved to Oregon. Missing the kids, he'd followed her to Oregon and convinced her that they should get together again although not in a married status. After a year or two of this experiment she'd decided he'd be better in some other domicile. He'd moved to a spare bedroom but not out. That was the status when I met him. He'd leave at four-thirty in the morning so he could be home to get the kids off to school. Even on weekends. Obviously, he was trying to stay in his ex's house as long as possible.

In late October Slopes went on a rafting trip on the Rogue River. Two in hard shell kayaks, three in inflatable kayaks, six in a raft and one with the cargo raft that carried all the food, clothing and camping gear. Baseball, the captain and sole crew of the cargo raft, was impressive. I saw rafts with six people get dumped, kayakers dumped, yet Baseball maneuvered that cargo raft through Class III and IV rapids with no mishap. With us was Ralph who was going to be kept ignorant of our relationship no matter what the cost.

I'd set up my 'two-person-if-they-were-midgets' tent on a slight slope as it was the only area left that overlooked the river and wasn't peppered with feces. (Manners were not high with rafters who had been there before us.) When I tested the sleeping arrangements there was no roll so there the tent stayed. Now I was 5'8" at the time (5'6½" now) and Baseball was about 6'3". With two of us in the tent the tight fit required lying in the tent differently than when I tested it. While it did encourage activities he had adamantly sworn were not to occur – but which he thanked me for in the morning – it also meant that someone was going to be rolling into, and possibly over, someone else throughout the night. This wasn't too bad at first but early in the morning it rained so the person on the bottom of the slope, in this case the male of the pair, started getting a little damp. Luckily he'd done a lot more wilderness camping than I and gallantly let me stay on the dry side.

Baseball had told his son that he was going to sleep under the overturned raft and waited until everyone was in the tents before coming to mine. He then left the tent first thing in the morning and started breakfast. Unfortunately the rain that night made his 'sleeping place' under the raft a mass of puddles. His son must have asked ten times how he slept in the rain and puddles and Baseball came up with a different answer each time. Others in the group had figured out what was going on and it was hard for most of them to keep a straight face.

That trip was memorable for other reasons.

Before, during and after breakfast, George, the trip leader, had temper tantrums. He was going with a woman from Slopes who attempted to make nice for him but the displays ranged from disgusting to hilarious. At one point he threw some of the plates in the river and various members of the group had to retrieve them. Many of us quit trying to help and packed up to leave. He had another tantrum because no one was helping load the cargo boat and he refused to listen to the reason. His tantrums.

Baseball's son was 16 but an accomplished kayaker. Another kayaker in the party was a 21-year-old college student who, while not as experienced, was definitely unwilling to take advice from some young kid. Then we hit Mule Creek Canyon. The river runs through a narrow, 18-foot-wide gorge for about half a mile and at some points the current sweeps through with no places to eddy out into calm areas. Ralph tried to give the college guy some pointers on how to run the canyon but college guy wasn't taking any instructions.

At the start of the canyon he was propelled out of his kayak. The kayak went straight up at the bow and then straight down until it was submerged. The rapids sucked his kayak under more than once, stood it on end, danced it in circles. Baseball, oaring the supply raft, tried to get an oar into the kayak cockpit but only broke the oar. Finally the kayak stayed on the surface but no one was hanging on to it.

Our raft had made it through the canyon and as we looked back at Baseball trying to maneuver the supply raft and kayak downstream the situation rapidly got tense. The college kid was missing. We feared he was trapped in a sieve.

We called, Baseball called. Finally a head bobbed up just upstream of our raft. We had to swing the raft out to catch him because once past he wouldn't be able to swim against the current. We hauled him in. Although he was talking he still needed a few whacks in the back to dispel some of the water he'd swallowed. After getting back his breath and self-esteem, he opted to get back into his kayak. I noticed that he was behind Baseball's son the rest of the day and listening intently to instructions.

One inflatable user, Ron, dumped multiple times. At one point the inflatable shot to the shore at which his girlfriend, Theresa, exclaimed, "Well, will you look at that. Ron's got his inflatable trained to go to shore and wait for him."

Another interesting incident was watching a group using ropes as they tried to get some of their rafters off a boulder in the middle of the Blossom Creek rapid. Not only had they wrapped their raft on the upriver side of the boulder, they'd basically sunk it. For non-rafters, the pressure from the river's current can plasters rafts so tightly to the rocks that the rafts have to be extricated with mechanical means such as winches and trucks or lots of people. Since this part of the Rogue was a roadless Wilderness area, it was either pay big bucks to get a truck into the area or find lots of people willing to be real busy for a while.

Unfortunately, my pictures of these interesting events, along with the Chinese watercolor morning mist hovering over the river at our Horseshoe Bend campsite, were for naught. The film in my camera had come off the reel.

As previously noted, high school football was big in the area particularly because Oregon had no major league football team and, at the time, the college teams weren't exactly contenders. So when Ashland, North Medford and Grants Pass were ranked in the top ten for the state, the level of excitement went up a hundred-fold. With about five percent of the state's population to have one-third of the top-ranked teams was pretty extraordinary. The Ashland/Grants Pass game was to decide the Southwestern conference championship. About 5,000 people showed up with many saying their friends had decided not to come because it would be too crowded. Grants Pass went down to ignoble defeat but since this was their first year in the local conference playoffs and Ashland's umpteenth year the results were not totally unexpected.

Some notable items that occurred:

Ashland did not want the Grants Pass marching band to appear because the Ashland band was so bad it would be humiliated. Grants Pass did come. Ashland had not set aside any seats for the band so Grants Pass supporters had to go into town and scrounge up chairs for the kids. Ashland's band, indeed, was really bad.

The only police action I saw was some kid getting his coat searched for cigarettes.

Outside of one loud-mouth Ashland supporter who was finally ribbed into silence, everyone was courteous and fair. Contrast that to today's high school football games.

The more I explored the area, the more I thought I'd run out of the spectacular. But I was continually surprised. In October I went to Crater Lake with Baseball and we drove the East Rim. While at one viewpoint a landslide down the slope of the crater kicked up dust that shimmered against the blue of the lake. Later he took me to an area where they hunt elk and showed me twin pinnacles called the Rabbit Ears. Two volcanic plugs, these pinnacles were sheer cliffs rising out of the mountain meadows with climbing routes ranging from 5.4 to 5.11 on a 5.0 to 5.15 scale. The red and gold rocks glowed from the setting sun in contrast to the deep green of the surrounding trees. My next door neighbor, a 40-year-old married to a guy who worked in the lumber mill, had been outside the city of Rogue River once in her life and had no desire to do it again. To me it was incomprehensible.

On another 50-mile bike ride that was supposed to be 30 I went past Gold Rey Dam. With a 200-foot or more spillway the water shimmered over the top like sparkling, liquid silver. Lower Table Rock's sheer red and black cliffs were in the background and the deep blue sky was above. Naturally, I didn't have my camera.

In November I went to the Annual Model Train show in Medford. The setups were far more sophisticated than any I had seen in San Diego. One modeler's display was a rail car with a 'skeleton crew' that were miniature skeletons. Another rail car was the 'Spotted Owl Express' with owls hanging off the sides. Two houses had the roofs removed. The ladies in red-sheeted beds and the men unbuttoning their shirts left no doubt what the houses were for. The modeler, who had been doing this for about 20 years, said his wife called him a dirty, old man even though some of the creations were from her suggestions.

INJURIES, BASEBALL AND BERNIE
Rogue River, Oregon 1993-1995

For months I had been doing conditioning exercises in preparation for ski season. This included racquetball, running with ankle weights, exercises wearing my skis and boots, squats, jumps, whatever the books recommended. On December 17 I had the chance to see the results.

Baseball and I, taking along Stanley and Ralph, went to Mt. Ashland on a Friday so we would have minimal competition for the slopes. He started grumbling on the way there. "We were supposed to leave at 7:30 (we left at 7:50). We'll be late." He repeated it. Often. I really didn't know how we could be late, the lifts didn't open until nine and Ashland was an hour away but he was convinced we'd be late. Baseball was fun when in a good mood. Which was not evident at this moment. However, after twenty years of living with renters and/or kids, I'd learned to put up with a lot.

We got to the slopes on time. Starting to ski he told me multiple times what I should do to avoid an injury. Along with numerous other lectures on skiing, skis, poles, lessons, etc. until my eyes crossed. Like I said this was not one of his better days.

My workouts had succeeded. I had good control that year and was able to negotiate an expert slope I couldn't ski the previous year. I skied much faster, which you must do if you're going to turn well. I wasn't tired and felt very confident that this year I was going to do well. We came off the lift, I barreled down the slope after Baseball watching where he was going, relaxed 'cuz I was doing so well and my skis crossed.

I usually knew when I was going to fall so I could be prepared. This time I wasn't. I slammed the ground and felt a snap in my right leg like when you snap a towel. My hand hit the ground and I could feel the thumb jam. I was going down the slope, head first, and couldn't dig my skis in to stop because my right leg was virtually useless.

Baseball had to get the rescue patrol. How humiliating, to be taken off the mountain in a sled. We got to the bottom and I rode the snowmobile back to the lodge. I half-walked, was half-carried into the lodge. I figured nothing was broken but my inner thigh and groin muscles had been stretched way beyond their limit. I hoped. Without medical insurance, I couldn't afford to go to a doctor so whatever was wrong with the old bod was going to have heal on its own. Bob came in and the fun began.

"I knew you were getting tired, that's why I kept saying I was getting tired, so you could say you were tired and quit."

"We'd only been on the slopes for two hours, how could I be tired? I wasn't tired, I wasn't paying attention."

"No, you were tired, that's why your skis crossed."

"Baseball, the ski instructors told me they have crossed their skis." These were the same instructors that when I took lessons had me go down first then yelled at the other students, "Don't do it the way she does."

Baseball continued, "No, you're wrong, you were tired."

This went on until finally I said, "Yeah, you're right. I got hurt because I was tired."

"See," he replied, "I told you that you were tired." I shook my head and rolled my eyes.

Baseball said he'd take me home but I could see he wanted to continue skiing so I told him to finish out the day. (This happened at noon and the lines closed at 4.) So he skied until about 3 p.m. Unbeknownst to me, before the 'accident' he had told Ralph that he could ski as long as he wanted and we would wait for him. Now that I was injured and Baseball was done skiing, the wait for his son became a problem. He started pacing, mumbling about how inconsiderate Ralph was. I couldn't figure out how Ralph's skiing until the time his father had agreed to was being inconsiderate but Baseball was not open to logic. I suggested he have signs posted at all the lifts to get Ralph in. He said, "That's no good, that's not going to help, that's ridiculous."

After about two hours, Ralph came in to Baseball's wrath. Viewed by about thirty people of course. Baseball turned to me, "See, I had the signs posted but it didn't do any good." Neither Ralph nor I could understand but somehow Ralph was getting blamed for my not getting home to rest.

Stanley, who was also skiing, came in. They carried me to the truck. I couldn't lift my leg or walk on it. The pain was incredible. Ralph and Stanley got in the camper shell and on the way back I asked Baseball why Ralph was in trouble for not coming in earlier. Baseball pointed out that Ralph ignored the signs posted at the lifts. I asked Baseball, "Have you ever noticed the signs posted at the lifts?"

We stopped at McDonald's. As they went in (I stayed in the truck) I heard Baseball say to Ralph, "About my getting upset because you didn't come in..."

We dropped Ralph off at his mother's house and Baseball got me home after saying that I needed to take Ibuprofen and that none of my pain medication would work to help keep the swelling down in my leg. Of course he had no idea what kind of medicine I had but whatever it was it wouldn't work.

"You're not going to be walking for at least a week."

"I'm going to a concert tomorrow night."

"You won't be going anywhere for a long time."

"I think I'll get better quicker because I am in pretty good condition." He kept insisting I wouldn't get better for at least a week until I conceded I wouldn't to shut him up.

At my house he and Stanley unloaded me onto the couch then Baseball got the ski equipment out of the truck. My gloves were missing. He called Ralph. Now it was his fault the gloves were gone because he must have knocked them out of the truck when we stopped at McDonald's. He hung up spewing how Ralph was inconsiderate and irresponsible. I pointed out that I'd lost my gloves in the past and I'm an adult. How could he blame a fifteen-year old kid for the same thing? He called Ralph back and told him it wasn't his fault but would he call McDonald's and Mt. Ashland to see if anyone turned in the gloves. His one saving grace was that when he blew it he might not admit he was wrong but he did right the wrong. Plus he at least listened when you told him he blew it. One of the few men I'd met who did listen.

He gave me a handful of Ibuprofen and an ice bag, got me into the bed and left with the parting shot, "You're not going to get much sleep tonight."

I crawled out of bed, got one of my super-duper anti-inflammatory pills that I have for my cervical arthritis and slept nine hours straight.

The next day I had to manually lift my leg to move in any direction. I spied a cane Josh left when he was here and, with the cane, if I moved reaaaaal slow, I could get from point A to point B. At this stage the points were the bed to the bathroom. The pain was from my waist to my right ankle and my hand was one blackened bruise. I made my bed and learned that the inner thigh was used in the bed making process.

I had planned to buy a used washer and dryer that day and I intended to do so. To drive my stick shift I had to manually lift my right leg with my hand to get my foot on the brake but I could drive. I pulled out of the garage and not being 100% on paying attention tore the molding off the side of my car. A discouraging word escaped my lips.

I found a washer and dryer for $100, got back home and called Don to a) rent me some crutches and b) help me get the washer and dryer back to my house. (I'd met Don, who also lived in Rogue River, through a personal ad in the local paper. At our first meeting he realized I was the woman who gardened in her bikini. He told me that when he first saw me he was on his bicycle and had ended up in a ditch.)

He brought some crutches over but I couldn't use them because they pulled on the leg muscles and made them hurt worse. As my attending angel he went with me to get the washer and dryer and to shop at WalMart for the hookups. He kept trying not to walk ahead because I had to move so slowly but you could see how antsy he was getting. At my house he and Stanley unloaded the washer and dryer and hooked them up. He had a headache, downed some of my Ibuprofen and went home to rest up for his cross-country skiing trip the next day.

That evening I went to the concert but there were few cars and I didn't feel like dragging myself into the building if the concert was that uninteresting. Grocery shopping I saw what the handicapped were up against. A third of the people were helpful. A third, seeing the cane and slow gait, wouldn't look me in the face. A third ran me over as if I were invisible. Thought-provoking.

When I got home I had a message from Baseball asking how I was doing. I called him back, told him about my day and could tell he was irritated. Maybe because I was walking and it had been less than a week?

At least the washer and dryer worked.

The next day, Sunday, December 19, I called Josh in San Diego. Recounting his ski accident when I had left him in first aid then skied until my lift ticket time ran out I concluded, "Remember that old saying about pay back? Well Mom got paid back for making you wait until I was done skiing." His laughter covered his expressions of concern.

Stanley had his kids over and the daughter, with her large candy cane filled with M&Ms, used it to imitate me and my cane. Stanley kept talking about going skiing again this week, how great the snow was, all those runs. I told him he might be the shortest term renter I'd ever had if he kept it up.

I putzed around the house, did some Christmas shopping and got to bed by nine. The pain in my leg was less but still stretched from mid-calf to my hip and pelvic area. I must have landed directly on the pelvic bone as it was untouchable. But I slept like the dead.

The next day I called Don to see how his skiing had been on Sunday. He was in bed all day with the flu. Not being able to ski was catching.

I went to work and had to suffer all day with the remarks.

"Here she comes. I can hear the clump-clump."

"And she's racing down the hall, she's into the backstretch, she's getting close to her chair."

"Wanna go skiing?"

I went to a plumbing store to order a washtub, got into a conversation with the clerk discussing injuries, motorcycling and skiing. He said, "Well, things can only get better."

I left the store, came back in, motioned the guy over, said, "Remember what you just said?"

He said, "Yes," and smiled.

I smiled too. "I have a flat tire."

I did more Christmas shopping. My kids would get their gifts after Christmas but I didn't want it to be too much after. It was amazing how big the Mall was when you had to walk slowly. It was also amazing how exhausted you could get from walking slowly.

I met a man in a cast. I looked at him, said, "Skiing?"

He nodded.

He looked at my cane. "Skiing?"

I nodded.

He said, "I can't ski again."

I said, "I'm lucky. I think I'll be back on the slopes by New Year's Day." But I wondered, was this an omen?

When I got home and no message from Baseball, I was ticked. He hadn't called to see how I was doing nor offered any help. He should have known I needed help. My thoughts were 'I can do it alone and we are just friends but why didn't you take care of me, you big jerk.' (One benefit of having been in counseling as I was during my divorce from Ray was that you could be totally irrational but at least you knew you were being irrational and you knew why.)

He called at ten-thirty that night. I was ready to blast him into the past.

"How's your leg?"

"Doing good, I can walk sometimes without the cane," I replied coldly.

"That's great, you're recovering a lot faster than I expected. You're in a lot better condition than I thought. I really wanted to come up and see you but I've been sick with the flu for two days and I didn't want to get you sick. I was going to call last night but I took some medicine and ...."

'Well, OK,' I thought, 'maybe I won't blast him into the past *this* time....'

On December 22 I went out without the cane or Ace bandage. Bad move. My leg hurt worse. I completed my Christmas shopping and returned home to wrap the stuff for mailing. Stanley had cleaned house that morning and it looked nice. Because I couldn't use my thumb I had a tough time wrapping. Getting frustrated I re-jammed my thumb, the post office was going to close in ten minutes and when I left the house it was a disaster with paper, tape, etc. all over. I made the post office but I stayed away from the house until he had gone to bed. I didn't want him jumping on me because I hadn't re-cleaned the house. (But I did the next day.)

My leg still hurt, I couldn't get around well yet but I was going to ski again. It was kinda like driving a car. When you got into an accident you didn't stop driving. You just figured out what you did wrong and tried to avoid those mistakes the next time. Life was filled with risks. Those who were afraid to take a chance may not lose anything but they missed out on a lot.

Given the choice, I think I would have chosen to miss out on this.

The Christmas party for the motorcycle club had about 20 people with one of the attendees being a lady who had advertised in our roster as being in her early 40s, good-looking, youthful, and interested in all ages and types of bike. The ad was much like mine at the time except by now my ad stated the late 40s. Real late. Before she arrived I mentioned to one of the guys that she was probably like me even in the looks department as she'd listed her height and weight. His response was, "I don't think so. When you see her you'll understand."

When she arrived my mouth fell open. Long, bleached, straw-like hair emblazoned with horizontal shades of blonde, orange and red down to her brown roots. A tight scoop-necked top showed off large, sagging breasts and a short tight skirt emphasized a protruding stomach and flabby veined thighs and legs. This contradiction to her ad was surpassed by a face on the far side of 50. After the guy looked at me with raised eyebrows and commented, "I took her for a ride. That's how I knew," I responded, "I think it's time to require pictures."

Baseball and I had planned a weekend trip for late December that he'd disguised to his ex and children as a fishing jaunt. The Friday we were supposed to leave a very distraught Baseball came into my kitchen while I was on the phone with Don. As Don and I conversed Baseball repeatedly stormed from my kitchen to the dining room and back shaking a toothbrush in his hand and muttering, "I can't believe it. She threw me out. She's going to destroy everything I own. I can't believe it."

After the fourth or fifth circuit I said to Don, "You know, Baseball seems a bit disturbed and he's waving that toothbrush in a lethal fashion. I better sign off and see what's up."

Don replied, "Well call me if he attacks. Although I don't know what damage he can do with a toothbrush but ya never know."

The upshot was his ex- had tired of his refusing to move and had the local gendarme's physically remove him from the house. Since she owned it he didn't have much ammunition against the eviction. His concern, aside from the indignity of some woman pushing him around, was that she'd sell or destroy his mementoes from his short but spectacular Major League baseball career. While he'd only been in the majors for seven years, two of those years involved him relief pitching his team to wins in the League Championships and World Series. He'd often said he would have made it to the Hall of Fame if it weren't for his leg injury but the truth was his alcoholism.

I got him calmed down and told him he could stay at my place for a few weeks until he found a place, emphasizing this was a temporary solution. While Baseball was great in bed and into the outdoors as was I he was a typical reformed alcoholic who lived at the local AA center. Each time he had an issue I tried to help him look at his options. But being a female who was not a former alcoholic meant my suggestions were worthless. The right way was what his AA buddies suggested and there was to be no discussion.

He was at my place five days. Between the abrupt end of sex by the third night to the constant moaning about issues that he really didn't want to resolve, he also liked to shake his bag of popcorn and change the TV channel every five seconds. Despite my pointing out how irritating it was he wouldn't stop. After he moved to the couch for sleeping purposes I subtly hinted his two-week residency was coming to an abrupt halt.

A week after he moved out he called and noted that he'd probably set a record by being thrown out by two women in less than a week. I suggested he discuss it with his AA friends. He noted that since his membership in AA he'd lost four girlfriends so maybe he needed to rethink his association with the group. I saw him again about six months later but he was still certain that his AA buddies were the greatest counselors since Freud.

The clinching blow was our discussion of the floor plans for a development he was investing in. My noting that the plans did not bode well for sales to older owners (a large part of real estate in the area) resulted in his saying that I didn't know anything about real estate. Notwithstanding my 12 years as a real estate broker. We had one more fling in bed before I said hit the road and don't call again.

Before he faded completely from my life he dug up my backyard with his bulldozer.

He really loved that dozer and hired himself out to many acquaintances so he could run around their property digging stuff up. My house had come with over a third of an acre but most was buried under waist high weeds. I spent so much time fixing the inside, the front lawn and the side yard (plus running around sight-seeing) that I'd been in the house two years before I finally got to the back of my property. By gosh that water I had seen glinting in the sun *was* Evans Creek. (As a note, a California creek was typically five to seven feet across and maybe five feet deep. An Oregon creek was typically ten to twenty feet across and as deep. So having a creek in your backyard in Oregon was significant.)

For the remainder of my stay in my house I could get to the plum and apple trees on my property and eat the blackberries that lined the back near the creek. I also cleaned up the grapevines that ran along the fence between my house and the neighbor's only to discover his back yard was a dumping site for car husks and parts. After he saw what I had done he drily noted, "There was a reason why the old owner grew those grape vines."

The night of New Year's Day I went to Medford for a concert, *Nirvana* with an opening act called the *Butthole Surfers*. At the time *Nirvana* was one of the top alternative rock bands in the country who typically played in 50,000+ seat stadiums. For them to come to Medford's 5,300 maximum-capacity facility was incredible. Bob Goldwaithe was the MC and he needed his mouth washed with acid. Reflecting the mind-set of the area very few of the 5,000 teenagers laughed and he was soon booed off the stage.

During the concert I called Josh in San Diego. Over the din he asked where I was.

"I'm at a concert in Medford. Bob Goldwaithe was the MC and they booed him off the stage."

"Wow," Josh exclaimed, "they must be real farmer types."

"Yeah, maybe, but they really seem to like the bands. One is called Bumhole Slipper or Butt Stomper. I can't remember the…"

"You mean *Butthole Surfers* Mom. I'm not too enthused about their music although some of the lyrics aren't too bad."

"Well, I can't hear them that clear anyway. And the other band is Nervy? Maybe it's Nerana? I can't…"

At that Josh screamed. "*Nirvana*? *Nirvana*? You're at a concert with *Nirvana*?"

"Yeah," I replied with a spring in my voice, "that's the name. *Nirvana*. That's who's playing."

"Damn it," yelled Josh jokingly, "I've wanted to see them in concert for years and my mother is sitting at one right now. My mother!" I heard his friends groaning and laughing in the background.

On January 4 I returned to working out. The trainer at the Fitness Center said, "One of the instructors saw you in the shower and we all agree you need to see a doctor. Whatever happened, you don't look so good."

Taking funds from my steadily shrinking bank account I had a doctor check me out. I was black and blue (and now yellow and purple) throughout my groin area and down the inside and outside of my right leg. I told him I thought my ski had snapped back and hit me in the groin although I didn't understand how it could without releasing from the binding or breaking my leg.

Looking at me with a jaundiced eye he diagnosed that I had torn my right hamstring, adductor muscle, the muscles that attach to the pubic bone and my thumb. The bruising wasn't from being hit by the ski it was from internal bleeding. Gulp. If things weren't better in three months he suggested surgery. But he agreed that I could work out, if only moderately, and maybe ski by the end of February.

At the end of January I went dancing with Bernie, a friend with whom I'd been discussing a business venture. He liked to dance very enthusiastically. He spun me around right into another couple. Twice. I got up the next morning and had a lump on my forehead. And we were drinking water most of the night!

The first weekend in February I planned on going skiing. I had been doing high-impact aerobics and my leg was fine. During the week I was teaching Continuing Education classes at night. Going to class on a Thursday night I was in a dark parking lot. Someone had broken up a cement parking block and pulled the block's rebar across the unlit pathway. I fell over it, smashed my knee and elbow to the point that I almost blacked out and pulled my hamstring again. At this point I had had more injuries in six weeks than I had in the last 20 years. This was not fun.

The next day I went to Don's because I was trying to arrange a white-water rafting party for Labor Day weekend. Since the permits were awarded by lottery each person in my party was putting in a request. I got Don's request, showed him my wrecked knee and elbow and he said, "Well, you know how it is when we get old." *He* now had a walking problem from my kick to his shin.

I'd planned a party for the motorcycle club for February 19 but the announcement in the paper had the wrong telephone number. I called the published number and an older woman answered. She thought it was a real kick that she and her husband, people in their 80s, would be getting phone calls about a singles motorcycle club. Particularly since her husband used to own a Harley.

Around this time I'd met Joe through a personal ad. He was a firefighter in his 40s and very reticent about his past relationships. I quickly learned that he lied about them so much he didn't want to discuss them in fear that he might not be able to remember what he'd said. On our last date I asked if he wanted to come in for a drink or something to eat. We'd been wandering around different towns that night for quite a while and I felt guilty that he hadn't had anything to eat. He interpreted this as an invitation for sex. I set him straight noting that his evasions were the primary cause for my lack of interest. He went into a rant that only ended when I threatened to call the police or scream enough that my next-door neighbors would investigate. Leaving, still screaming at me, he tore ruts in my dirt driveway during his exit.

I saw Bernie a few days later and his tale of a woman he'd met through the personals was almost unbelievable until the last line.

When he called to arrange a meeting she suggested he crawl through a window she would leave open at her house. He demurred and suggested perhaps a meeting at a public place. She insisted it be at her house and finally conceded to his entering her house by an unlocked door. While he realized she was a little loopy he agreed and the following night entered her house.

He found her, all 350 pounds, in a red negligee and seductively arrayed on her bed. While he was grossly overweight he didn't like overweight women, a hypocritical attitude we'd discussed more than once. But he wished to be kind and after a brief discussion made his fond adieus. She, while disappointed, pointed out that she had a date with someone else later that week who would no doubt better appreciate her. He was a firefighter in his late 40s and his name was Joe. With proof of the veracity of his story I said, "Wow, small world."

Writing this book brought back memories and one was an image I have held in my mind from that time. The City of Talent, population 3,100 and three miles north of Ashland, was (and still is) home to the Minshall Theater, a venue that seated 85 people and put on 10 productions a year. Their Christmas season production *The Lion, the Witch, and the Wardrobe*, based on C. S. Lewis' Narnia stories, had among other otherworldly characters a lithe person dressed from head to toe as a white deer. The deer entered from the back of the theater and flitted from row to row down the aisle to the stage. After 17 years I can still see that deer.

A trip helped me realize how being countrified and citified can affect a person. In early February I went 250 miles north to Salem for a meeting. As soon as I hit Eugene where Interstate 5 widened to three and four lanes on each side of the freeway I felt tense, irritated and just wanted to get out. Coming from San Diego it still amazed me how quickly I had changed to a small town attitude. One woman at the meeting agreed with my feelings but another, from Portland, said she got nervous when the freeway narrowed to two lanes on each side.

In March a shopping mall in Medford had a vintage motorcycle show where I left off flyers for the Singles Motorcycle Club. On the way home I thought, 'I'd like to get some unusual rocks for my fireplace hearth and this *Southwest Oregon Recreation Map* shows a 'Rock Collecting Point of Interest' near Butte Falls. Maybe I'll take a quick run over and see what they have.' I checked the *Recreation Map* against a regular road map and saw that the road leading to the rock collecting area went all the way through from Butte Falls to Highway 62, a main highway. I thought, 'I can go in by Butte Falls, come out on the main highway and head home. Great.' I trusted the highway maps. Bad move.

The road into the rock collecting area is called Obenchain. For about two miles it is two-lane highway. Then it becomes one-and-a-half lane smooth gravel road. Then it becomes one-lane unsmooth gravel road. Then it becomes ruts with low spots filled with water. Then it becomes mud. Real deep mud. Mud a 4x4 would get stuck in. And I was in my Mazda 626.

Good car. Gets me where I want to go. Also gets me out of where I don't want to go. After three miles of ruts I hit the mud and realized this was the end of the line, rocks or no rocks. So I had to turn around. On a one-lane rutted trail with woods on one side and about three feet to the edge of a sharp drop-off on the other. I couldn't just drive backwards because I couldn't see the ruts and some of them were deep enough that I could get hung up on the axle.

But the old girl did it (the car, not me). I'd back up a few feet at an angle, go forward at an angle a few feet, back up, go forward. At least I had enough clearance in the wooded area that I could go into the bushes for the width I needed to turn around. When I got home, I had to wash down not only the inside of the car but the inside of the tailpipe that was clogged with mud. Interesting side trip.

In April I was at the Pear Blossom Festival in Medford with a Rottweiler whose name was Rocky. He belonged to a new renter and liked to stick his head in my car window for treats when I came home from work. We quickly learned how pervasive the movie *Rocky* had become. Calling his Rottweiler back from trying to nip the parade horses' hooves, about ten other Rotties came to attention. Originality in naming evidently was not Oregonian's strong suit.

This guy was an incredible sculptor with an incredible drinking problem. I have one of his pieces and pictures of others. After I left Oregon I tried to track him down because after people saw what he had created they wanted to buy. He could work with stone and wood, crafting sculptures ranging from a one foot high piece to others more than six feet high. As he handled a piece of wood or stone you could see him envisioning the end product with every highlight of his material shining through. According to him he had tried to show his works at the various artist fairs in the area but because he had no education or sponsor he continually met with failure. Sadly I never was able to contact him.

In April I wanted to show some property. The conversation with the realtor about access illustrated the area's laid back attitude. "We don't have a key and it doesn't have a lock box. Actually, we don't have a client, he's been gone since last Friday and no one knows where he is or when he'll get back. We've left messages at a lot of places but no response. If he doesn't show up soon we may have to check the house to see if he's in it but not moving. I don't think he's in jail but he might be. You could try the tenant in the mobile but he doesn't have a phone. He might have a key to the house. There's also a rumor that the owner hid a key somewhere. If you can find it, you can use it. You could walk around the property and peek in the windows. Actually it's not my listing. The listing agent is on our graveyard shift. He has another job where he works until midnight then comes to the office. We have the only office in town that has someone here at 2 a.m. Good luck."

After three months the knee I had injured when I fell in the school parking lot still had not healed. If I bumped it the pain was sharp and lasted for hours or it would bruise and swell. A minor fall skiing had resulted in my knee turning into a large grapefruit. At the doctor's office he again suggested I use ice packs and go to physical therapy. I had been working out for months so that solution was obviously not a good one. I demanded, "Operate on this knee and find out what's wrong. I am sick of this."

After a few more minutes of arguing he conceded to my request. I had out-patient surgery. The bursa, a sac that covers the kneecap and provides lubrication and protection against blows, had been crushed by my fall. All that remained was the equivalent of a half of a cup of scar tissue that he removed. With the scar tissue gone the bursa could now recover. The doctor later noted I was right and he should have operated soon after the accident. They wanted me to stay overnight but my kitty wouldn't have had anyone to sleep with. She had a very strict bedtime. If I tried to read in bed she pawed my book until I turned the lights out.

I walked out on crutches and in a thigh-to-ankle brace. Not fun. The crutches resulted in my re-herniating the disc in my back and straining my hip. I had the staples out May 26 and went off the crutches but I still walked funny. When I went into the bank where everyone knew me I dragged my leg, waved my arms, made like a hunchback and started slavering. At least I got some fun out of it.

At the bank I observed that with my semi-broken thumb and unhealed hamstring tear from my December ski injury, my knee and elbow from the parking lot, my semi-healed eye due to a major infection in May and my back and hip I had to get out of Oregon before I ended up in a wheelchair. (My eye infection had manifested itself the day before the weekend I planned to scrape and paint the outside of my house. The intense pain when light hit my eye resulted in my wearing an eye patch while I worked. Up on my ladder I looked so jaunty people waved as they drove by.)

Right after my knee operation I was busy. I had decided to move to Medford for more job opportunities and potential real estate business so I was trying to finish fixing my house. I visited Josh in San Diego and John in Los Alamos, New Mexico while taking in some more Southwest parks. From the time of my knee operation until Wednesday, July 13 when I saw my doctor I put in 100 hours on the house, drove 4,000 miles on my trip and rode a motorcycle for 7 hours. Looking at me with a jaundiced eye his only comment was, "When do you expect to give your knee a chance to heal?"

At the time property values in San Diego were falling. My $280,000 house was now worth $220,000. I pulled it off the market and on my trip cleaned up the yard that had not been worked on for at least a year. Josh and his friends had been renting the house but none were much on gardening.

Unfortunately there was something in the weeds that caused an allergic reaction. I took off for Los Alamos and on the way through Arizona the rash got worse. Little bumps covered my arms and legs and brought with them a burning sensation akin to a severe sunburn. In an area where there were no motels I had to car camp with my Calamine lotion that was only making the rash itch and burn worse. My car floor looked like a pink flamingo nesting area.

In Los Alamos I toured the area around Santa Fe with John and visited with his two kittens who liked to drink out of water glasses instead of their bowls. By that time I was on Benadryl for the rash. I needed to take a pill so I just whisked the glass away from the cat and drank. John said, "Gosh, Mom, I can get you some clean water," but I figured whatever was giving me the rash was surely more dangerous than what the cat could give me. At the time both kittens were the same size. Within a few months Grif had grown to twice the size of Pumpkin. John told me the vet asked if Grif was part mountain lion.

The rash finally began to subside and I continued on my journey taking in Arches and Canyonlands National Parks and the clouds of gnats that went along with the spectacular scenery. Driving home I ended up in Lakeview, Oregon without enough gas to get to Klamath Falls where they had the only 24-hour gas station within 100 miles. Lakeview did not have 24-hour stations. Car camping is not fun.

While I was still pre-ambulatory with my knee the Sierra Club had a hike to the 'Hanging Gardens' about twenty miles north of Rogue River off West Fork Evans Creek Road. By August I figured I could hike again so I got the directions to the Gardens from the Club and set off.

The directions were good but my following them wasn't. Somehow I meandered onto some Forest Service roads all unpaved but in good condition. After a few hours of driving I stopped to check the scenery. I could see Mt. McLoughlin, Mt. Shasta, and Mt. Thielsen. Considering how far Thielsen is from the city of Rogue River and the mountain ranges that intervene my first thought was, "Where the hell am I?" Since no one was around to answer my question I continued to drive and out of nowhere appeared a shelter with a picnic table. A trail across from the shelter said 'Cow Creek Trail.' Now Cow Creek is in Douglas County which is about forty miles north of Rogue River on the freeway. I was really on the wrong road.

I started to hike the very steep and downhill trail then thought, 'I've just started hiking again. What if I fall and tear my knee? How many months would it be before someone came by this road?' I returned to the shelter, drove a few more miles and saw a sign saying 'Red Mountain' pointing back the way I had come. Now I knew why I could see Thielsen. I had stumbled up a mountain. I continued following service roads for a few more hours, saw an eagle and some other big birds then came out on a highway that pointed to West Fork Evans Creek. Following it I at least found out where West Fork started – at least 90 miles less than what I had driven. The amazing things about this summer weekend trip were passing a campground with no one in it, not seeing one other car on any of the roads and finding the shelter in the middle of nowhere.

A hike in late August with the Sierra Club to Devil's Peak in the Sky Lakes Wilderness solidified my love for this part of Oregon. At least the scenery part. Twelve miles, half up hill, but what beautiful views. At one point the trail opened to a canyon. As you walked along the canyon ridge towards Devil's Peak you turned a corner and below were three alpine lakes like huge teardrops among the green. Further on a small mountain peak came to view with another alpine lake nestled at the top. More mountain lakes appeared in the valley and the ridges were massive slabs of red and black rock. Someone mentioned they had spent a honeymoon at one of those lakes. In the far distance was Klamath Lake. At this point I got lost and didn't make it to the top of Devil's Peak but I was within 500 yards.

On the way back I walked with a man who looked to be in his late 50s although his face was quite lined and his leg muscles ropy. He had had knee replacement surgery two years ago but was now playing tennis and walking as fast as I was after eleven miles. He was 76. His comment about his youthful appearance? "Hair dye does wonders." He attributed his physical condition to having always walked or biked to work all his life. Exercise does wonders.

OREGON AND DAVE (AGAIN)
Rogue River, Oregon 1994-1995

Right after my hike Dave came up to stay with me for a while. I can remember Dave sitting in my kitchen one night staring at my wood front door.

"What's the matter, are you in a trance?" I asked.

"There's something wrong with that front door and I can't figure out what it is," he replied.

"Well, I installed it by myself so it may be a little off but it looks OK to me."

"It's not OK. Now I know what's wrong."

"What?"

"You installed it upside down. No wonder it looked weird."

With some wood putty and repositioning he was able to re-install it correctly. Dave always admired that I did most of the work myself but he did have a habit of sighing a lot when he looked at some of my results. On the other hand when he saw what the house looked like before the renovations he had to give me a plus for the results in total.

The first of September Oregon's injury trap hit again. My front tooth broke. This could have happened anywhere but with my knee, leg injuries and other physical problems I'd encountered I was beginning to wonder. Luckily the dentist saw me right away since I was presenting an offer the next day but Oregon struck once more. About an hour before I was to present the offer the temporary crown broke and I had to glue it together with Super Glue then glue the whole mess back on. Got my upper lip stuck to the tooth for a while. After all that the offer was rejected.

Two days later Dave and I rode from Rogue River aiming towards Happy Camp along the Klamath River then north to O'Brien. We intended to stay on paved roads since Harley owners didn't like dirty bikes. Another Harley owner's girlfriend assured us the road between Little Applegate and Talent was paved. We ate dust for about twenty-five miles. In between the dust puffs we saw a lot of beautiful country with views of Mount Ashland, the Siskiyous and the Marble Mountains.

When Dave stayed with me he got pear duty. I had run out of pear recipes (although I did make some super pear chutney) and Dave was to get rid of the extras. He dug a ditch at the back of my property that he filled up within a few weeks. As he dragged the drums to the backyard he'd note that he was going to the 'Pearatorium.'

On Labor Day Dave and I hiked in the Wild and Scenic Rogue area to Whiskey Creek Canyon. Keep in mind every time I hiked with Dave I ended up with poison oak because he liked to 'explore.' On the way we meandered off the path to the river to cool off and ended up climbing a very steep hill to get back on the trail. At Whiskey Creek we meandered off again to cool off. Then we got separated. A typical hike with Dave. Three days later I could definitely tell Dave was back. I had poison oak.

The weekend of September 17 Dave and I went on one of our adventures. Normally when you go somewhere, you go, you walk around seeing things and you return. However it was never that way with Dave.

I said, "Let's go to Hell's Canyon this weekend." In the far northeast part of the state and home to the Snake River it was the deepest river canyon in the United States. "The trip should be 10 to 12 hours. If we leave early Friday night we can be there Saturday to hike then drive back Sunday." Sure!

We didn't get out of Rogue River until 7:30 p.m. (I had planned 5:30.) I had gotten home late and Dave dithers. By 3 a.m. I pulled off on a fire service road to sleep. Dave got the ground and I got the car. Incidentally from Redmond to 395, about seven hours of driving, there is one rest area. Thank heaven I brought toilet paper.

The next morning Dave was comatose until we found a restaurant where he could get coffee. His return to normality took so long I had the chance to have a long conversation with a local lady about all the fires in the area and the Pendleton Round-Up. She suggested that when we got to Hells Canyon we might like to go to the local annual snake and bear barbecue. We said we'd think about it.

When we got to Enterprise we were told the best sight was at Hatpoint Lookout. I wasn't too sure about the actual name since, as usual, I had left my maps at home. As we took the twenty-three mile, one-and-a-half lane gravel road to the top I kept wondering, 'Why is this car overheating so much?'

The view, 6,800 feet above the river, was pretty but little of the Snake River was in it. After the Grand Canyon and Canyonlands it was not that spectacular. We stopped at another viewpoint where we had to walk after I almost hung the Mazda up on some rocks. It was a good little car-pretend-truck but it had its limitations. Dave, whose stamina level due to lack of sleep was about half of mine, slowly trudged up the hill. Hiking was out of the question. On the way down I started noticing signs: 'Use low gear, stop and cool brakes, 16% grade.' No wonder the car was overheating going up!

We camped by the Imhana River that I called a babbling brook and Dave commented, "So tell it to shut up." The next day we went to some more viewpoints than headed for home.

Dave helped drive part way but after stalling the car on a railroad track with a train coming his drive sharing was limited.

I visited places to decide if I wanted to return. While the scenery from on-high wasn't that great, on the Idaho side was a two-lane highway running along the river that followed the whole canyon. That would have been worth driving. Plus the Snake had many Class III and IV rapids. Now that my knee was better, returning there next summer for a white-water trip was in the plans. Never made it back.

Dave was a college football nut. He adored University of Michigan, which he never attended, while I graduated from U. of M. and cared less about their football. Michigan played Colorado and I was teasing Dave about Michigan losing. He ran out in the last minute of the game, "Ha, ha, they won it." About 30 seconds later he walked out, stunned. "They lost it. Colorado threw a 'Hail Mary' and they lost it." I could not contain my laughter. He almost got back at me the next day when the Chargers were trying to snatch defeat from the jaws of victory but the quarterback, Stan Humphries, came through for me.

My doctor had sent me to physical therapy for my knee and it had gotten worse. I went to a health club and it started feeling better although still not strong. Very painful when kneeling. In late September I returned to the doctor who he said I'd never be able to kneel or squat or put a lot of stress on it. This was said to someone who rode a bicycle 15 to 20 miles three times a week, hiked 5 to 10 miles a week, sometimes with ankle weights, did high-impact aerobics five times a week, skied, rafted, played racquetball, you name it. So them's were fightin' words. I decided to work out more and within a few months I was back to normal. Never take a doctor's opinion about what you can do until you prove to yourself that you can't.

At the end of September Josh came up from San Diego to take care of some business (traffic tickets). He rode AMTRAK and we both vowed never again.

The train left San Diego around 6 a.m. Thursday and was scheduled to arrive at Klamath Falls at around 7:45 a.m. Friday. I had no idea why Amtrak was scheduled into Klamath Falls with a population close to 15,000 rather than Medford the center of a metropolitan area of 260,000. At least the drive to Klamath Falls was beautiful with mist and fog drifting in the valleys and forest as cows and deer grazed in the early morning light.

I got there at 8:15 a.m. "When did the train from San Diego arrive?"

"Well," said the station manager, "if you're still here at 9:15 you can greet it."

The train finally pulled in at 9:30 and no Josh. Walking outside the train I heard, "Mom! I must be in Klamath Falls." The train had stopped so often in the middle of nowhere he thought it was another unscheduled stop and had just gotten off for a cigarette.

On the way back to Rogue River a wolf crossed the road. As usual the 80-mile road had one sign to tell you what highway you were on. In Oregon, if you got lost you were lost forever. When I took Josh back Monday we were just on time after a tire screeching run. The train was an hour late.

In late October I attended a football game between Grants Pass and Ashland high schools. Grants Pass was now number two in the state with no losses. Ashland, who had gone to the state playoffs four of the last five years was 3-2 in the conference. However, Ashland had beaten Grants Pass the last seven years. Not this time. The score was 34 to 15.

The announcer was hilarious.

"Blanchard *(the quarterback)* had to run for his life."

"And, as usual, another flag on the play."

"Appears the five-yard penalty is one of the Caveman's (Grants Pass) better defensive moves lately." I couldn't keep track of all the funny remarks but he was good.

In October I went to one of the strangest Halloween parties that I have ever attended. Not because of the costumes but a guy I met. I was dressed as a fortune-teller with a veil and my state-of-the-art crystal ball, a light-bulb. The party was all couples so I decided to leave. On the way out I ran into a good looking man who I'll call Jeff. After learning why I was going he said, "Hey, don't leave. I'll go back with you."

On the way in Jeff asked, "That's not a mustache I see under the veil is it?"

I laughed showing him it wasn't. Using the stamp mark on the back of my hand we stamped his hand and sauntered in where he introduced me to many of the party-goers. He was very friendly and seemed interested in me. Then he asked, "You're not a man are you? I mean this isn't *The Crying Game* is it?"

(For the uninitiated, *The Crying Game* is about a cross-dresser who fools another man right into the bedroom. *Naked Gun 33 1/3* did a great take-off on that scene.)

I replied "No," with a little irritation. I have a husky voice but not that husky.

About an hour later he suddenly looked at me and said, "You're a man, I know it," walked away and refused to talk to me the rest of the evening.

When I told Dave about this he laughed. "I've known you for five years and I've never mistaken you for a man."

Josh said, "Now I understand why you're talking about moving back to California. All the California fruitcakes have moved to Oregon."

This guy owned a Bed-and-Breakfast in Ashland and in answering a personal ad a few weeks later I learned he had lied about his name (and, in the ad, his age). As we talked I determined he was the same guy at the party. When I pointed this out he denied it but got tangled up in this third lie so he was outed. Hopefully his weirdness didn't extend to his cooking. As an aside they had fortune cards at the party. Jeff's said, "It may be that your whole purpose in life is simply to serve as a warning to others."

Starting in 1992 Tim Behrens had been performing a one-man stage play of Patrick McManus' humor. On November 12, 1994 I went to Medford for his performance of *A Fine and Pleasant Misery*. Based in Spokane, Washington at the time Behrens noted that the show couldn't play big towns because of the advertising expense but in the intervening years I have never understood why more theaters haven't booked this guy. The humor is G-rated and kids and adults in the audience were literally falling out of their chairs from laughing. The stories revolved around McManus' made-up childhood in a small Mid-Western town and Behrens portrayal of the multitude of vignettes was hysterical. Had I been in San Diego I never would have seen him. (Tapes of his shows are available online.)

The Medford paper related the following tale by a local motorcyclist. As a young boy moving to Oregon he thought it such a wild place that you could ride a deer. While riding his Honda dirt bike thirty years later he got his chance. He collided with a massive, four-point black tail deer whose horns became entangled in his bike's handlebars. The deer pinned the rider's leg to the bike and the deer's face was against the headlight. Besides crashing the rider feared going over the front of the bike and being impaled on the deer's antlers. Finally the deer steered the bike into a ditch and deer, rider and bike all parted company. The rider's helmet saved him from losing half of his face. And he sure had a story to tell.

With the best record they'd had since 1976 Grants Pass won the Southern Oregon Conference title and made it to the state playoffs that included all major state high school teams. Unfortunately they lost in the second round in overtime. The quarterback, Jimmy Blanchard, was a junior and the coach's son. (The coach, Tom Blanchard, played professional football as a punter for the Giants, Saints and Buccaneers.) That year and for years after at Portland State University Jimmy broke many state high school and college records but never made it to the NFL.

The last nine seconds of regulation play the other team attempted a field goal, had it blocked, advanced it beyond the line of scrimmage and blew the officials' minds. None of the referees could agree on what to do. Coach Blanchard had to be restrained. Five to seven minutes went by while they debated. A guy behind me yelled, "Come on, refs, I gotta go to work on Monday." We all wanted the game to get on. I had heard the temperature was supposed to drop to 20 degrees that night and I think it got real close before the game ended. A sad loss but pretty funny.

That year the University of Oregon Ducks went to the Rose Bowl. The broker I worked for had a friend who bet $20 with Vegas odds makers that the Ducks would smell the roses. The odds were 1400 to 1.

The excellence of the Grants Pass band program was demonstrated at the 1994 University of Oregon's Festival of Bands contest. With 16 other bands this contest was considered the Pacific Northwest's top band showdown. Several of the judges from across the country said the band was top ten material on the national level. The next year they were to start competing nationally. Yet this was the same city that closed their libraries and wouldn't pass school levies. It demonstrated to me that money wasn't always the only way to achieve excellence.

LOGIC, SOUTHWEST OREGON STYLE

1992-1995

When I first put down Oregon roots I envisioned that with the country coming out of the 1990 recession and Clinton's election in 1992 the unemployment situation in Southwest Oregon would soon be a memory. However in 1992 the Grants Pass libraries were open part-time with volunteers because the locals had refused to pass a parcel tax to pay for librarian staff. That should have given me a clue. (A year later the parcel tax passed. After numerous closings and openings due to defeated tax measures the libraries were closed permanently in 2007 and are now privately run.)

Every month my newsletter had an article about some political action no sane person would condone or some societal value no one could understand. After writing my newsletter for a year I began to realize I was repeating the same strange happenings with only the town or county names changing. For this book it just seemed simpler to put it all in one place.

Societal Values

Southern Oregon had the highest rate of drug abuse among high school-age students of any area in the state. Josephine County led the state in methamphetamine production. The two counties had the highest state-wide ratio of unwed mothers on welfare and they were not minorities. It was not uncommon to meet unmarried women under 25 with at least three children. A state report indicated Jackson County's federal Women, Infant and Children program had the highest percentage of reported drug or alcohol abuse by pregnant women in Oregon. Jackson and Josephine counties had one of the highest spouse and child abuse rates in Oregon; I had been told the highest in the United States.

One of the school superintendents said, "Education is not valued here. Between the retirees who do not want to educate other people's children to the people who have lived by the timber industry which did not require education, there is little support for the schools." Josephine and Jackson counties spent close to the lowest amounts per child in the state and these amounts were based on tax rates passed by the voters. The community colleges spent as much time in preparing students for GEDs as college instruction. Local employers indicated at least 25% of their job applicants could not read. Another 25 to 40% couldn't pass the drug screenings.

Yet some of their school districts produced winners.

Ashland middle school (6th - 8th grade) students in an academic contest stressing creativity and team problem solving placed eighth nationally. Rogue River students won or placed high in several state speech contests. The Central Point Crater High Brain Bowl team finished sixth against teams from 42 other states. The Ashland High School speech team won the National Forensic League competition at Stanford University in California. Four local students were selected from 2.5 million seniors nation-wide for the 1994 Presidential Scholars Program. Two were made Scholars.

Government Employees, Elected and Otherwise

The Josephine County Parks Director wanted to sponsor a weekend rock concert to raise money for the parks system. The Board of Commissioners said, "O.K., you can spend $8,000." The Parks Director spent $42,000. The concert earned $4,000. The Parks Director was fired.

Community leaders started a campaign to pay back the money and get the Parks Director rehired. The Commissioners refused. The county was now out the money plus had to spend more money recruiting a new Director. At least the Commissioners never had to investigate how he was able to get the $34,000 over what he was allocated.

The Oregon Legislature set up $3.5 million to fund pilot projects in the Rogue River basin area for stream-improvements designed to save fish such as the salmon. To get the money Curry, Jackson and Josephine counties had to form volunteer watershed councils to review and recommend projects. These projects impacted how much river water land owners could take for irrigation, how close to the streams timber companies could log, how much mining would be allowed, etc. Josephine County commissioners appointed land owners who represented irrigators, loggers and miners as their representatives then couldn't understand why their team was rejected by the state.

The Grants Pass Board of Realtors recommended area Realtors back a resolution on in-stream water rights passed by the Josephine County Farm Bureau. In-stream water rights meant that the stream and the fish it supported had more rights to the water than irrigators. The resolution wanted to use 1988 as the base year, a year that due to a ten-year drought had recorded the lowest number of fish on record and water-flows about 50% of normal.

In the winter of 1992 Gold Hill faced penalties for sewage plant violations that included discharging sewage sludge on the plant grounds and falsifying water treatment plant records. The newspaper headline read: 'Gold Hill in deep doo-doo for faked sewer reports.' The public works director was fired and the recently-hired sewer plant operator quit. My question in a letter to the editor was, "Why didn't the mayor or a city council member or even a citizen see this? I mean, in a town with 1,000 people sludge on the plant grounds would be pretty hard to miss."

Rogue River hired a Fire Chief whose driver's license was revoked because he had failed to pay tickets. Note that in rural areas the Chief had to be at all fires and, in some cases, had to drive the fire truck.

Phoenix hired a Police Chief who had been fired from a California police department for using government property for private business and pleasure and a host of other illegal actions.

Eagle Point hired a City Manager whose primary responsibility was to be planning. The new employee had never done any planning or supervised a staff or prepared a budget or a host of other things he needed to know to be a City Manager. He was fired before he ever got a chance to work even though he had already quit his other job and had been replaced.

The new Finance Director at Central Point had never held this level position. Six months after his appointment he had yet to report to the City Council on budget versus expenditures because he a) didn't know he had to and b) didn't know how. He also didn't know he had to prepare an annual proposed budget. (Despite seven years of government budgeting and monitoring experience my application for the position was rejected because my experience wasn't 'local.')

Gold Hill was considering raising water and sewer rates to keep the city's creditors at bay. Bond agreements used to finance utility improvements contained terms requiring that the utilities earned a profit. Both the water and sewer lost money for the 1993 budget year, losses revealed during the annual end-of-year audit. No one could explain why it took the Finance Director 12 months and an audit to discover they were losing money?

Rogue River had a problem with parking downtown. Note downtown was exactly four blocks on one street but business owners were complaining to City Hall. Even the Grants Pass paper had addressed the issue. Personally I never found parking a problem but I guess when you were used to parking right in front of a store walking around the block might seem a major inconvenience.

Two Jacksonville volunteer firefighters decided to drop their drawers in front of a woman firefighter.

During a public event.

In the presence of others, including tourists.

The results? They were suspended and she quit. (This was not the first form of harassment she had encountered.) Now why was this notable? Because the suspended firefighters sued Jacksonville claiming the suspension was unnecessary and 'overkill' for the offense. The topper? They had the support of many Jacksonville citizens.

Rogue River residents turned down a levy that was needed to avoid layoffs. The reason? City residents resented a police policy of going outside city limits to support other officers and respond to calls for assistance. They had no objection to other officers helping out in Rogue River.

The only tax increases approved in two years in the two counties were the Grants Pass levy for the library and the Ashland levy for the schools. The citizens repeatedly turned down levies for police and fire protection then complained that crime was increasing.

Talent hired two police officers. One had been fired from Medford for sexual misconduct including forcing a woman to have sex with him and sex while on duty. The other officer had been fired from the Jacksonville force during his probation.

The challenger for Rogue River mayor, who had held that office in 1975-79 and 1984-90, said the ballot levy for the police force was unnecessary because the city could find the money elsewhere. The levy, designed to ensure 24-hour coverage by increasing a budget that had not been changed since 1983, failed.

This same man also opposed the bond issue for a new sewage plant. This was in light of an engineering study that stated repairing the existing plant would cost as much as building a new one. His opposition also ignored the Oregon Department of Environmental Quality telling Rogue River to stop polluting the Rogue or DEQ would build a new plant and make Rogue River citizens pay for it. (The condition of the existing plant was underlined when Rogue River residents received a plea in our water bill to not flush toenail clippings down the toilets as they clogged the treatment equipment.)

The bond issue passed. The mayor's job was still undecided due to a tie vote. They flipped a coin. The no-sewage-treatment guy won and immediately started work on overturning the bond vote. And people wondered why I was selling my house.

A Jackson County commissioner candidate opposed a criminal justice levy that would employ more prosecutors, investigators, etc. because it might strain county jail facilities. (The levy passed.)

A Medford parent requested doors be installed on the boy's toilets at the schools where 85 doors were missing. Some boys were embarrassed to use the toilets causing bladder and constipation problems. After six weeks the parent again approached the school board. A board member said, "I suggest we stop talking about the crappers. I'm really tired of wasting time now on bathroom doors."

Paying for Government

The passage of Measure 5 in 1990 severely reduced property tax revenues for all counties in Oregon. The concept was to even out school and other funding between rich and poor counties by having the state distribute funds from a state sales tax that would be passed to provide the necessary monies. No such sales tax was ever passed. The real intent was to starve counties and the state to force them to cut salaries and employment while maintaining the same service levels.

As a result local government salaries got so low that Gold Hill could not get a supervisor for their wastewater treatment plant because they didn't pay enough. One city offered $18,000 for a full-time Public Works Director. This was the same area where I was earning more than $12,000 a year working part-time jobs in sales, real estate and substitute teaching.

Teachers who were negotiating for increased salaries were told they should take whatever was offered for the privilege of working in Southwest Oregon.

One ballot measure that passed reduced the Jackson County Commissioners' salaries by 50% from $42,000 to $23,000. Someone running an entire county was paid the same as a sanitation employee. The voters didn't think that was illogical.

By this time the anti-tax measures were starting to take their toll. A measure to build a new jail was voted down. Due to jail overcrowding, people (including a major drug dealer) charged with anything less than a major felony were set free within one day of arrest. The Josephine Juvenile Center construction was voted down. Juveniles who committed any crime less than murder or attempted murder were arrested then let go.

The numbers told the tale. By 1993, Josephine County with a population of 67,000 had 364 felony crime juvenile offenders with only one secured bed available in Medford in Jackson County. The rest were free. The felonies ranged from attempted murder to assault, sex crimes, burglary and drug offenses.

Between 1992 and 1993 reported crime increased by 12.8 percent in Jackson County compared to a 1.1 percent increase across the state. By 1994 the trend continued. The greatest increases, at 14.2 percent and 13.8 percent, were in drug offenses and assaults and sex crimes. The county was continuing to see dramatic increases in rural crime and an influx of people wanted for crimes in other areas. Knowing they would never go to jail why wouldn't they move there?

Josephine County's reported crimes dropped by 9.1 percent. However the Sheriff noted that they had less people available to respond to or investigate complaints. Bias crimes stayed about the same although the state saw a 50 percent decrease. Since most of the state-wide anti-gay referendums started in Josephine County the stability in this statistic was inevitable.

The results of this stupidity were rapid. Ashland's Lithia Park had a 1915 fountain with a bronze cherub and marble bowls. Restoration in 1987 cost $35,000. In 1993 it was vandalized to the point that they were considering a video system. Park bathrooms in Josephine County were vandalized with toilets ripped out and sinks destroyed.

Many blamed the damage to the increase in population. That felons were released the day they were arrested had nothing to do with it.

After five rejections, Josephine County voters finally approved building a juvenile facility. The citizens finally woke up

Anti-Gay and Anti-Minorities

The anti-gays were so vehement against any laws promoting equality they almost shut down city government.

The Grants Pass City Council passed a resolution advising County voters to study Measure 17-1 because it was discriminatory. (The measure prohibited government bodies from passing legislation stating homosexuals can't be denied their rights.) The head of the anti-gay group, John Tetweiler, challenged that if the city passed the resolution his group would 'vote down every levy and leave the City of Grants Pass with no money with which to operate.'

The consequences of passage included defeating two levies, spearheading seven recall campaigns for ten commissioners and passing legislation that prevented the

County from being in debt for anything including capital projects. Already operating with millions less than the previous year, the County had to divert one million to pay off existing debts to meet the new requirements. The group placed a measure on the ballot where the County couldn't buy anything considered capital equipment without voter approval. This included tables and chairs. 17-1 passed.

In late February I saw the movie *Philadelphia* in Medford at the early-bird rate. *Philadelphia*, a story about gay rights, was not available at the Grants Pass Theater until after the Oscar nominations. Even then it was only shown after 8 p.m.

When the comic series *For Better or Worse* addressed the homosexuality of one of the strip's characters, the strip was moved to the opinion page in the Medford papers. In Grants Pass it was canceled until that part was over.

The Oregon Citizens Alliance that initiated and helped pass numerous anti-gay rights propositions was heavily represented in the Grants Pass – Josephine County area. Grants Pass had a County Taxpayer's Association. You all know what a Taxpayer's Association does – it studies government budgets, makes expenditure recommendations, fights tax measures. Well, not in Grants Pass. They had a picnic to honor local heroes. Like the local director of the Oregon Citizens Alliance whose sole objective was to pass anti-gay laws. What that had to do with taxes was beyond me.

While working in real estate I had numerous clients tell me that they were moving to the area because few blacks lived there. Blacks, gays and other minorities were pretty safe in Ashland and kind of safe in Medford but beyond that it was questionable.

Recalls

The Commissioners, the Sheriff, the Health Board, you name it, were so busy fighting recall petitions they didn't have time to govern. Saying nothing was a mode of political survival.

Phoenix, between Medford and Ashland, had put their police chief on administrative leave because the chief's employees complained to the City Council about his management practices. Some citizens submitted petitions to recall whoever voted to put the chief on leave. They felt the employees did not follow procedure, i.e. take their grievances through the proper chain of command. The chain of command was the police chief.

Butte Falls had a small school and was in the back country. On Fridays when athletic teams played away games with other schools classes were decimated. In 1993 substantial money had been cut from the schools so reductions had to be made. Since half the school was gone on Fridays anyway the school board decided to lengthen the other four days and eliminate Friday as a school day. The parents didn't like it because it interfered with their schedules so the entire school board was being recalled.

Rogue River needed a new water treatment plant so they were thinking of raising connection fees for new housing to $9,500 a house. For houses that would probably sell for $90,000 without the fee increase. They were afraid to raise fees for everyone served by the new plant because, hey, you guessed it, they might get recalled.

Gold Hill residents started a recall campaign to rid themselves of their elected council and mayor. The reasons? First, the council fired the city clerk, a popular employee who was trying to unionize city employees. Second, they 'wasted money.' According to the person heading the recall campaign two of their 'wasteful and unnecessary expenditures' involved removal of leaking underground fuel tanks to comply with federal regulations and paying an attorney to defend themselves against a lawsuit brought by the fired public works director (see previous 'doo-doo' incident).

Since 1983 the city had had five recall elections. Of the 22 people who served in city government less than half finished their terms. The constant turmoil had affected property values and even with an average of 5,400 cars per day passing through town businesses were failing. (P.S. The recall failed.)

Timber

Because the local economy in many parts of Oregon was so entangled with the timber industries a lot more related to logging appeared in the papers. It was educational.

While Pacific Northwest Federal congressional representatives declared that timber jobs were a dominant part of the Northwest economy an economics study published in 1992 showed timber employed 4 to 6 percent of the 1.4 million workforce in Oregon.

According to the timber industry the 17 percent (13,500 jobs) decline in industry jobs was all due to environmentalists stopping logging. In reality it was due to the timber industry changing production methods. From 1979 to 1989 the number of workers needed to mill one million board feet of lumber dropped from 4.5 to 2 due to industry automation. In addition the industry had built finishing plants in other countries or sent logs to other countries to be finished creating the unemployment they blamed on environmentalists.

In the Medford paper a logger lamented that many of his brethren were filing out of the woods forever. Logging had been a family tradition since his grandfather – it was in his blood. He contrasted the money and steady work with today where work was irregular and he couldn't pay his bills. Nothing was mentioned about training for a new occupation. The newspaper published my letter where I noted buggy-whip makers were probably pretty miserable when cars made their jobs no longer viable. Maybe we should have eliminated cars so they could continue in their chosen field instead of facing reality. My next-door neighbor, a mill worker, agreed.

A 75-acre timber sale was designed as a clear-cut before the Forest Service was legally enjoined due to a lawsuit from environmentalists (spotted owl habitat which the Forest Service knew was spotted owl habitat). Several years later the same sale reappeared as a 'meadow restoration.' The Forest Service representative explained the sale thus, "The meadow restoration can be misunderstood. While we're going to sell some timber from this project, that's not its purpose." Of course not.

The enormous loss of lives, timberland, and buildings due to forest fires prompted Congress to propose 'emergency measures' such as massive increases in timber sales to reduce 'the unnatural buildup of fuel in the forest.' To the uninformed public this looked like a good way to reduce the loss of lives. However, living near the forests being targeted I learned the truth from ex-loggers and people who worked in fire suppression.

Much of the 'unnatural buildup' in the forests was logging slash. The worst fires either started or 'blew up' to firestorms in untreated logging slash. Logging the 'unnatural buildup' would only create more buildup and perpetuate not reduce major fires. These truths eventually came out but I wouldn't have paid attention if I hadn't been so close to the issue and actually seen how the politicians, forestry officials and timber industry heads lied.

Redevelopment

The inability of residents to understand simple economics was mind-boggling. In Grants Pass the unemployment rate of 10.5 percent was fueled by job losses in logging, construction, service, durable goods and trade jobs. Elected officials were afraid to offer tax breaks and other incentives to businesses because a fringe group would start another recall or put another measure on the ballot to further reduce government's ability to negotiate. The long-vacant position for economic development had been filled for six months. When the incumbent quit in frustration the Southern Oregon Regional Economic Development organization had to put one of their people in the position because the county couldn't (didn't want to) fund the position.

In Oregon some lottery money went to economic redevelopment. The counties were grouped and each group chose three strategies to pursue. Many counties, including Jackson and Josephine, chose tourism and wood products as strategies. Now tourism brought money into the area but it did not create high-pay jobs. And wood products needed wood which was in short supply due to the decreased logging on public lands. Realizing this, the Portland counties changed their strategies to biotechnology, high-tech and metals. Jackson and Josephine did not pick these or aerospace, film and video, plastics, watershed improvement (with the Rogue River running through the area), fisheries or other high-pay strategies. Then they wondered why the average income kept dropping. (Note: Jackson County had Southern Oregon College, now a university, so other strategies would have been viable.)

Another problem was the resistance companies encountered from government when the companies wanted to expand. In Central Point a company expansion would have generated 200 more jobs. However the expansion was outside city limits and the Medford Water District, which supplied Central Point, wouldn't service firms outside city limits. Unless, as pointed out by Paul Macomber of the Medford Tribune, the firms were connected to the timber industry. To build a new warehouse the company was required to store 65,000 gallons of water on the premises in case of fire. Since the company was being wooed by other states, the problem was resolved by the state stepping in with a grant for the water main and forcing Medford to back off. But what did that say about local leadership?

I'd been warned that Oregonians hated Californians. I found out why. The Planning Commissions, composed of ex-Californians, consistently made decisions to prevent anyone else from moving to the area and, in the process, hindered economic growth for Oregonians.

THE LAST TANGO IN OREGON
Oregon 1995

Christmas was spent in San Diego with Josh and his friends. They had been renting the house since June and he was noted for his lack of initiative in cleaning or gardening. A vacation it was not. But it did have some interesting memories.

We didn't have time to get a Christmas tree so we had a Christmas wrench. Josh's friend Matt brought over a six-foot wrench he had built from plywood and cardboard so we decorated it with ribbons and bows. Josh got a large wrapped gift of 50 rolls of toilet paper. I never got a straight answer on why he was so thrilled.

Josh worked at a game shop on the Mission Beach boardwalk. One day he saw a motorcycle go down the boardwalk with a skateboarder attached. Followed by two motorcycle police. The police started to write a ticket for the motorcycle being on the boardwalk – except the biker asked why he had to obey the law and they didn't. They then started to change the ticket to reckless driving when the biker pointed out he was on the right side of the line that divides the boardwalk so skaters, etc. won't run into each other. So they changed it to speeding which the biker accepted. When they started to write a ticket for the skateboarder, they got hung up on routine items such as Make of Vehicle and Vehicle License.

Also observed from his boardwalk job Josh watched a guy drive his motorcycle into the water. His reason? He wanted to see if it would run underwater.

Many schools in San Diego are on the edge of a canyon. At one of the high schools a kid was doing donuts in the parking lot. The first donut he hit the chain on the canyon rim. The second his rear tire went over the rim. The third they needed a crane to get the car out of the canyon.

The Ashland Forest Conference was held from January 13 to 15 at a large conference center in the city. The attendees numbered over 400 and I was charged up to learn more about clear-cut logging, why trees did not grow back in clear-cut areas and what legal issues were being pursued. At the same time the San Diego Chargers were playing in the AFL conference playoffs with the winner going to the Super Bowl. The opponent was the Pittsburgh Steelers who were so confident of their victory they had developed videos of their soon-to-be trip to the Super Bowl. While I was intensely interested in saving the forest I was more intensely interested in the Chargers. The forest would be there another thousand years but the Super Bowl was a once in a lifetime occurrence. At least for the Chargers.

I kept running into the small room in the basement that had the television. By the fourth quarter I was hoarse from screaming my incentives to my team. The minutes ticked down to seconds. We were ahead 17 to 13 and the Steelers were at our three-yard line. The Steelers threw the ball and Dennis Gibson, the San Diego linebacker, tipped it away from running back Barry Foster. We had won the game and were going to the Super Bowl! The quarterback, Stan Humphries, and I jumped up like kids and screamed in unison.

I returned upstairs to the conference room where all 400 attendees were having lunch. As I walked into the loudly buzzing area one of the organizers met me.

"We don't need to know who won. We could hear you all the way up here."

While I knew the probability of our winning the Super Bowl was slim to none, I wanted to be in San Diego when the game was played. By this time Dave was living in Chico, California a few hundred miles south of Rogue River. As we eagerly discussed over the telephone what San Diego would be like with the Chargers in the Super Bowl Dave piped up, "I'll pay half the gas if you want to go."

I picked him up in Chico and we drove all night in a blinding rainstorm to make it to San Diego by Saturday. The cop who pulled me over outside Sacramento noted that he understood the urgency but I needed to slow down from the 95 mph he had clocked. When we got to San Diego we bunked with a couple who I had helped find a house. Dave slept most of Saturday while I toured the area.

Almost every office building had the Charger bolt draped outside often three to six stories tall. Bolts were on garages and houses in the residential areas. At Ocean Beach the surfers were painted half blue, half gold with lightning bolts down their faces and bodies. At a Target store where every shopper was dressed in Charger gear I spotted a man in a 49ers jacket.

"You have guts," I said.

"Yeah, but I'm not stupid. I'm going home to change right now."

We lost because we were outclassed and because the players were so stunned that they had made it that far they didn't play as they had when we beat the Steelers. When Dave and I left San Diego it was like driving through an area that had been hit by an earthquake. No sound except the soft swish on tires on pavement. No radios blaring. Nothing. But it had been worth the drive.

Sometime in early spring of 1995 I had some kind of attack that I later diagnosed as passing a kidney stone. Or a gall stone. Or stones. Whatever it was I was miserable. It started at night with pain spreading from my crotch to under my breasts. No matter what position I assumed, standing or lying down, nothing stopped the pain. Then my body started to swell. By the next morning I looked like I was seven months pregnant. The swelling was from my rib cage down to my hips. The pain had lessened but the swelling hadn't so I had to go to work in a very loose skirt and blouse. People at work asked what was going on. I guess they had never seen an overnight pregnancy before.

Within a few days the swelling disappeared. I didn't go to a doctor because I had no health insurance and was earning little money. About a year later after moving back to San Diego it happened again but the pain didn't last as long nor was the swelling as bad. Again, no insurance, no diagnosis. In 2010 my doctor (yes, insurance) said it sounded like gastroenteritis but the symptoms of that condition included vomiting and diarrhea neither of which I had during my two attacks. At any rate if I did pass gall or kidney stones I felt proud that I could do so and still work. The old work ethic, do or die. And I certainly felt like I was dying during both attacks.

During the same time period I read the tax codes on selling my house. I was 51 by that time and if I could wait it out until I was 55 I could sell my house and not have to pay taxes on the equity. Nor would I have to buy another house to avoid the taxes. However I had been renting the house for three years and at that time you had to be in your house for three years to claim it as your main residence for gain exclusion purposes.

My credit cards were maxed out on dental and car expenses, I needed to be in the Cather house for three years before I sold it and there were no decent paying jobs in Southwest Oregon. So I decided to sell the Rogue River house and move back to San Diego. However selling did have a few hiccups.

An agent called and said her buyer, a woman working for the post office, was really interested. But she would need me to clean up the workshop area and guarantee it would not back up again. 'Back up?' I thought. 'Again?' What did she mean?

The house had a fifteen-foot breezeway between the garage/workshop and the house. I rarely went into the workshop and due to the size of the breezeway the entry to the workshop wasn't visible from the kitchen door. (At one time my cat had dragged a dead bird bigger than she was across the breezeway, stopping every foot or so to spit out feathers. After she finally got the bird to me at the kitchen door her bright look of triumph was quickly squelched when the bird ended up in the garbage.)

The L-shaped workshop sat at the back of the garage with the long part of the L being maybe fifteen to twenty feet by seven feet and opening through a door to the breezeway. At one time there had been a toilet near the door but the toilet had been removed and plywood covered the hole.

Over the past six months water and debris had backed up into the hall bathroom tub a number of times. Drain cleaner and vigorous use of the plunger had cleared the clog so I thought no more of the problem. When I got home that afternoon I realized why the clogging problem had gone away. It had gone away into the workshop.

The mess was probably two to three inches deep along the entire length of the workshop. It had seeped into every corner and crevice. And where had it come from? From the open pipe where the old toilet had been. This needed more than a shop vac. I thought about calling in one of those tankers that cleaned septic systems. But first I had to call Roto-Rooter to clean out the drains.

The guy determined that the grease the former renters had poured down the kitchen drain had finally congealed with the other debris going down the drain to the point that the pipes were clogged from the kitchen to the main in the road. Luckily when he roto-rootered it out most of the debris in the workshop found its way to the main. Hosing it down for three days eliminated the need for a tanker truck. Unfortunately by the time I got the workshop cleaned up the prospective buyer had lost her job with the post office so I was back to square one.

Then another realtor brought some prospective buyers but noted that I needed to get the electrical meter where it belonged, on the side of the house rather than on a fifteen-foot pole that was situated to the right of the driveway. This pole often caused visitors to either attempt parking on my lawn or to grip the steering wheel tightly as they maneuvered between the house and pole to the back parking area. When they had run the gauntlet I praised their nerves of steel and excellent driving skills. (It was pretty tight.)

The electrician who replaced the meter said that the pole was usually erected when the house was under construction. It had been illegal through maybe four homeowners and I was getting stuck with the bill. Such was Southwest Oregon.

The house sold and I disposed of the furniture I had brought from San Diego including a dining table that even with the base removed required two or three people to move it. It was time to lighten up. I needed to make a few trips to the Cather house in San Diego to move all that was left. At the time I had a cat who had been given to me by someone who'd found her, cold and wet, in their yard. I'd hoped Annie wasn't going to be a repeat of Silver who had picked a new owner after we moved into Cather but, alas, that is what she did. However she did leave a lasting memory.

Driving south on Interstate 5 the exit at Ashland is the last until you get over the Siskiyous. From there you have maybe twenty to thirty miles to any bathroom facilities. I had the van stacked to the top as usual and did not want my cat in a cage for the fifteen hour drive to San Diego so I had a plan. The plan was to let her roam around the van, use her litter box as needed, eat and drink when she wanted and maybe take her for a short walk at some of the rest areas. That was the plan.

Unfortunately she was not in on the plan. I hadn't driven fifty feet past the Ashland exit when she draped herself around my neck and urinated. An hour later I was able to get into a rest area bathroom where I had to remove my clothes, although not all at once, and rinse off the urine. I got a lot of attention from the women and children using the bathroom. I also got my explanation down to very few words since I had to repeat it for each aghast look when people walked in.

For some reason I can't remember I had to take her back with me to Oregon after my first trip. On the way right after the last exit on the California side before we hit the Siskiyous she pooped in the center console ashtray. I had to live with the smell for another thirty miles before I could get to a restroom.

During the move back and forth I stayed at Vern's. His girlfriend didn't like the idea of another female in his mobile home so I camped out on his land. One day I was going to his house to use the telephone when his girlfriend showed. I was flabbergasted. She was a female administrator for the community college where I'd taught. They'd met while he was taking courses to get his GED. In her working mode, she wore conservative clothing with hair pulled back in a bun and used very formal, reserved syntax in conversations. With Vern she was a different lady. So to speak.

Hair frizzed to a halo, heavy makeup, tight jeans and a very tight Harley tank top that showed off a bosom a lot bigger than the one discernible under her conservative clothes. Rings bedecked her fingers as well as numerous studs in her ears. My mouth fell open and Vern, standing behind her, shrugged his shoulders and smiled. I was once again convinced that some women will do anything to ride a Harley.

ANOTHER WHIRLWIND TOUR
Oregon, Washington, Vancouver and Idaho, 1995

Before settling in San Diego I took a grand tour of the Pacific Northwest. I had *The Waterfall Lovers Guide to the Pacific Northwest* and to this point I had bagged about twenty waterfalls. I targeted only falls over 50 feet high. Some had involved little more than driving somewhere on a two-lane highway and taking a short hike. Others had required driving on dirt roads and taking hikes of one to three miles one-way. Many of these out-of-the-way falls were on trails where you might see three people the whole day, even on a weekend. While I visited close to 50 waterfalls, this chapter only touches on the highlights, i.e. weird or wonderful.

At a rest area off Route 126 coming out of Eugene I sat with two men and a woman from Portland looking across the deep valley at the 200 feet of Rainbow Falls. One of the guys said, "I was told there's a four-mile trail to the bottom of those falls. Maybe from there we could get to the top."

Looking in my guide book I noted it distinctly said you would look at the falls across a valley. "If there's a trail I think it would be in this book. So you'd be going on a trail that no one's been on for a while."

The guy looked at me, his two companions, back at me then said, "I'm game if these two are."

Off we went. There was a trail, barely, and we had to backtrack a few times when we meandered off on a deer track but finally we neared the foot of the falls. I was scared 'expletive.' The slope to the bottom of the falls was steep, covered in slippery pine needles and at least 50 feet to where the water was boiling up as it pounded the moss-covered boulders. We held on to exposed tree roots to work our way down. One slip and you would be gone. Remember what I said about the size of Oregon creeks.

Our intrepid leader said, "I'm going to see if there's a way up." At this point I was hoping there wouldn't be an accidental way down. We waited a few minutes, clinging to our roots and praying the root and tree wouldn't decide to pull out and hurtle us down the slope. He came back and yelled over the noise of the falls.

"There's no sign of a trail. The way looks pretty crumbly in some areas and pretty steep in others. I wouldn't want to chance it."

As I struggled back to the trail we'd come down I was saying silent prayers of thanks. I would probably have tried to follow if there was a trail to the top of the falls but would have been near heart failure at the end. Assuming there would have been enough light for the end. By the time we got back to the overlook, it was nearing dusk. Getting to the bottom of something that looked like a thin ribbon across a valley? What a gas!

Koosah Falls on the McKenzie River is located at the Ice Cap Campground. Benches lining the river provide the best view of the 70 foot falls that stretch about 50 or 60 feet from shore to shore. The middle of the falls is split by a rock outcropping with some spindly trees growing through the cracks. As I walked along the river towards the falls I noted two things. First, it was totally quiet. No one on the benches was chatting. Second, everyone was looking at the falls but the air was filled with tension. I stopped at one bench and asked an older man sitting there, "What's going on. It's like everyone is waiting for a bomb to explode."

He pointed at the falls. "See that outcropping there?"

"Yeah."

"And see that little tree right at the edge of the outcropping? Right where the water goes over?"

"Yeah."

"Well if you look real close you'll see a leg on each side of that tree. A woman is sitting on that rock with the tree between her legs to keep herself from being swept off."

My mouth hanging open I raised my camera with the telephoto lens and aimed at the falls. I could see her legs and moving upwards, her terrified face.

"Jesus," I responded. "How the hell did she get there?"

"Her dog jumped in upstream and she jumped in to get the dog out. River's pretty heavy this time of year. Swept both of them over the edge. The dog's gone but she was able to grab some tree roots sticking out of the outcropping and pull herself up. Been there maybe two hours by now."

I later heard on the radio that it had taken the local police and fire departments, the county sheriff and fire departments, the state police and two or three other agencies seven hours to get her off that outcropping. In a state with hundreds of swift-flowing rivers and creeks none of the agencies had training in white-water rescue. I always wondered what happened to her after her brush with death.

At Lemolo Falls on the North Umpqua I passed a couple coming back up the trail as I went down. They had the same guidebook and said not to bother because the falls were very short and not that interesting. Their description certainly didn't match the 100-footer in the book. Re-reading the passage I realized there must be two falls, one about a third of a mile in and the other farther down the steep trail. The author often passed over really short drops if they were on the same river or creek as a big one. The extra walking was worth the trip. Also in the area was Warm Springs Falls and based on the trail undergrowth I was probably the first one there in a number of years. I almost thought I heard fairy songs through the sound of the water.

Between two sheared off 1,000-foot cliffs the Crooked River Gorge is a wide, green plain bisected by the river. Further on are the jumbled blocks of mountains at Smith Rock State Park. Both were breathtaking. So breathtaking that I ran over two parking abutments while trying to park and take in the scenery at the same time.

All during this trip I was camping. To save money I often primitive camped, sometimes with a shovel to dig my own latrine. In later years when I told people about my camping adventures they wondered how I had avoided bears. God knows but if I were to do it today I'd be camping *in* the car. I had YMCA and 24-Hour Fitness memberships so it only meant an hour or so until I got to the nearest town for a shower and clean clothes. Traveling on the cheap meant I could go farther.

East of The Dalles and across the Columbia River in Goldendale, Washington was Stonehenge and Maryhill, a monument to World War I dead and a museum in the middle of nowhere. Both were built by Sam Hill a Seattle financial baron. Maryhill was to have been a Quaker community with Hill's mansion, started in 1914, as the cornerstone but the people did not come. The population for the 2000 census was 98. Hill couldn't finish due to a lack of funds but was persuaded to turn what had been built into a museum. The structure was completed in 1937.

Stonehenge kind of resembles the English Stonehenge but the real draw is the museum.

Being a close friend of Queen Marie of Roumania, who dedicated the museum in 1926, Hill received many donations from her of furnishings and paintings. Another friend, Alma de Bretteville Spreckels of San Francisco, also donated numerous art objects. Loie Fuller, a pioneer of modern dance and close friend of Auguste Rodin, was able to bring some of his creations to the museum.

I have rarely seen comparable art in more illustrious museums in big cities. At least 50 chess sets ranging from a few inches tall to three or four feet. A complete floor for Dale Chihuly's glassworks. (In 1995 Chihuly was big. How his art got into a museum in an area where nobody lived was mind-boggling.) A huge collection of Native-American baskets from probably every tribe in the 50 states. Ancient Russian religious icons. It was like finding waterfalls in the sand dunes.

Fall Creek Falls was many miles up Route 30 and required a mile or more walk. I had been in so many dense forests that I was starting to hear voices. While the sounds may have been from babbling brooks they were taking on a distinct vocabulary. At the same time I kept fearing attacks from cougars or bears and watched the trails for signs. Since I couldn't distinguish bear and cougar tracks from large dogs or mountain bike skids watching the trails was probably a waste of time.

This was a waterfall I was inclined to forego not only due to the length of the walk but because it was clouding over, getting cold and starting to sprinkle. Arriving I was glad I had pushed on. Falls Creek was three cascades totaling over 250 feet with the middle angling off from the top and bottom. Very unique. On the way back I met two men with two big dogs who must have scared off the cougars and bears.

At Mt. Rainier I hiked to Comet Falls in the Nisqually drainage, 1.9 miles straight up through mud or over stair-like rocks and boulders on very steep slopes. This is not a hike for agoraphobics. Of which I am one. I get nervous standing on ladders or the roofs of houses. But letting it get me was not allowed.

On the way up the Nisqually River had many more falls then mentioned in the guide. Van Trump Falls was described as a double but looked more like a triple. I had been climbing so long I'd forgotten the description of Comet Falls so thought Van Trump was Comet. Turning to leave I noticed the trail going further up was pretty worn. So I climbed some more and was awed by the sight. Over 320 feet of shimmery plunge then another 70 feet of fan. The mist made the top of the falls somewhat hard to see but it was worth the extra climb.

At this point the light mist had turned to light rain and it was cold. On the way down I put my camera under my sweatshirt to keep it dry. Coming around a bend and seeing a particularly beautiful series of small falls in a gorge I whipped my camera out for a shot and stood silently as I watched the wide-angle lens slowly roll down the slope. The lens coming loose had happened before when I had the camera under my sweatshirt but a) I forgot and b) it wasn't on a steep slope above a crashing river. Debating the $79 lens against my bones or possibly my life I said a silent goodbye to old faithful and went on.

By the time I got back to my car I was drenched. The quandary was momentous. Do I get in the backseat of the car and try to change my clothes under cover of ensuing dusk and blankets thereby getting the seats wet and wetting my new dry clothes? Or do I just open the car door, stand behind it only visible to those approaching my car from the rear, pull off everything on top, replace, then everything on bottom, replace and get into a basically dry car. Option two resulted in the other vehicles slowing to a crawl but was much quicker.

I had washed my other tennis shoes and the ones I was wearing were soaked. I had to put on dry socks and plastic bags over the socks to use the shoes. The plastic sticking out of my shoes got a few curious stares particularly from the Japanese touring the area.

Still in the park I viewed Clear Creek Falls falling through a rainbow to the bottom of the chasm. I returned to the parking lot to hear two women tell their children to go to the bathroom.

"Let's get going, you don't need to explore any trails." They had no idea and probably didn't care about what they'd missed.

Leaving Mt. Rainier I had the choice of driving late into the night to an open campground, paying a significant fee for a nearby campground or car camping at a picnic area. I chose the picnic area. It was pretty dark when I parked and the next morning I woke to a panorama. Across a narrow chasm the sun slowly turned the cliff from shades of buff to deep reds and ochres, a cliff of fractured spires much like Devil's Postpile at Mammoth Mountain. What a way to wake up!

I targeted Tacoma for a new lens using Route 410. At one point you crest a hill to see a vast blanket of forest with little villages and farmhouses that ends with the city of Tacoma floating on a plain like someone's vision of a fantasy kingdom. Breathtaking.

Going to Tacoma meant I had to car camp because I couldn't afford a motel. After buying the lens I drove around for an hour and found a wooded area behind some warehouses. I had settled down when I heard stones hitting the car. I thought maybe they were from some animal on the hill above the warehouses but the stones increased in frequency and size. It took another hour to find a second spot where I again heard noises. Finally I found a roadside rest area to complete what was left of the night. A little scary but no expense and my limited funds would last a little longer.

The Olympic National Park and Forest seashore is incredibly beautiful with tendrils of mist turning the monoliths in the water into gigantic monochrome ships, silver-toned driftwood littering the shore and trees with huge burls on the trunks. The latter was something I had never seen before. Imagine a tree trunk sprouting huge rounded growths one to three feet thick and maybe three feet around or even encircling the tree. The next time you see something carved out of burl you'll know what it looked like in its natural setting.

I soon realized the wide-angle lens wasn't the same as the one I'd lost so I drove down the peninsula through Bremerton to get back to Tacoma. As I crossed the Hood Canal suspension bridge I looked up and almost hit another car. There was Mt. Rainier looming so large it was as if I could reach out and touch it. The bridge was bumpy and other cars quickly got out of my way as I wrestled my camera to get a picture of the view. In Portland Mt. Hood is a beautiful backdrop to the city but Mt. Rainier dominates the Seattle/Tacoma skyline as a presence. It is there.

My camera was busy. Everett to Bellingham along the coast, seeing a refinery near Birch Bay State Park all aflame in the late night, taking the ferry to Vancouver Island, Butchart Gardens and the exceptional architecture in Victoria (one of the oldest cities in Western Canada), the Northern Cascades. When I thought I'd seen all the moving, beautiful scenery or waterfalls or architecturally unique buildings or towns something else would pop up. I never hit overload. This was turning into one hell of a trip.

The ferry ride had something I'd never seen out in the open in America. In the brochure racks for tourist attractions were colorful pamphlets for companies such as *The Rubber Rainbow* and *A World of Condoms*. The brochure for the first company included, '*This fun shop features CONDOMS from all over the world and you will be delighted and amazed by the presentation and selection available. The enthusiastic staff at The Rubber Rainbow are happy to provide assistance or answer questions you may have.*' I would have gone to see what kind of 'assistance' they provided but didn't have the time.

Near Mt. Baker I stopped at a small grocery store. A van with an organization name for disadvantaged youth pulled into the parking area. Two adults emerged, a man and a woman. The man said, "Well, is it like you thought it would be?"

She replied, "I didn't think they could get that rowdy. Next time they all get tranquilizers before we leave."

On the way out, I again overheard them. The man laughed and said, "So, you were the one who wanted to go to Mt. Baker." I understood his laughter because the route we were on did not get you to Mt. Baker. They were about fifty miles out of the way.

The Northern Cascades ranged from stark pinnacles to aquamarine jewels such as Diablo Lake set in deep canyons and surrounded by forested slopes. In Spokane, another city in the middle of nowhere, I worked out at the YMCA on a treadmill that overlooked a waterfall on the Spokane River. What fun to be getting healthy while bagging another waterfall.

Getting there had taken me through miles of rounded mesas interrupted by deep canyons. I think it was part of the Channeled Scablands, a run-off area for an ancient lake in Montana where breaks in the glacial dams resulted in floods that flowed to the Pacific. How cool to see unusual geologic formations that have a unique history millions of years old.

My last stop before heading to Chico to visit with Dave was Steens Mountain in Southeastern Oregon. I had seen pictures of the mountain's face but after 66 miles of gravel road, 16 of which were so heavily rutted and strewn with rocks that I couldn't go over 3 miles per hour, I never made my destination. Still the area was beautiful with its craggy peaks, deep gorges with dark green meadows and beautiful vistas of the nearby desert. With no toilets and a road described as 'rough' instead of 'almost impassable in some areas for passenger vehicles particularly a Mazda 626' my appreciation of the view was significantly lessened.

In Chico, Dave, his girlfriend and I went to her place where I slept on her daughter's bed amid grunts from her pet sow-bellied pig. My dreams were of ham sandwiches with a lot of fat and barbeques. When I went to the bathroom, I had to stomp my feet at the pig because she was trying to nip me.

THE LAST STAND IN SAN DIEGO
Cather House, 1995-1998

While Josh and his friends rented the Cather house they had another 'Steve' incident. When they had parties Josh always notified and invited the neighbors. A number dropped by and when they complained about the music, it was turned down. Steve, of course, complained about the music from the time the party started. After a while the police resorted to drive-byes so they could prove they had answered his call but found nothing illegal. The crushing blow however was Steve's girlfriend.

Steve was in his early twenties when we first met him but we'd never seen a lot of women around. One had been on scene for maybe three or four months but not many after. One night when Josh was having a party Steve, as usual, came out to complain. With him was a pretty girl who asked Steve about the party. Steve went off on a rant about how rotten Josh was and the girl turned to him and said, "I don't think he's so bad. And it looks like a fun party. See you later." Josh said Steve almost went through his own front door without opening it when he saw his date sitting in Josh's lap.

When I returned from my trip I asked where my cat was. One of Josh's buddies said he had seen a little boy carrying her around and after that she didn't come home again. Talk about loyalty.

With the proceeds on the Oregon house Josh started paying off the fines he had accrued from minor traffic tickets that turned into major license suspensions and revocations when they weren't paid. As he ran through the morass someone asked him about the drug paraphernalia warrant. Since Josh had never taken drugs he was a little confused.

While in Oregon Josh had returned to his legal name of Mitchell. We soon learned that a Josh Samuels whose mother's name was Mitchell had been picked up for drugs. When the other Josh Samuels had not appeared for the drug bust, a warrant had been issued. Because most of Josh's tickets in San Diego had been under the name of Samuels the court clerks, alert as always, had not bothered to check the social security number. The other guy's warrant was tossed in with Josh's and into the online system.

He went to court and got the paperwork exonerating him of the warrant. However he had not gotten all the traffic warrants cleared up and, at the same time, made an enemy of a San Diego police officer. The officer decided to make an example of a civilian who didn't kowtow to his authority. I came home from work one day (yes, I had found employment) and his friends gave me the bad news. Josh was in jail.

But it wasn't just the fact that he was in jail. The officer had gotten some of his buddies to come along and they had tossed the house trying to find something to charge the other guys with dealing drugs. Josh had been arrested and not allowed to get the court paperwork to show he was not who was being arrested. After four hours handcuffed in a police car, the cops determined he couldn't be held for the drug warrant but with the outstanding traffic warrants he was sent to the hoosegow.

I can't remember what we did to get him out but when we picked him up at one o'clock in the morning he was pretty chipper. The county had recently opened a new jail and he had the privilege of being one of the first occupants. Beds were a little uncomfortable but neat and clean. With no other inmates he had no problem sleeping. The only problem was he had started smoking. And has never quit except for short periods of time.

The warrant problem kept recurring. If he was playing his car radio too loud and was stopped by the police, they tried to arrest him on the warrant. I can't remember what caused the last arrest but I had had it.

First I went to the San Diego County Jail downtown to learn he wasn't there. This took a little talking on my part because the deputies wanted me to wait until the next morning before they would even tell me if he was in the County jail. When I pointed out all the crap that had gone down because of the bad warrant the officer took pity and determined Josh was still at the Central Division jail.

By the time I got there the front doors were locked so I went to the back door. As some officers left for the night I entered. An officer saw me and told me I had to leave. I sat at the table next to the door, folded my arms and said I was not moving until my son was with me. Not wanting to create an incident one of the officers asked me the problem and I explained. Another officer started muttering that Josh probably had been doing drugs and he was probably some slime who had faked me out and I was probably too stupid…. Well, you get the drift.

The officer who had been trying to help saw me starting to clench my fist and get up. He then suggested to the other officer that he leave the room. After that the good guy noted that they probably had the original booking papers for the other Josh Samuels so sit tight he'd be back.

About a half hour later he was back with Josh. He said that while both were close to the same age, the eye color wasn't the same nor the height or social security numbers. The desk Sergeant gave Josh a 'get-out-of-jail-free' card that Josh could show to officers if he should be stopped again.

That wasn't good enough for me. I wrote letters to the Chief of Police, the District Attorney, the State Attorney General, the Mayor and all the City Councilmembers. I noted that some clerk's stupidity was making both my son's life and mine a major headache. The DA responded the only way he could. He dismissed the charges against the other kid to get it out of the system.

A few years later Josh was stopped for speeding. The officer took his driver's license, went to his car then returned to Josh's car. "You the guy who had all the problems with the drug warrant?"

Josh nodded in assent. The officer then handed him back his license and told him not to speed any more. Josh told his friends that he was really impressed. The San Diego police were afraid of his mom.

My back had been achy since I'd returned to San Diego. Sometime in October or November, the bad luck furies struck. The night Princess Di was killed I had another attack like the kidney stone one I'd had in Oregon. A few days later I was moving storage boxes when stabs of pain suddenly shot down my legs – my disc had gone again. The turbo-charger and catalytic converter on my Mazda went out. I was out of work.

With my back I could walk less than 100 feet before having to sit down. The pain was paralytic, my legs incapable of movement. It wasn't too bad when I was home but when I went grocery shopping, I had to sit down in the middle of every aisle in the store. After the first few times the store manager knew the drill so when people would rush to my aid he'd just shoo them away understanding I would eventually be up and moving again. Josh wanted to help but I wouldn't let him. This problem was not going to run my life.

With no insurance I had to go to a community clinic where X-rays revealed a herniated disc. Only this time it was lower in my back than the one I had when married to Ray. A suggestion that swimming would ease the pain only resulted in my almost drowning in the 24-Hour Fitness lap pool. The pain was so bad I couldn't move my legs. The clinic gave me a prescription anti-inflammatory but that was the extent of their mandate. No insurance, no operation.

The car issues had stemmed from someone telling me how much better my car would run if I used synthetic oil. They forgot to mention not on old cars. Along with the back problem I came down with a bad case of the flu. So here we were. I couldn't walk, could barely stand from the flu and we're running all over San Diego looking for a used turbo-charger. Found one but then I learned the catalytic converter had to be new. My credit card was on its last gasp.

Prior to this tsunami I had joined a ski club and bought tickets to a package ski trip in Salt Lake City. As the departure date approached I prayed my back would recover. But it didn't. I went anyway hoping I could go down some of the gentler slopes. Besides, the tickets were not refundable and at least I would see Salt Lake City. Skiing was not in the cards and I faced the real attitude of people in singles ski clubs. If you can't participate you are on your own including going out for meals, sight-seeing, etc. (I experienced this again when I moved to the Bay Area.)

While a lonely outing I did see the city including Park City where they were holding the Sundance Film Festival. Didn't see any movie stars but did mingle with people who evidently had. And, of course, got lots of pictures.

When I returned it was back to the gym, exercising through the pain as I forced its retreat. I remember the day I once again could get through an entire Step class. Tears were rolling down my cheeks.

At least I had a kitty.

One of Josh's friends, Mark, had gotten a kitten. He was not too assiduous in cleaning the litter box and after a while the kitty expressed her displeasure by using his bed. Rather than learning a lesson Mark banished the kitty outdoors. Food was left in the garage but other cats often got it before she did. Basically she was being treated like a feral cat.

She was a cute little thing with big paws. I felt sorry for her so I got a litter box and food bowls and started training her to come to my room. Soon she was with me all the time so I had her spayed and notified Mark she was now my cat. She grew into her big paws, about 11 pounds worth. A date took one look at her and pronounced she was part Maine Coon. Checking out the breed, it was definite. Big with a rough coat, tufted collar at the neck she resembled the pictures.

Unfortunately she was not gentle. Trying to brush her, rubbing her belly, a variety of other verboten actions resulted in flying claws and slashing teeth. No amount of discipline or attempts at training worked. I had a kitty but not one I could trust any farther than I could throw her, which happened more than once when she bit me.

I've never been an indoor cat person and she preferred the outdoors to her cat box so she became an indoor-outdoor cat. Unfortunately she displayed her ill-mannered personality to other cats and I had to take her to emergency twice. Once time she came in, cuddled on my bed and I noticed ants crawling on the bedspread. She had an abscessed slash on her belly that required stitches and medication.

The next incident she had been a little lethargic for a few days. As she came into the house on the third day a veterinarian assistant, who was Josh's friend, saw her.

"Your cat is really sick. You need to get her to the vet as soon as possible."

This time she had five abscesses in her behind above her tail. As the vet noted he could see how she reacted when other cats wanted to fight. He had to insert drains and to keep her from licking the wounds, install a collar. To prevent her from draining onto my bed I overlaid it with plastic sheeting and then a few towels where she could snuggle. Unfortunately it was winter so the plastic sheeting was also overlaying my heating blanket. A few hours later I woke with a start as the droplets of water under the sheeting soaked into me and the bed.

Ah I remember it well. But knowing my history with cats I figured she was just passing through and when gone I could get another cat a little more amenable to being touched and less likely to get injured.

She's still with me. Seventeen years in August 2012. Seventeen years that have included three infections from her bites, operations because she ran away from other cats but not in time and grooming appointments every three to six months to get the mats out of her hair. I once calculated she's cost me over $3,000. And she still bites. Lucky me.

In June of 1996 my high school graduating class had its 35th reunion. I didn't have the money or inclination to go back but did have my picture taken in a bikini. I sent it back via an old school chum who not only pinned it on a corkboard at the reunion but sat close by to hear the reactions. I had been about thirty pounds more in high school and not as physically active in the exercise area. He said the gasps of disbelief were pretty funny.

I found work as an Executive Assistant to a guy who had developed a popular software program. But he was sleazy. He would have me book car rentals for his trips then badger me to use outdated coupons to get price reductions or upgrades. Not outdated by a few days but often a few years. He was vehemently opposed to upgrading his software from DOS-based to Windows-based. If people liked what his software could do they would take it the way it was offered. The real reason was he didn't want to spend the money for the upgrade. When customers started using other programs he blamed it on me and other employees because we weren't marketing the product aggressively enough. When I advocated for the upgrade, he fired me. Since he's still in business, someone must have gotten a clue.

Prior to the parting of the ways, he asked me to fly to Oregon to pick up his new SUV. Seemed he had a friend who lived in Oregon where he could register his cars and not have to pay sales tax at purchase (Oregon had no sales tax). In addition, the insurance up there was cheaper. I was flown up to Portland, met his dealer and drove back to San Diego. At a rest stop, despite parking as far as possible from other cars, an even bigger SUV parked next to the car and dinged the door. So much for saving money on taxes.

Based on my photo album I must have visited Dave on the way back because we took a hike to the top of Feather River Falls, at 640 feet the sixth highest in the continental United States. Dave had noted that it was all uphill both ways. After I pointed out it couldn't be uphill coming down he backed off a little from his statement, saying it was uphill from the bottom of the falls to the start of the trail at the parking area.

This also may be the time when he bought his four acres of heaven. The acreage included lots of trees and a small stream bisecting the property. He had sold his beloved Harley to get the down payment. (A guy he worked for later bought him another Harley in exchange for doing renovation work on his motels in King City and some other out-of-the-way burg near Interstate 5. Dave said only a Harley was worth the utter boredom of staying in places like that for months at a time.)

The property also included a broken down two bedroom trailer that only a hobo could love. Being part hobo Dave was happy. His intent was to build a two or three bedroom cabin on the site and the trailer would do in the meantime. When I stayed with him over the years I pointed out that a few minor fix-ups, like at least cleaning the place, would not be a betrayal of his original intent.

He told me about the time the pump to his well broke. He didn't have the money to get it fixed but he still needed water for bathing and toilet flushing. So one night into his no water situation he scooped water from the stream for a bath. The water was evidently warm enough that it didn't need excessive heating because Dave said he shared his bath with all kinds of little wiggly critters who seemed copacetic with the soap and shampoo. Since they were not returned to the environment except through the septic leach lines I guess they probably weren't that happy.

In late 1997 a temp agency assigned me to format and edit procedures for a medical device sterilization company trying to get ISO 9000 certified. My capabilities being a lot higher than editing I began to question some of the procedures. One in particular dealt with a failure in the radiation equipment used for the sterilization process. In the emergency procedure the operator was instructed to notify the supervisor, note the problem in the log then turn off the equipment. I asked the Quality Assurance Manager at what point in this process would the equipment melt down before being turned off? Observations and questions of this nature led to my writing a large part of the procedures. They gave me a certificate of appreciation for helping them obtain their goal.

John was now working in San Jose, California so for Mother's Day in 1997 he invited me to go white-water rafting on the Cal-Salmon in Northern California. The put-in was off Highway 96 in the Trinity Alps. I can't remember if I flew up or drove but this was the first rafting I'd done since Oregon. I had turned 53 in April.

We camped with two of his friends and boarded the bus for the trip up the mountain to the put-in. As we sped along the narrow dirt road bordering the river below John kept glancing out.

"That looks a lot higher than last year." He'd turn to one of his friends who evidently had gone with him on this run a year or so before. "Isn't this higher than last year."

His friend would look out the window then nod his head. "Does look higher."

They kept this up until we reached the put-in. I figured he was just trying to scare me so I laughed at them. I told others in the party, "Most Moms get flowers and brunch. My son takes me on a trip where I might get killed."

The head guide then began his talk on how the river would be run, who was guiding each boat, paddling, how they would scout each rapid, etc. Somewhere in this talk he mentioned that the river was much higher and faster this year than in former years and therefore much more dangerous since there were more hydraulics. I turned to John with the comment, "Well, this is a fine mess you've gotten me into." The guide thought I was in earnest and offered that I could bow out.

"Nope, I'm here and I'm going. My will is made out and he only gets half."

That sucker was one scary run.

The Cal-Salmon has numerous Class IV rapids as well as three Class V. Based on that it is generally classified as a Class IV+. So it can get hairy. Bloomer Falls can be run straight or through a side fish ladder. The river was so high that year, they used the fish ladder. When a river is high, the force of the water (cfs) is greater. When it hits boulders rather than running over them, it can reverse on itself causing hydraulics. As I noted before hydraulics tend to push you down not up. Getting caught in one can result in drowning.

In a paddle raft everyone paddles. If someone doesn't pull their weight the raft can go the wrong direction at the wrong time and capsize. When that happens, particularly in a rapid full of boulders and hydraulics, lots of damage can result. So paddling in unison, responding instantly to the guide's commands to paddle left or right or back or forward is paramount.

The final rapids are Last Chance and Freight Train. Last Chance is reached through a shoot that drops you into a hydraulic. Before we ran it the guides lined up at the bottom of the hydraulic with ropes stretched across the bottom and throw bags that could be aimed at those who fell out of the rafts to prevent them from going down Freight Train.

John was in front of me in the raft. I can't remember how we arranged it but I think at these last rapids I was holding onto the raft straps and John was making up for my lack of participation in paddling. (John was 6'4" and solid muscle from the gym and sports.) I had been on other rivers but not one this violent. In later years I was able to pull my own weight but this was a first time and I was given some slack.

Freight Train is a long, steep, fast, and powerful rapid that ends in a narrow chute. In high water perfect aim is important or you will be hurtled out of the raft and down the rapid with no way to get out until the end. As one guide book noted, 'This is one of those rapids that you will never forget whether you have a perfect run or swim it from top to bottom.'

Obviously I didn't die or get injured. But the one thing I did get was an overwhelming urge to try new runs. I knew I was going to move after I sold the house and this rafting trip had solidified where. The Bay Area would give me a slew of rafting opportunities plus its nearby ski resorts had once been the site of the Winter Olympics.

Back home I went to the ballet. Escondido had a beautiful new auditorium but whoever designed the balcony seating needed some tips. The seats had great clearance but they were up so high from the row below it felt like you were falling out of the seat. This design also made the aisle steps steep. In short, it was not a place for fast exits.

On the night in question the ballet performance consisted of five pairs of male and female dancers from five of the elite ballet companies in the nation. The tour was limited to maybe two or three cities in each state and the performances were magnificent. One of the duets was set to the song *Fire* by the Pointer Sisters. The song started, the dancing commenced, it got to the point in the song when the word 'Fire' is first spoken and the fire alarm went off. We all had to stumble down those steep stairs to the areas providing entry to the seating. The alarm was silenced, we all trooped back in and were assured the alarm had not been part of the performance.

Although I have had many renters who were memorable during this time period one topped the list. The renter was Chinese and he was in America to attend school, run an Internet business and tell me how worthless America was compared to China. I didn't think to ask why he was here if China was so great.

His 'manners' left a lot to be desired. Male visitors and he would wander around the house in their underwear. No amount of telling him this was unacceptable worked. I finally evicted him. But that too didn't work. He would leave when he felt like it.

All the rooms had separate phone lines. At the outside box I took his line out of the jack, cut the wire then glued it back into the jack. It would look OK but, of course, not work.

He went into a frenzy. First he accused one of the other renters of interfering with his line demanding entrance to her room. She told him to buzz off. Then he went next door to Steve to accuse him of taping into his line. This went on for four days with him demanding each day I call the telephone company to fix the line. I refused reiterating that he had been evicted and it was time to move. Every day meant he was losing money on his web business.

The day he moved he sat in his car at the corner of my street. I figured he had pulled something and wanted to see the results. What he had pulled was to change the lock on the bedroom door then keep the key.

The bedroom was on the second floor so I had two options. Break down the door, meaning I would have to replace the door and probably the frame or go through the outside window. I figured as intelligent as he was he probably had forgotten to lock the window.

Putting my extension ladder up I determined he was, indeed, an idiot. I got through the window, opened the door, went downstairs and approached his car. He rolled his window up leaving just a crack.

"You forgot to lock the window asshole. I'm in so you might as well leave."

His tires left scorch marks.

At least he wasn't like the two 'nurses' from Australia who I found out were prostitutes. This revelation came from attending a party a Marine was giving for two friends leaving the service. He had parked his RV in front of the bar where the party was located. My two renters appeared, quite shocked at finding me there. Soon one left with one of the guys at the party. She returned and the other left with another guy. I asked the Marine where they were going and he indicated to his RV. I told the Marine and the renters to hit the road.

My bills outran my earnings and in 1996 or 1997 I declared bankruptcy. At the time housing prices were so depressed that there was not enough equity in my house to satisfy my creditors so I was able to keep it. I settled back in waiting out the golden age of 55 so I could sell without paying taxes on the profit if any existed. Luckily, with Bill Clinton's election in 1996, the new tax laws would let me get out sooner.

But not before I had another medical crisis. Without insurance any medical problem was a crisis.

I was driving to the gym when someone dropped a piece of black Spanish lace over my head or so it seemed. My left eye was awash with black, spidery lines. I got to the gym and tried to wash out the eye but no luck. Since it was late (I think I was on a temp job at the time) I went home. The next day at work I used my lunch hour to call ophthalmologists because this definitely was not dirt.

I described the symptoms and office after office refused to see me because I had no insurance and no money. By the fifth or sixth office I was in despair. One or two offices had said it sounded like a retinal tear and needed to be looked at as soon as possible. They just wouldn't do it.

Finally the last place I called gave me the number of an ophthalmologist in La Jolla. Keep in mind, La Jolla is the second highest income zip code in San Diego County. Any doctor there is going to have exclusive clients and charge very high rates. They don't do charity in La Jolla. But I had hope.

I wish I could remember his name as he should be nominated for sainthood. He agreed to see me that day. After the examination and the diagnosis of a retinal tear I said, "My house is for sale. When it sells I can pay you. How long can I go with this before it gets dangerous?"

He took up something to numb my eye and said, "You can't wait. The tear could cause a detached retina and you could go blind. I'll do it now."

He had faith in me and, of course, was paid as soon as I got my escrow check. Years later I was examined by an ophthalmologist at Kaiser and she said the repair was so well performed she could barely see the scars. But think what could have happened if I hadn't been persistent, if I had just given up. Or he hadn't been there when I needed him.

In February of 1998, two months shy of my 54th birthday, the house sold and I moved to the Bay area.

I've never wanted to leave.

ADDENDUM

While I wanted this book to demonstrate how you can face and overcome adversity, for my children I want them to know some of their relatives (even if most of them are dead). After my mom died and I was putting her pictures in albums I realized I was my son's last living relative who knew who these people were.

My Mom told me she was born Marguerite Lillian Petoskey but at some point she may have switched her last name to Haines, my grandmother's last name from her next- to-last husband. I think her last husband was Hayner.

Mom told me some of her childhood. Evidently due to a lack of work my grandmother's husband could not keep Grandma's kids so they were sent back to Great-Grandmother Petoskey who may have lived in Manistee, Michigan. My Mom said that at the time she remembered Mr. Haines dyeing his hair in order to appear younger for job interviews. According to her, she was responsible for raising all the kids because Grandma Petoskey couldn't handle it but I don't know if she really was the oldest or that responsible. She was pretty good at shaving the truth to get people's sympathy. At any rate, she always carried an animosity toward that period of her life that she was responsible for all. She also mentioned that during that time she fell from a truck and broke both arms plus losing skin from her arms and legs as a result of the accident. She never showed me any scars so this may be anecdotal. (When she died I found duplicate lists scattered throughout the house noting her injuries and medications throughout her life. No idea why she did it.)

She told me that when she was fifteen she moved to Detroit and was a hatcheck girl at a club run by the Purple Gang, a rum-running offshoot of the Mafia. Sometime during this period she met Jack, whose last name is in my picture albums. They married at 17 but Jack's well-to-do Detroit family managed to annul the marriage. She had pictures of him at West Point.

From there she went to New York with her sister Florence after whom I was named. She became a cold cream model and eventually a runway model for furs. During this period she met and married a man named Bill who died in an air crash. She kept many pictures of their life together and newspaper prints of his death. According to Mom she was pregnant when he died but suffered a miscarriage.

Some of the stories she told me of her time in New York were pretty funny. She and her friend Fern would go to Florida and when they ran out of money would send telegrams to male friends saying 'Love and Kisses, send me $50.' She said they never ran out of money. Another story was of her and Fern, both bleached blondes, being stopped going the wrong way on a one-way street. When Mom fluttered her eyelashes and responded to the officer, "But officer, we were only going one way," he shook his head in disgust, exclaimed "Blondes!" and waved them on.

My Mom had a suitcase filled with letters from my Dad during the war and portraits from many big name musicians such as Gene Krupa, Tommy and Jimmy Dorsey, Benny Goodman and others, all autographed to her. When we sold her house in San Diego (MiraMesa), California in 1991 the suitcase was lost. I don't know if the new owners found it and didn't realize its worth or Josh lost it but I would really love to get it back. It had many memories of her youth.

My Aunt Florence evidently had a boyfriend who left her and she turned to alcohol. She owned a wire-haired fox terrier, perhaps the source of my mother's love of that breed, and she and the dog were killed one day in a traffic accident. It wasn't until I was in my twenties that my Mom said she thought it was suicide. She cried when she described the scene with her sister and her sister's dog lying dead in the street.

My Aunt Noni married into the Pudduck family and had, I think, five children. She was told not to have any more as it would kill her and her last pregnancy did indeed result in her death. My mother never forgave her husband.

My Uncle Dick lived near us and at one time lived in the basement apartment in our house. He had a drinking problem but it was finally controlled, to some extent, when he started going with a woman named Evie. I think she moved him to Traverse City, Michigan but I did not keep in contact with them.

My Uncle Bart lived his whole life in Manistee and married a woman named Nana. They had one son, Kenny, who I believe still lives in the area. Again, I did not keep in contact with them. I will always remember Uncle Bart as a very taciturn man who said little but when he spoke it was often a dry, funny remark. Aunt Nana was like my Aunt Joy, a wonderful person who loved everyone.

Aunt Joy lost her fiancée who was on the Arizona during the Japanese raid on Pearl Harbor. She married my Uncle Floyd (Evilsizer) and had a daughter names Shelia. My Uncle Floyd was a slow reader and kept weeks' worth of newspapers in a pile by his chair. My Dad used to say that one day Floyd would pick up a paper and exclaim, "My God, we're at war in Korea."

On my Dad's side I am bad on names. He had an older sister Bella who died of stomach cancer. On his return from the funeral he said he never wanted to go back because he couldn't stomach the prejudice in his family and their friends for anyone not Jewish. His twin sister Sara (or Sarah) married a man who owned a dress-making business that specialized in high end party gowns, particularly prom dresses. I remember when I visited he gave me a fur stole from his stock.

The funny thing about their marriage, aside from their not keeping kosher and having to do the run around when Dad and Sarah's kosher parents visited, was the genes. My Dad and his sister had small noses. In fact when she, her son and I stood in a line, our profiles were the same. However, the man she married had a very prominent nose that was inherited by the daughter. I'm sure she didn't think it was funny but I thought what a trick to play on someone.

I remember one thing about one of the relatives. An Aunt, her name is gone by now, had a son who was going to medical school in Michigan, I think the University of Michigan. He was trying to find a low-calorie substitute for flour so tried some cellulose concoction. He had received a sample of pancakes made from this compound and his comment was, "It was like eating a soggy edition of the New York Times."

I have never made an effort to track down his relatives but I am sure they were Yormarfsky. My Dad said that when his parents went through immigration they spelled the family name as Jharmark, resulting in him and his Dad being the only Jharmarks in the New York telephone directory. This is confirmed by records on the internet. (And it also confirmed that my Dad lied to my Mom about his age saying he was two years older when he was five years younger. When he died he was not eligible for a pension but his popularity was so great the rules were bent so my Mom could have some retirement income and health insurance.) At one time I found a person named Jharmark on the internet but after months of searching finally learned it was a misspelling of his name (Jahrmarkt).

At any rate, as noted in my book, my grandparents wanted nothing to do with my mother and, as a result, had nothing to do with me, the only child of their only son. According to Bella and Sarah pictures of me wearing a small cross were routinely destroyed. I doubt my mother even thought of the significance since we practiced no religion. Prejudice comes in all forms but when it cuts off your children and grandchildren because of religion, it's a stupid move. Don't let it happen to you.

ABOUT THE AUTHOR

Flo Samuels has had a diversified career interrupted numerous times by her making organizational functions more efficient and eliminating her own job. She has been a teacher, computer and software support technician, trainer and manager, systems administrator, drug program data analyst, government budget analyst and construction contracts administrator. While employed she has had three husbands, two sons, six stepchildren and six homes that she bought and renovated. (Though she hates to dust.) To fill her spare time she took up skiing, hiking, white-water rafting and started and ran the Singles Motorcycle Club for 17 years, the only such club in the United States. The group inspired a number of women to purchase bikes of their own and to organize their own motorcycle clubs. The club also inspired some marriages and long-lasting relationships. She lives in Hayward, California with three renters and her 17-year-old cat Mow.

Printed in Great Britain
by Amazon